THE ULTIMATE
BOOK OF KNOTS

THE ULTIMATE BOOK OF KNOTS

More Than 200 Practical and Decorative Knots

by Peter Owen

THE LYONS PRESS
Guilford, Connecticut
An imprint of The Globe Pequot Press

The Lyons Press is an imprint of The Globe Pequot Press

10   9   8   7   6   5   4   3   2

Printed in the United States of America

ISBN 1-59228-160-5

Library of Congress Cataloging-in-Publication Data is available on file.

CONTENTS

FISHING KNOTS

CONTENTS

INTRODUCTION

A fishing knot is a vital link in your tackle system. If that knot is faulty or tied incorrectly, it becomes the vulnerable weak link of the system.

Every fisherman pursues that "fish of a lifetime." Imagine when that moment finally arrives—the rush of adrenaline as the epic battle begins—and then "ping," the weak link of the system breaks, and the fish is lost through knot failure. This is just one example of how very important fishing knots are.

This book does not aim to cover every known fishing knot, but it does look in detail at the knots that have been tried and tested by generations of fishermen. If your fishing knot is tied correctly and you are fully confident with it, you have eliminated the vulnerable weak link in your tackle system.

Effective Knot Tying

Fishing knots of one kind or another have been in use for thousands of years. Since ancient times and in all societies, human beings have been devising ways of securing hooks and baits to lines. Today we can take advantage of all the imagination, ingenuity, and searching for perfection done by fishermen through the ages. We have state-of-the-art tackle, including strong, flexible monofilament nylon fishing line that comes in breaking strengths of up to 100 pounds. In fact, in many of today's tackle systems, the only components that are totally reliant on the fisherman are the knots.

Effective knot tying is more than just following the instructions detailed in this book; rather, there are set, routine maneuvers that you need to implement into the tying of every knot. If you want to tie consistently strong and efficient knots, the following routines should become second nature to you.

• Choose your line carefully, buying only quality line from established manufacturers. When tying two lines together, keep in mind that lines of the same brand will tie more secure knots. This remains true whether the lines being joined are of the same or different diameters. Lines made by different manufacturers differ in degree of stiffness, and this can affect the knot. Many fishermen find line that they trust and have confidence in, and stick with that particular brand.

• Before tying any knot, always check your line for any signs of damage. Line that is already in use can easily become damaged on rocks and snags. If you are in any doubt, safely discard that section of the line. Since monofilament line exposed to the ultraviolet light in sunlight will weaken, it is advisable to change it at least once a year, regardless.

• Before completing a knot tied in monofilament, lubricate it with saliva or water, which helps draw it up tight and seat it correctly with a minimum of friction. Do not use a chemical lubricant, such as silicon; it may stay in the knot and increase the risk of slippage when the knot is put under tension.

• Draw the knot together slowly and evenly with a minimum of friction to ensure that it seats correctly. Some knots may have more than two ends to draw together. For example, the surgeon's knot (see page 46) must have all four ends drawn at the same time to ensure full strength.

• Continue to draw the knot together as tightly as possible. A knot will begin to slip just before it breaks—so the tighter it is drawn together, the more force it can withstand before it starts to slip. It is impossible to achieve maximum tightness with your bare hands, but the finer the gauge of line you use to tie a knot, the easier it will be to draw up tight and seat securely.

• Once the knot has been tightened and firmly seated, its end should be trimmed. Use a pair of sharp line clippers or fisherman's scissors to trim the knot ends at an angle of 45 degrees, as close to the knot as possible. It is important that the tag end does not stick out. If it extends, it can get caught up on rod rings, hooks, or weeds. Do not burn off the tag end; you could easily damage the knot and line.

All fishermen should have a pair of good-quality scissor pliers. Among their many uses are trimming knot ends, crimping lead, flattening barbs, and removing hooks. Keep them within easy reach by attaching them to a retractor secured to your fishing vest or clothing.

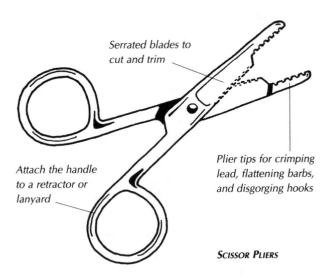

Serrated blades to
cut and trim

Attach the handle
to a retractor or
lanyard

Plier tips for crimping
lead, flattening barbs,
and disgorging hooks

SCISSOR PLIERS

• Visually check your knot—good knots look good. If you are not confident that the knot has been tied and seated correctly, don't risk it! It will only take a few moments to cut it off and retie it, which is far more preferable to losing that fish of a lifetime. How a knot seats down is particularly important. Where a series of turns is involved, make sure that all the turns lie neatly shouldering each other, and that there's no slack line within the knot.

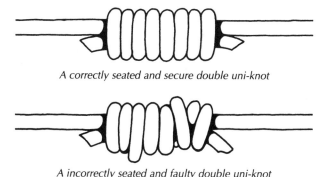

A correctly seated and secure double uni-knot

A incorrectly seated and faulty double uni-knot

• Finally… the riverbank in half light with a gale-force wind blowing is not the place to practice your knots. Practice in the comfort and ideal lighting conditions of home until your knot tying becomes second nature. Like most fishermen, you will find that you'll rely on a small number of knots to cover most situations. It is vital to be able to tie those knots quickly and confidently in any conditions.

Hooks

Tying a knot to most terminal tackle—swivels, lures, sinkers, and the like—is done by attaching the line to an eye. But this can be slightly different with hooks, because some hooks do not have eyes. In such cases, the line is knotted directly to the shank. Some knots described in this book, particularly dry-fly knots, attach the line to the shank even though the hook has an eye.

In fact, there are innumerable types, patterns, and sizes of hooks on the market today, in response to the many different methods of fishing. Here is a quick overview of the types of hooks that will affect the tying of the knots featured in this book.

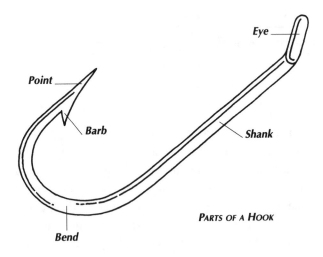

Eye

Point

Barb

Shank

Bend

PARTS OF A HOOK

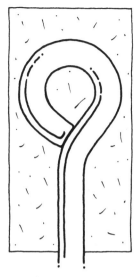

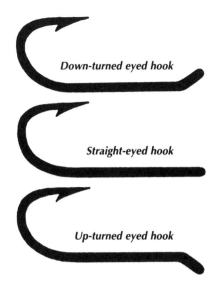

Down-turned eyed hook

Straight-eyed hook

Up-turned eyed hook

Round or Ring Eye
This eye is formed from the shank of the hook; it's the most popular type of eye.

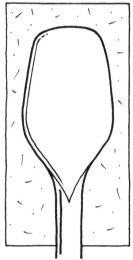

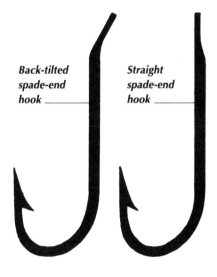

Back-tilted spade-end hook _____

Straight spade-end hook _____

Spade End
This is formed by flattening the shank of the hook.

How to Use This Book

The step-by-step illustrations and instructions are precise, so try to follow them exactly. There are arrows to show the directions in which you should push or pull tag ends, standing parts, and loops. Reversing or changing the steps could result in defective knots.

Because of the wide variation in the types and manufacture of fishing lines, the suggested number of turns are only recommendations. A certain amount of experimentation may be required to find the optimum number of turns required for the line and knot you are using. For example, four turns may not be enough to stop your knot from slipping, rendering it defective, while six turns may prevent the knot from drawing up and seating correctly; in this case, five turns would be the optimum number.

A simple way to test knots is to tie your test knot in a separate piece of line, attach one end to a post, then, wearing a pair of strong gloves to protect your hands, pull on the other end. If you vary your pulls between a steady and a jerking action, you can test the knot under different types of strain.

Fishing Knot Terms

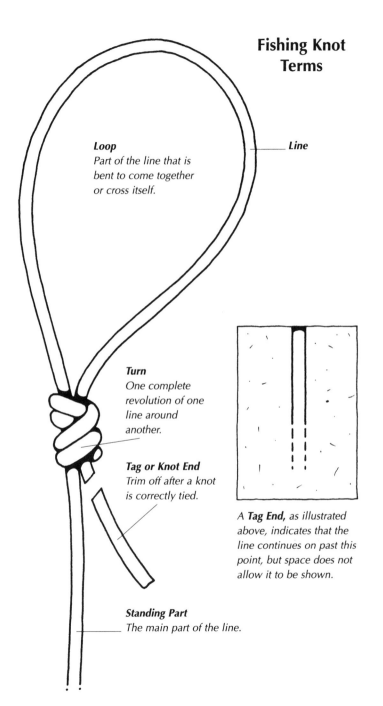

Loop
Part of the line that is bent to come together or cross itself.

Line

Turn
One complete revolution of one line around another.

Tag or Knot End
Trim off after a knot is correctly tied.

A **Tag End,** as illustrated above, indicates that the line continues on past this point, but space does not allow it to be shown.

Standing Part
The main part of the line.

13

1

HOOK AND TACKLE KNOTS

The knots in this section are for attaching hooks and flies to a leader or tippet, and attaching various items of tackle— lures, swivels, and sinkers—to a line.

An important aspect of choosing which knot to use is to feel fully confident with that knot. The knot you eventually choose will be a vital link between you and your quarry, so practice and experiment with it until you feel confident.

Arbor Knot

This strong but simple knot, also known as the **reel knot,** is used to secure one end of the line to the spool arbor of the reel, hence the name.

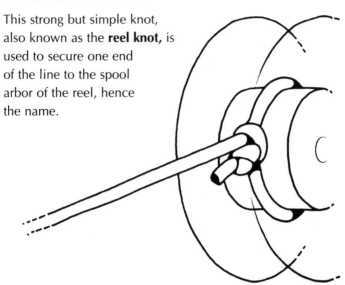

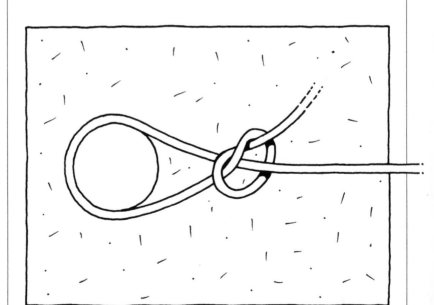

1 Take the line around the spool arbor of the reel. Then take the tag end around the standing part and tie an overhand knot.

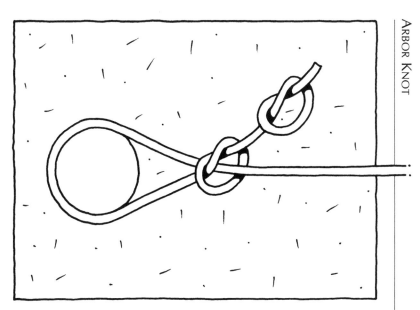

2 Tie a second overhand knot in the tag end as close as possible to the first overhand knot.

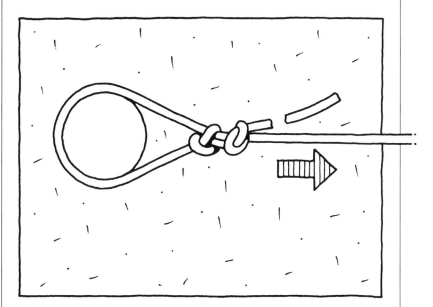

3 Pull on the standing part of the line, and the two overhand knots will jam together against the spool. Trim the knot end.

17

IMPROVED CLINCH KNOT

This is one of the most popular knots for tying line to a hook, fly, swivel, or lure. It is known by some fishermen as the **tucked half blood knot.** It is quick and easy to tie, and it's particularly effective with fine monofilament.

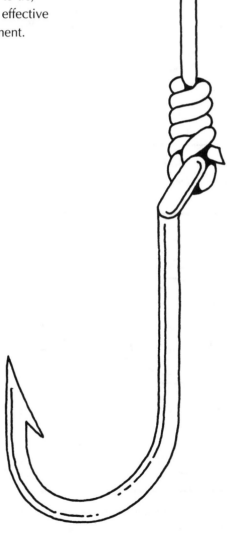

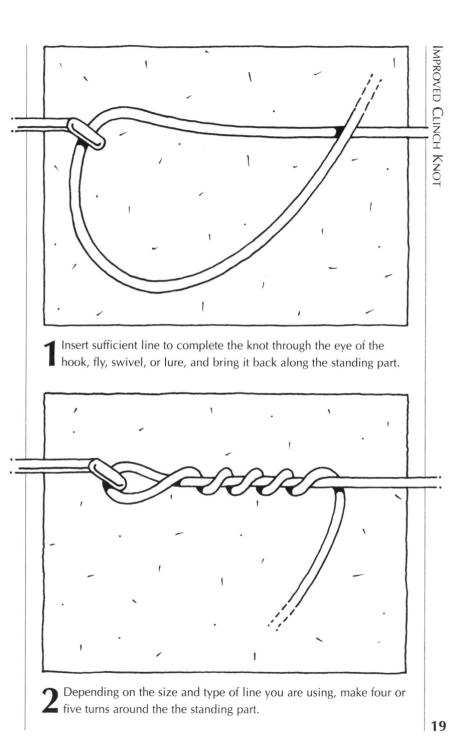

1 Insert sufficient line to complete the knot through the eye of the hook, fly, swivel, or lure, and bring it back along the standing part.

2 Depending on the size and type of line you are using, make four or five turns around the the standing part.

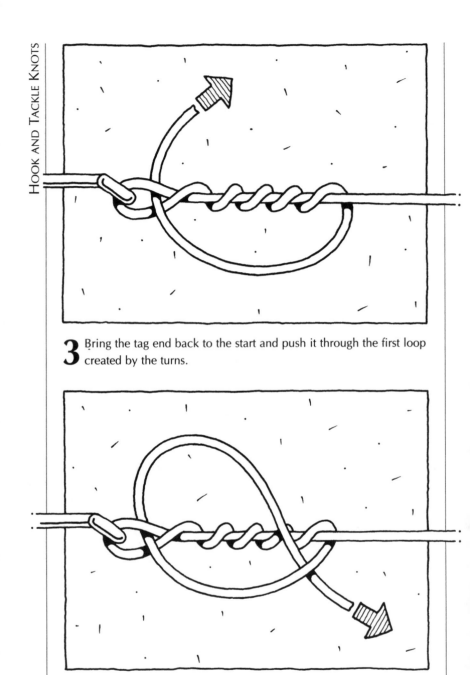

3 Bring the tag end back to the start and push it through the first loop created by the turns.

4 Bring the tag end back over and then push it down through the large loop.

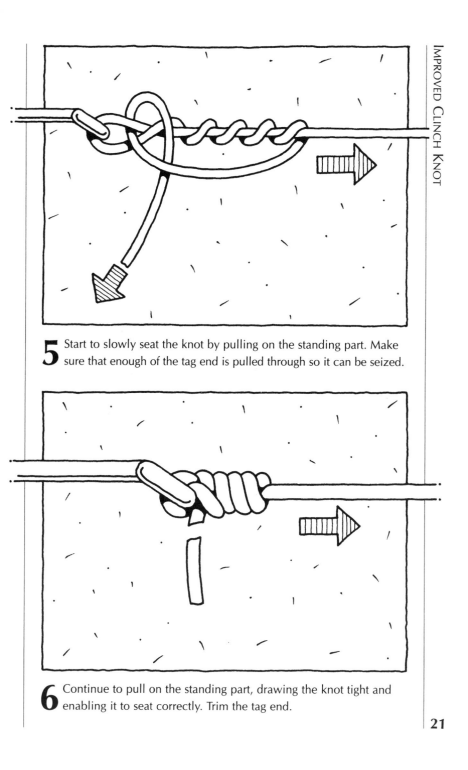

5 Start to slowly seat the knot by pulling on the standing part. Make sure that enough of the tag end is pulled through so it can be seized.

6 Continue to pull on the standing part, drawing the knot tight and enabling it to seat correctly. Trim the tag end.

UNI-KNOT

This knot, also known as the **grinner knot,** is one of the most reliable knots for tying an eyed hook or fly to a leader or tippet. It can also be used to tie line to a swivel, sinker, or lure, and is effective with most types and sizes of line.

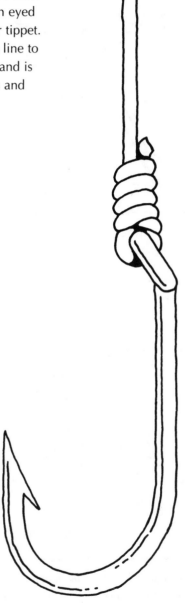

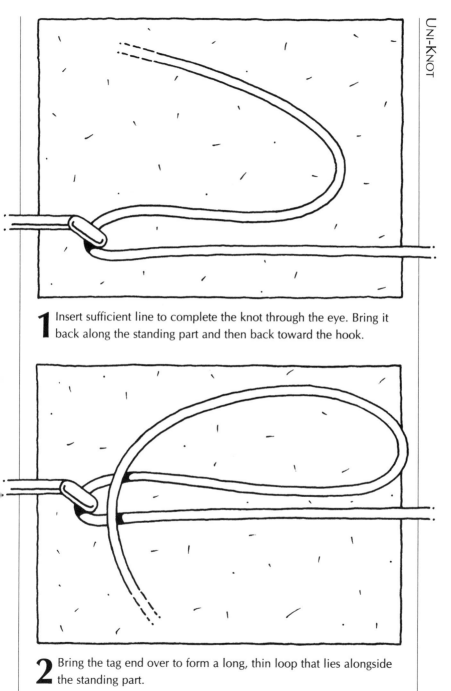

1 Insert sufficient line to complete the knot through the eye. Bring it back along the standing part and then back toward the hook.

2 Bring the tag end over to form a long, thin loop that lies alongside the standing part.

23

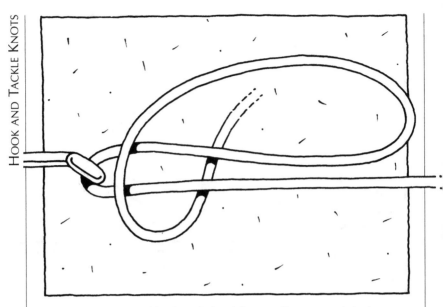

3 Bring the tag end back up behind the standing part and the lower section of the loop.

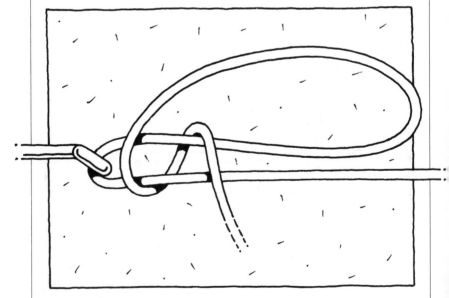

4 Bring the tag end out through the loop, to make the first turn around the standing part and the lower section of the loop.

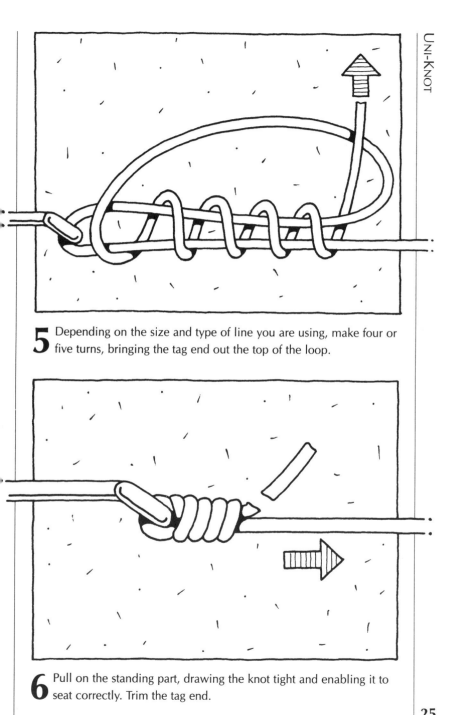

5 Depending on the size and type of line you are using, make four or five turns, bringing the tag end out the top of the loop.

6 Pull on the standing part, drawing the knot tight and enabling it to seat correctly. Trim the tag end.

DOUBLE TURLE KNOT

This knot is used exclusively for tying flies with up- or downturned eyes to tippets. It is not suitable for straight-eyed hooks. It is designed to allow an excellent fly presentation by keeping the fly in line with your cast.

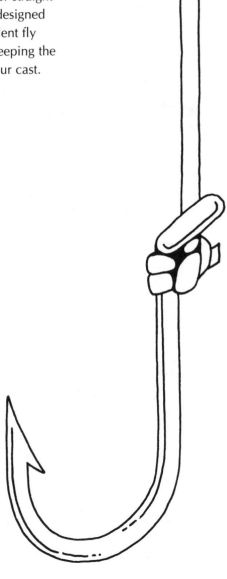

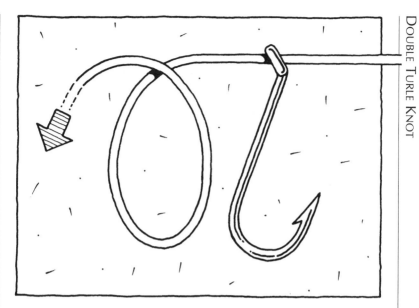

1 Insert sufficient line to complete the knot through the eye of the hook. Form a small loop.

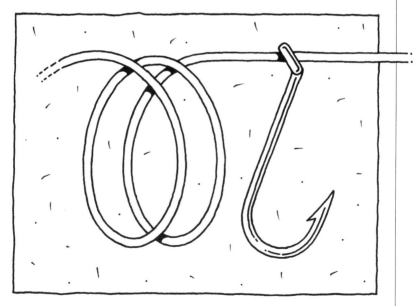

2 Bring the tag end around to create another, identical loop. This loop sits on top of the first one.

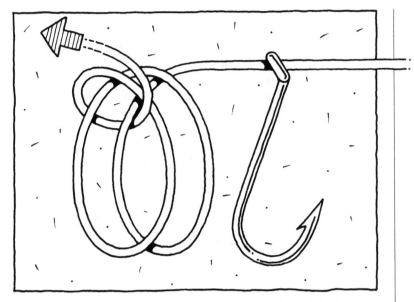

3 Continue bringing the tag end around, taking it through both loops and bringing it out at the top of the loops.

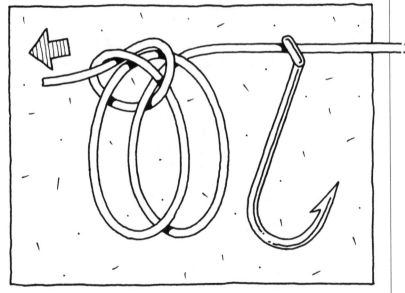

4 Tie an overhand knot around the the two loops, but don't tighten it completely. (This will allow for final adjustments.)

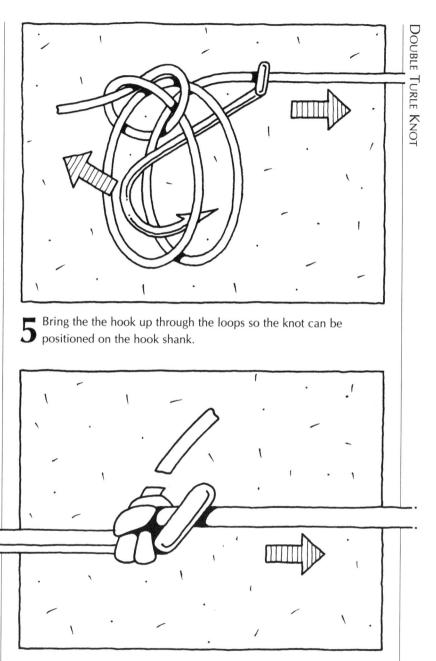

5 Bring the the hook up through the loops so the knot can be positioned on the hook shank.

6 Pull on the standing part, drawing the knot tight and enabling it to seat correctly on the hook shank. Trim the tag end.

GEORGE HARVEY DRY-FLY KNOT

Developed by fly-fishing
expert George Harvey, this
knot is specifically designed
for attaching a dry fly to a
tippet. Tied correctly, it is a
very secure knot that will
help you make a precise
and delicate dry-fly
presentation.

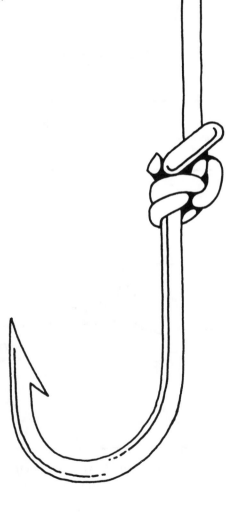

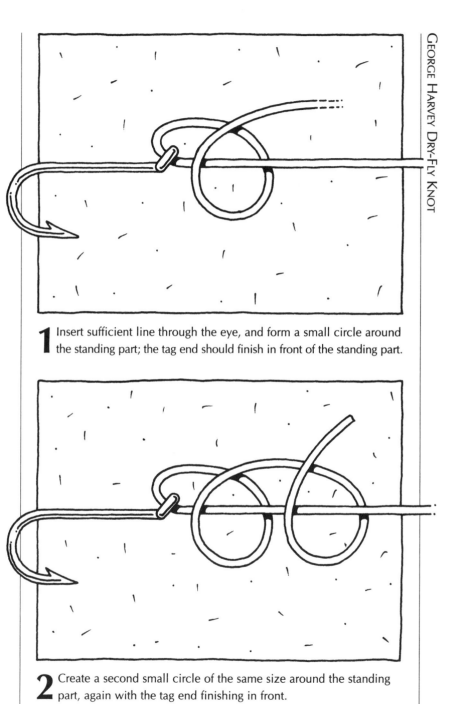

1 Insert sufficient line through the eye, and form a small circle around the standing part; the tag end should finish in front of the standing part.

2 Create a second small circle of the same size around the standing part, again with the tag end finishing in front.

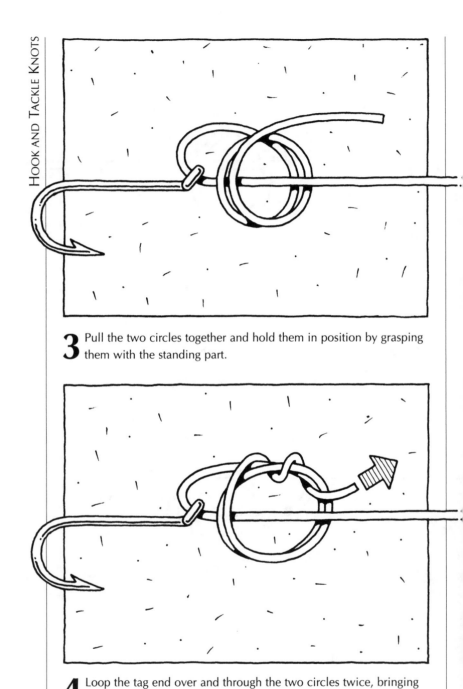

3 Pull the two circles together and hold them in position by grasping them with the standing part.

4 Loop the tag end over and through the two circles twice, bringing the tag end out in the opposite direction to the hook.

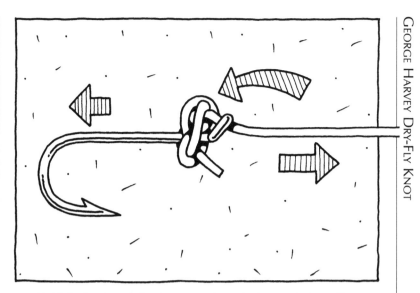

5 Hold the hook and slowly start to draw the knot tight by pulling on the standing part. If the knot is tied correctly, the loops will slide back and jump over the eye of the hook as it is drawn up.

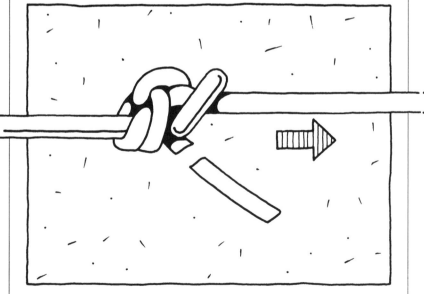

6 Continue to pull on the standing part, drawing the knot tight and enabling it to seat correctly. Trim the tag end.

NONSLIP MONO KNOT

This knot is designed to give artificial lures a more attractive action in the water. The knot forms a loop that doesn't slip, and allows the lure to move around more. The number of turns required when tying this knot will differ with various types and sizes of line. Try seven turns for fine monofilament, fewer turns with heavier line.

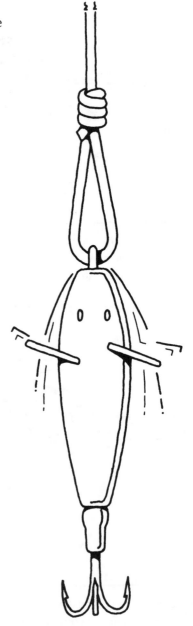

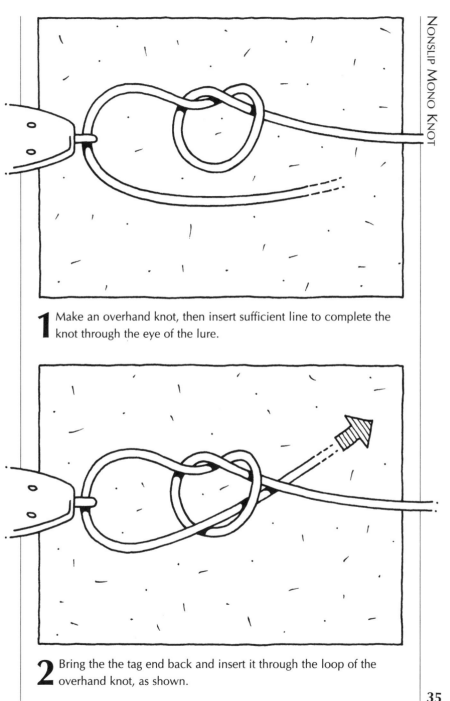

1 Make an overhand knot, then insert sufficient line to complete the knot through the eye of the lure.

2 Bring the the tag end back and insert it through the loop of the overhand knot, as shown.

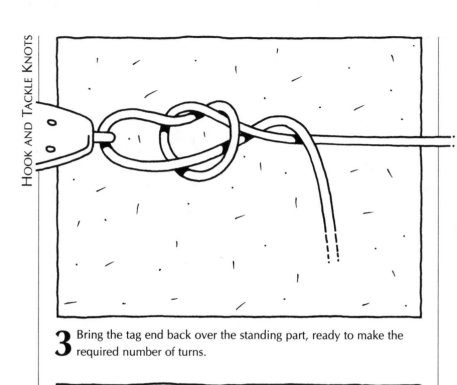

3 Bring the tag end back over the standing part, ready to make the required number of turns.

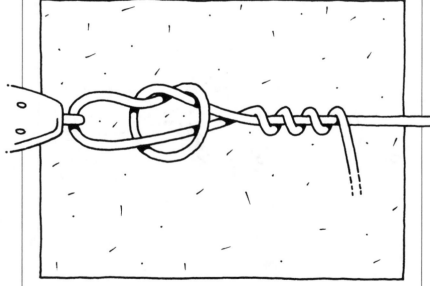

4 Depending on the size and type of line you are using, make the required number of turns.

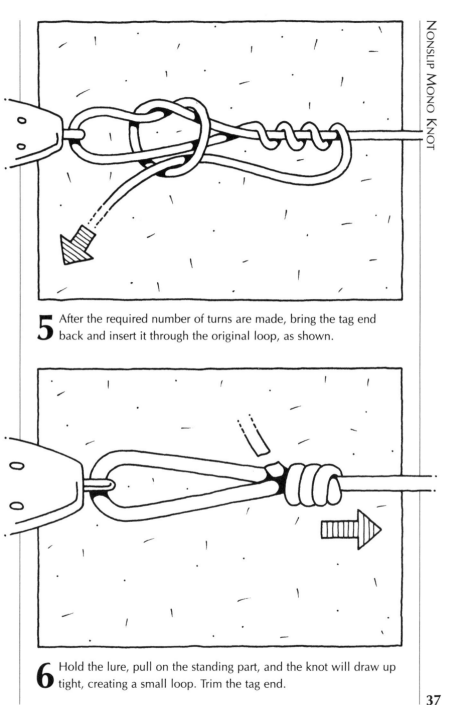

5 After the required number of turns are made, bring the tag end back and insert it through the original loop, as shown.

6 Hold the lure, pull on the standing part, and the knot will draw up tight, creating a small loop. Trim the tag end.

PALOMAR KNOT

This is a quick and effective knot for tying onto swivels, lures, and sinkers. It uses more line than other knots; allow for this when tying.

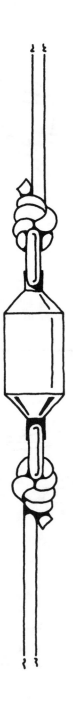

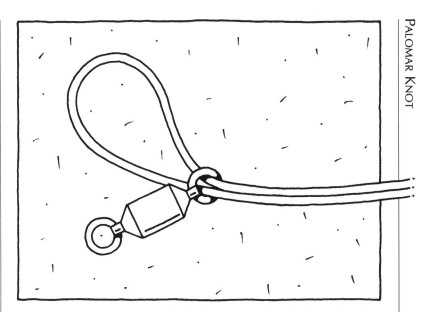

1 Insert a loop of sufficient double line to complete the knot through the eye of the swivel, lure, or sinker.

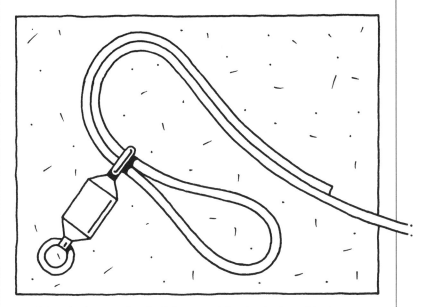

2 Bring the loop and swivel, lure, or sinker back alongside the standing part.

39

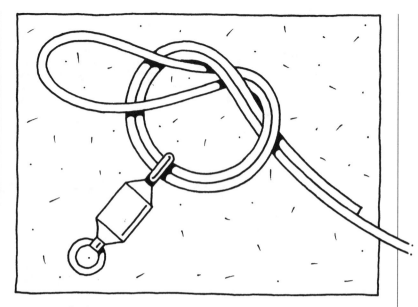

3 Bring the loop around and make an overhand knot, as shown above.

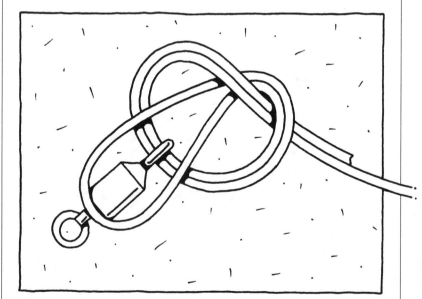

4 Bring the loop back down and position it over the top of the swivel, lure, or sinker.

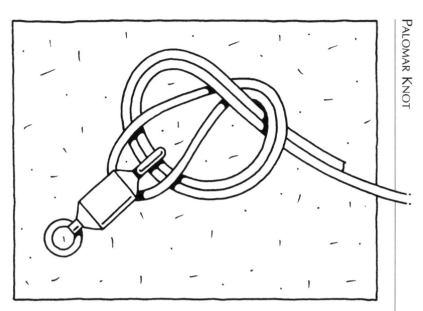

5 Hold the tag end and the standing part together, and pull the swivel, lure, or sinker out through the loop.

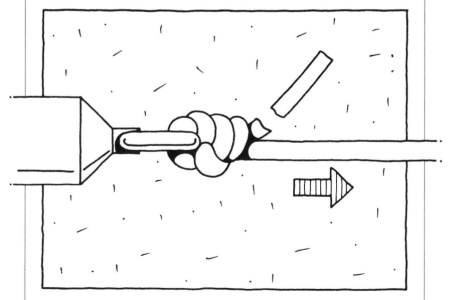

6 Pull on the standing part and the tag end together, drawing the knot tight and enabling it to seat correctly. Trim the tag end.

41

SNELLING AN EYED HOOK

The snell is still widely used by saltwater fishermen, but is often overlooked by other anglers. Tied correctly, it is a very secure knot for attaching an eyed hook to a line.

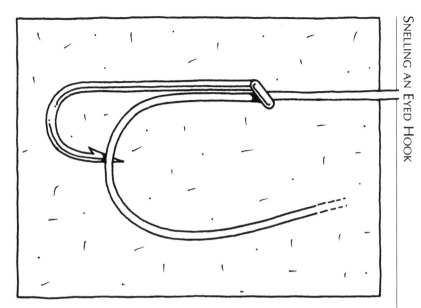

1 Insert sufficient line to complete the knot through the eye, and then turn it back in the direction of the standing part.

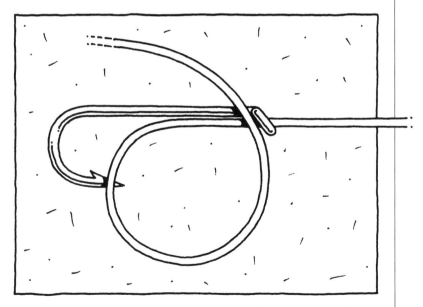

2 Bring the tag end up to form a large loop. This loop needs to lie along the hook shank.

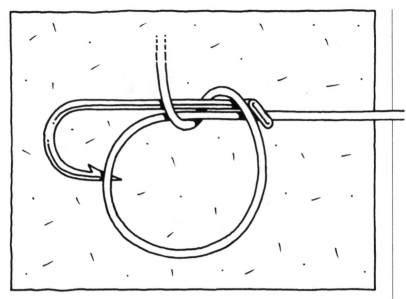

3 Bring the tag end down to create the first turn around the loop and the hook shank.

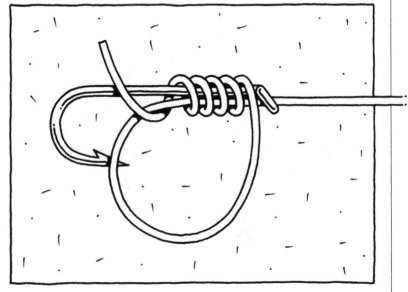

4 Depending on the size and type of line you are using, make five or six turns away from the hook eye toward the hook point.

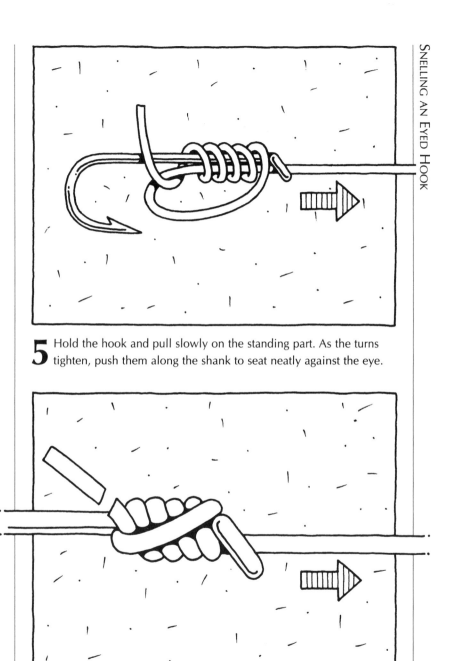

5 Hold the hook and pull slowly on the standing part. As the turns tighten, push them along the shank to seat neatly against the eye.

6 Continue to pull the standing part, drawing the knot tight and enabling it to seat correctly. Trim the tag end.

SPADE-END KNOT

Still a popular alternative to an eyed hook is the spade-end hook. This knot is designed specifically for tying this type of hook to a line. Take care to seat the knot correctly around the hook shank.

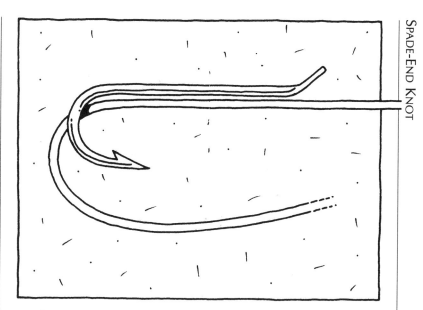

1 Place sufficient line to complete the knot alongside the shank of the hook, and bring the tag end back toward the standing part.

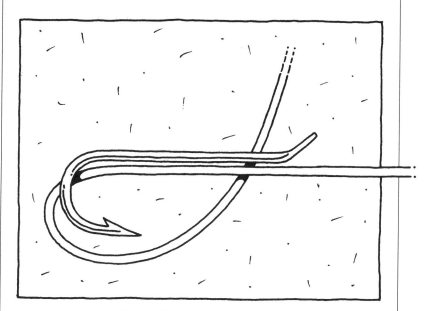

2 Bring the tag end up and behind the hook shank and standing part to form a large loop.

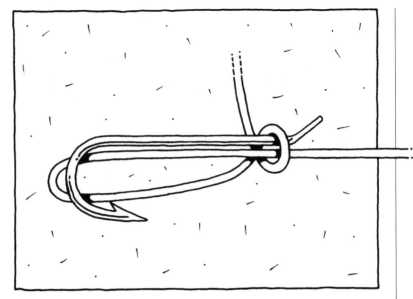

3 Bring the tag end over to form the first turn. This first turn also tightens the standing part and the loop against the hook shank.

4 Depending on the size and type of line you are using, make five or six turns away from the spade end, and bring the tag end out of the loop.

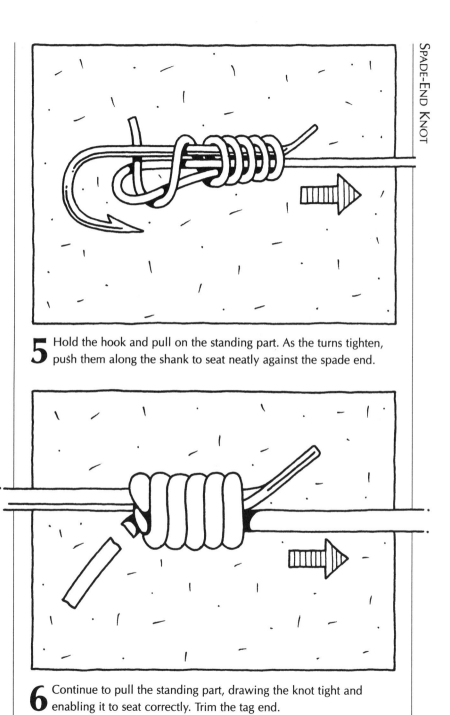

5 Hold the hook and pull on the standing part. As the turns tighten, push them along the shank to seat neatly against the spade end.

6 Continue to pull the standing part, drawing the knot tight and enabling it to seat correctly. Trim the tag end.

49

2
JOINING LINES

The joining of two lines is one of the most important connections in a tackle system.

The four tested and reliable knots in this section, when correctly tied, will provide secure connections. Because of the wide variety of line materials and sizes available, the number of turns required in each knot will differ. A general guideline is given, but a certain amount of experimentation may be required for you to achieve the optimum number of turns.

BLOOD KNOT

This longtime favorite fishing knot is still one of the most effective ways to join two lines, especially monofilament lines that are of the same or similar diameters. Having an equal number of turns on both sides of the knot helps absorb strain and shock.

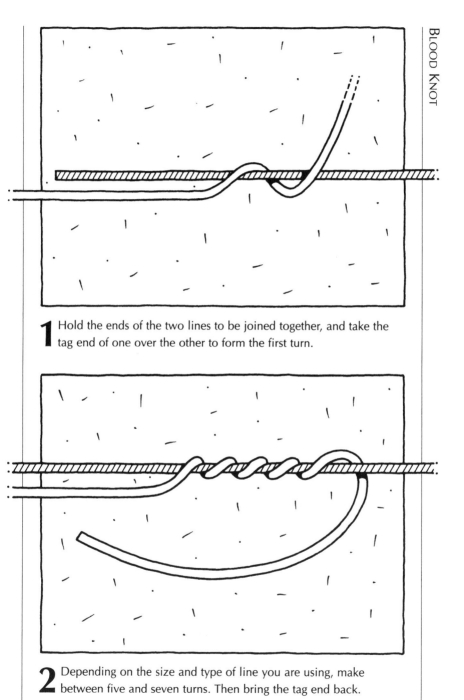

1 Hold the ends of the two lines to be joined together, and take the tag end of one over the other to form the first turn.

2 Depending on the size and type of line you are using, make between five and seven turns. Then bring the tag end back.

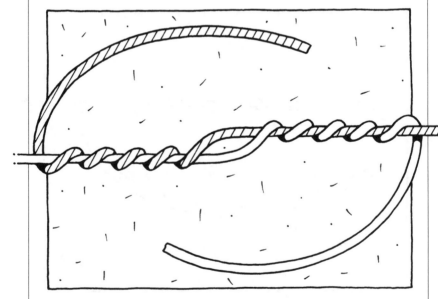

3 Holding the lines and turns in position, take the tag end of the other line and start to make a turn, as shown.

4 Make an equal number of turns, taking care to leave a clear division between the two sets of turns.

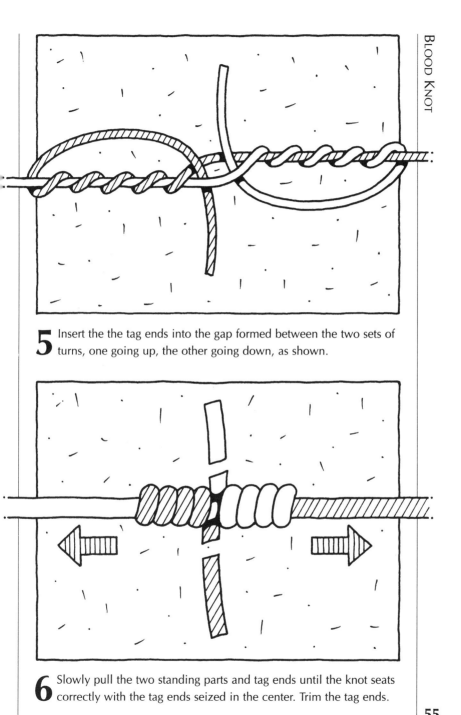

5 Insert the the tag ends into the gap formed between the two sets of turns, one going up, the other going down, as shown.

6 Slowly pull the two standing parts and tag ends until the knot seats correctly with the tag ends seized in the center. Trim the tag ends.

DOUBLE UNI-KNOT

Also known as the **double grinner knot,** this knot uses the tying principle of two knots tied back to back and then seated together to form a strong connection. With practice, it is easy to tie and very effective.

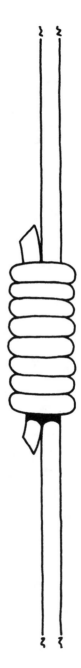

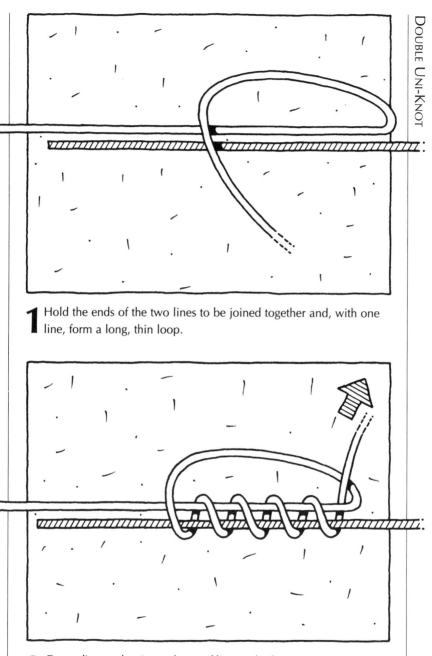

1 Hold the ends of the two lines to be joined together and, with one line, form a long, thin loop.

2 Depending on the size and type of line, make five to seven turns around both lines, bringing the tag end out the end of the loop.

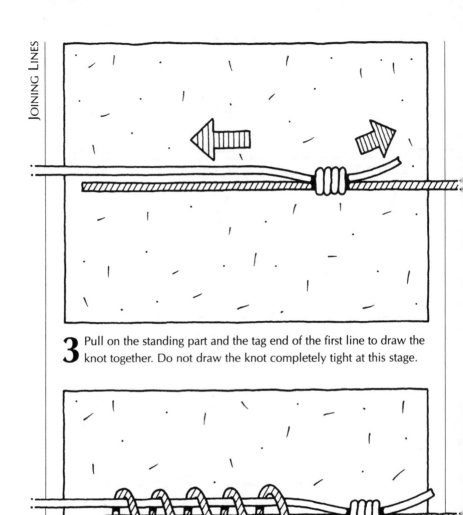

3 Pull on the standing part and the tag end of the first line to draw the knot together. Do not draw the knot completely tight at this stage.

4 With the second line, create a knot identical to the one you created with the first line, except the other way around.

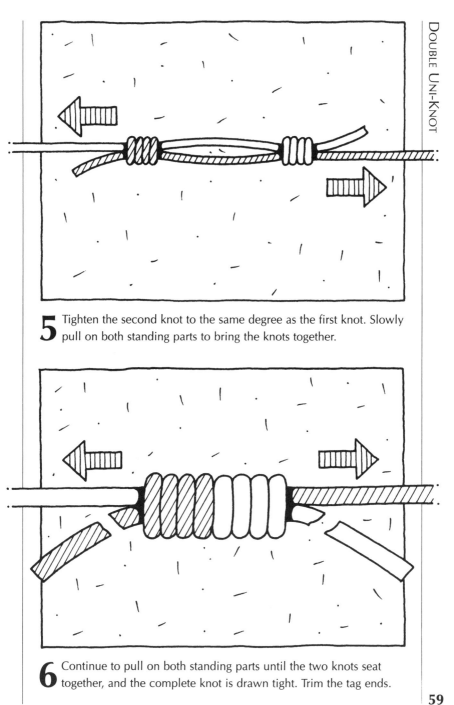

5 Tighten the second knot to the same degree as the first knot. Slowly pull on both standing parts to bring the knots together.

6 Continue to pull on both standing parts until the two knots seat together, and the complete knot is drawn tight. Trim the tag ends.

Surgeon's Knot

Also known as the **water knot,**
this is one of the best all-around
knots for joining two lines. The
lines need to be of the same or
similar diameters and types for
this knot to be effective. If you
find it difficult to tie from the
diagrams, just remember that
one of the lines—in most
cases the leader—needs to
be short enough to pass
through the loop.

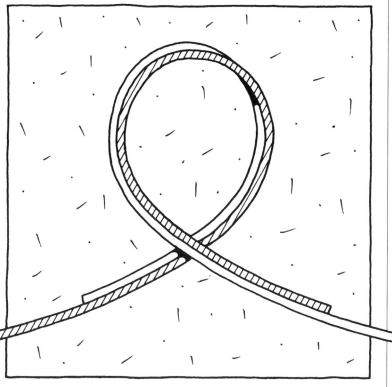

1 Hold sufficient lengths of the two lines side by side. In the illustration above, the unshaded clear line is the shorter one.

2 Hold both lines together and twist them over to form an open loop, as shown above.

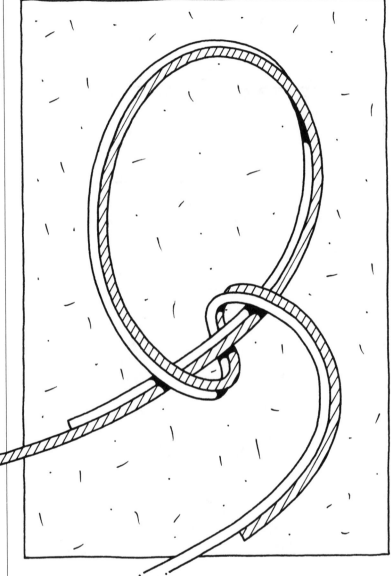

3 Make a first turn as shown. The unshaded clear line is short enough to pass through the loop. It is important to keep the loop open at this stage in order to make more turns.

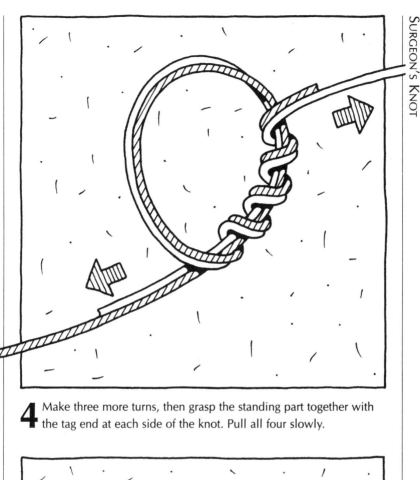

4 Make three more turns, then grasp the standing part together with the tag end at each side of the knot. Pull all four slowly.

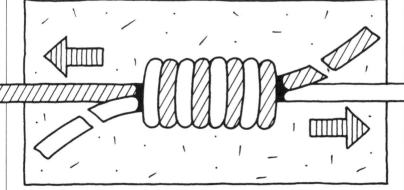

5 Continue to pull the standing parts and the tag ends, drawing the knot tight and enabling it to seat correctly. Trim the tag ends.

ALBRIGHT KNOT

This is one of the most reliable
fishing knots for joining two
lines of unequal diameters and
different materials. A good
time to use this knot, for
example, is when you're
connecting monofilament
backing to a fly line.

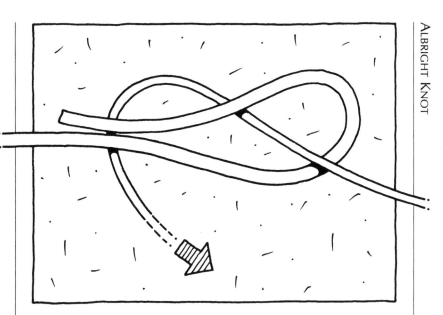

1 Create a loop in the tag end of the heavier line, then feed the tag end of the lighter line through the loop.

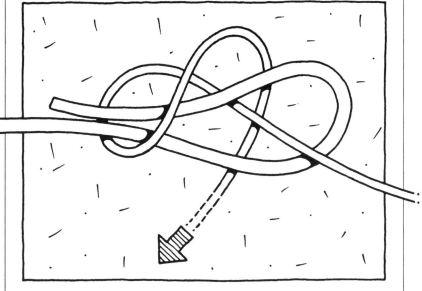

2 Bring the tag end up and over the loop to create the first turn, as shown above.

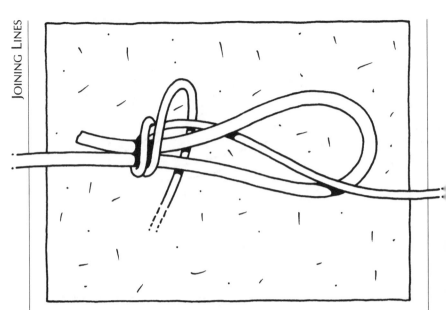

3 Make a series of turns around all three strands from left to right.
Keep the turns as tight as possible.

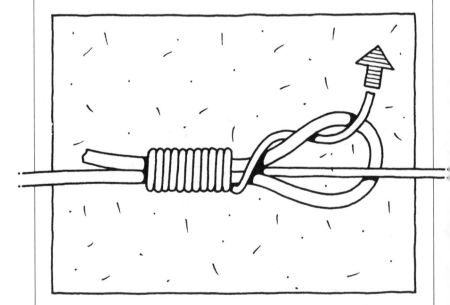

4 Depending on the size and type of line, make a minimum of 10 turns,
bringing the tag end out the end of the heavier line's loop.

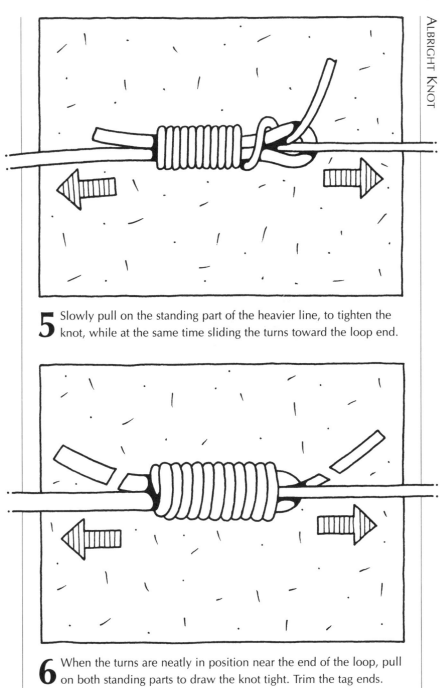

5 Slowly pull on the standing part of the heavier line, to tighten the knot, while at the same time sliding the turns toward the loop end.

6 When the turns are neatly in position near the end of the loop, pull on both standing parts to draw the knot tight. Trim the tag ends.

67

3
LOOPS

Correctly tied loops are exceptionally strong, and for many anglers the interlocking-loop system (see page 56) is an integral part of the tackle system.

Loops have a wide range of fishing applications, and the interlocking-loop system provides the perfect answer for any line connection that needs to be changed frequently. A good example is being able to change a premade leader quickly and efficiently while fishing. Because no actual knot tying is involved, this can be a real advantage in adverse weather conditions or poor light.

SURGEON'S LOOP

This reliable and widely used loop uses the same tying method as the surgeon's knot (see page 60), except it is constructed from a single length of line. It is also known as the **double loop.**

An interlocking-loop system created with two surgeon's loops.

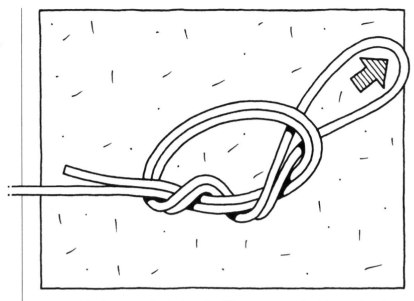

1 Double the tag end of a length of line, create a double overhand knot as shown above, and then slowly pull the loop through.

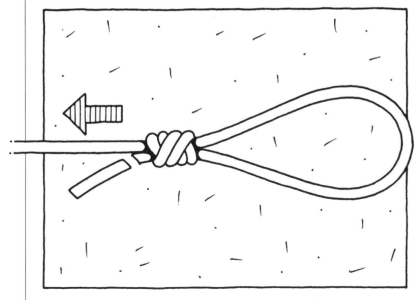

2 Finalize the size of the loop required, then draw the knot tight by holding the loop and pulling the standing part. Trim the tag end.

DROPPER LOOP

This extremely useful loop is used by a wide range of anglers; to many, it is known as the **blood loop.** It creates a loop at right angles to the main line. Fly fishermen use it to attach additional flies, known as droppers, while other anglers use it to attach sinkers and extra hooks to a line.

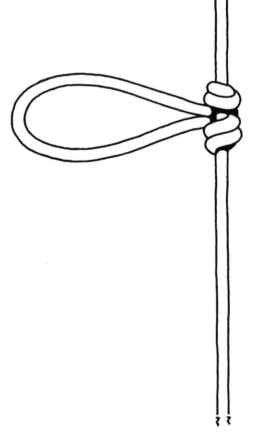

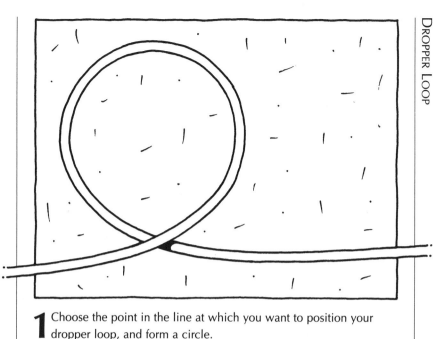

1 Choose the point in the line at which you want to position your dropper loop, and form a circle.

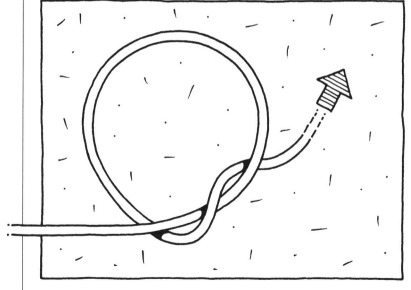

2 The size of the circle will determine the size of your dropper loop. Create the first turn with an overhand knot.

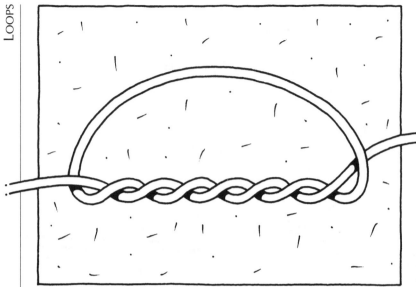

3 Depending on the size and type of line, make three or four turns in total, and position the knot as shown above.

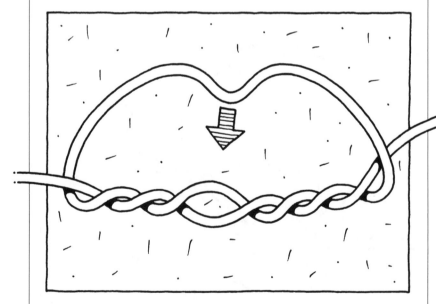

4 Create a slightly larger gap in the center of the turns, and bring the top of the main loop down to form the dropper loop.

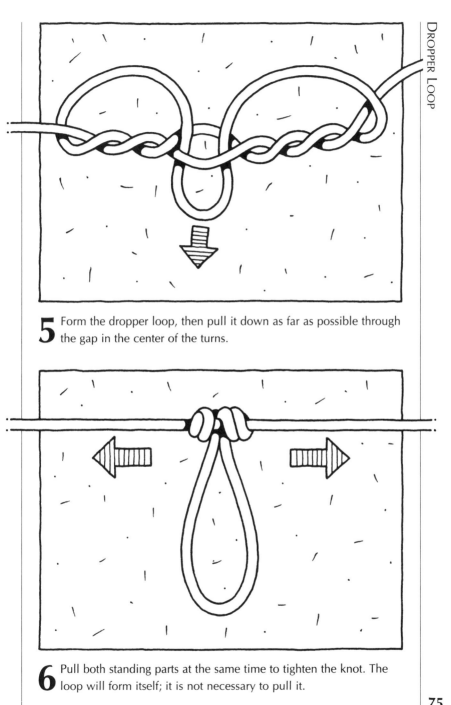

5 Form the dropper loop, then pull it down as far as possible through the gap in the center of the turns.

6 Pull both standing parts at the same time to tighten the knot. The loop will form itself; it is not necessary to pull it.

PERFECTION LOOP

This knot creates a very strong
and reliable end loop; leaders
and tippets can be easily
attached to it.

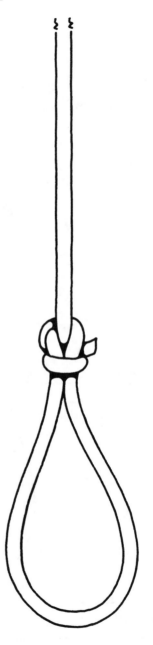

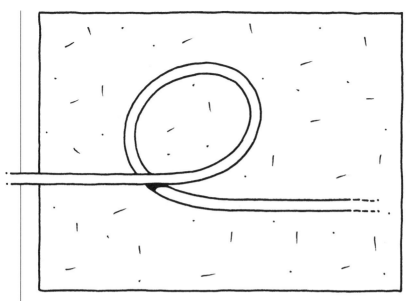

1 Create a loop near the end of the line, as shown, then hold that loop in position.

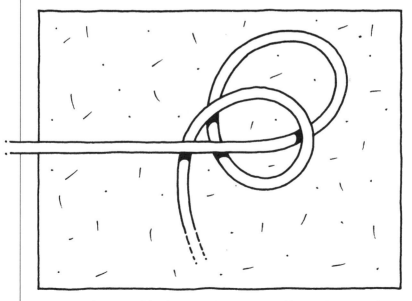

2 Bring the tag end back over to form a second loop. The tag end should now be positioned behind the standing part.

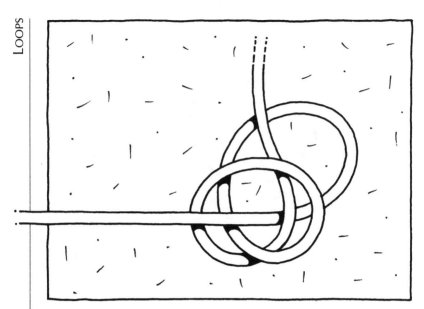

3 Bring the tag end back up and position it between the two loops, as shown above.

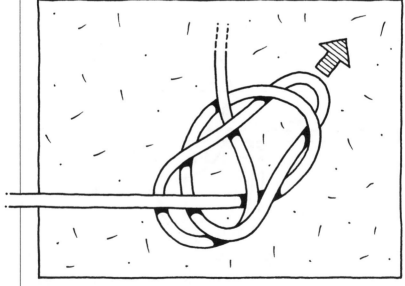

4 Grasp the front loop, form it into a narrower loop, and then push it through the rear loop.

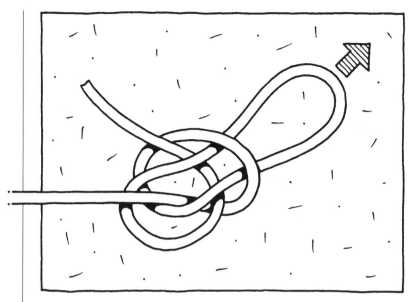

5 Pull the loop through as far as possible. You can still adjust the size of the loop at this stage, if desired.

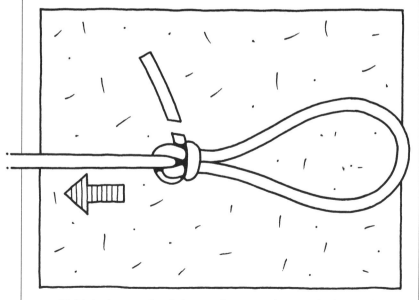

6 Hold the loop and pull the standing part, drawing the knot tight and enabling it to seat correctly. Trim the tag end.

Bimini Twist

This knot creates a loop that will give 100 percent knot strength. It is tied at the tag end of the line to form a main connection that other line or tackle can be secured to. It may take a little time to perfect, but once mastered, it provides one of the most secure loops possible.

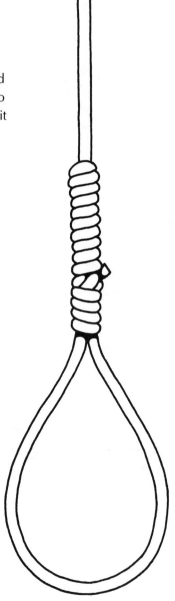

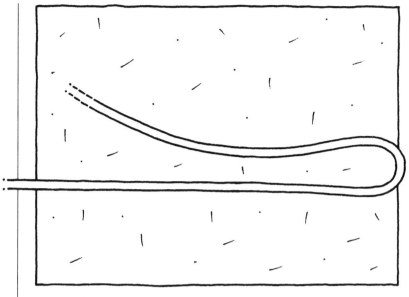

1 Double the line back against the standing part. Depending on the number of turns used, this knot will require a long length of line.

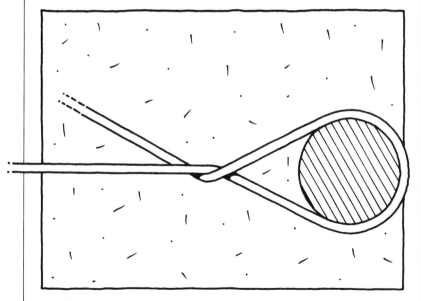

2 The first stage of this knot is best tied around a solid object. Take the line around the object and create the first turn, as shown.

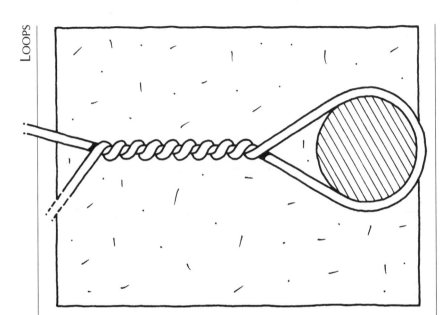

3 Depending on the line you're using, make between 8 and 20 turns. Fifteen turns are recommended for regular monofilament.

4 It is very important to keep pressure on both the standing part and the tag end, to keep the turns as tight as possible.

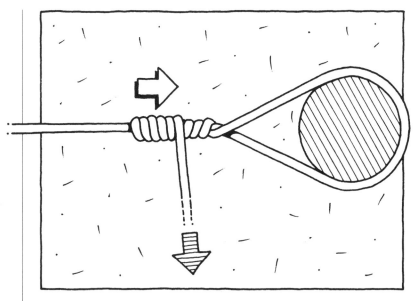

5 Make approximately the same number of turns back over the original turns in the direction of the solid object.

6 At this point, remove the loop from the solid object, and create a holding knot with the tag end.

7 Still keeping pressure on the standing part and the loop, tighten the holding knot and bring the tag end out.

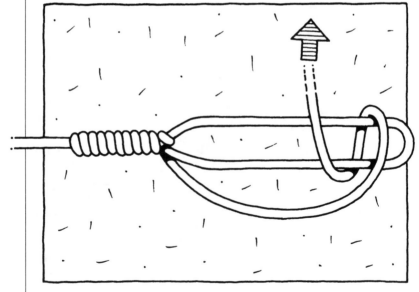

8 Holding the knot in the position shown above, make a turn around the narrowed loop with the tag end.

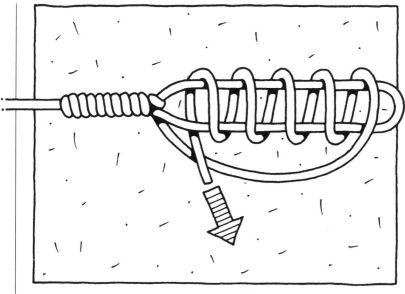

9 Make four or five turns, and then pull slowly on the tag end to seat this series of turns back against the original turns.

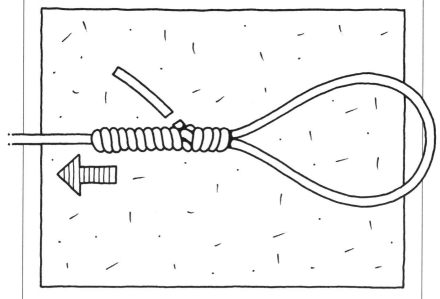

10 With the second series of turns seated correctly, hold the loop and pull the standing part to finalize the knot. Trim the tag end.

85

4
FLY-LINE KNOTS

A fly line requires a secure knot at both ends—to attach the backing line at one end, and to attach the butt section of the leader at the other.

This section covers various methods of tying these knots, some of which can initially prove difficult. Follow the instructions closely and practice before tying the final knot. If you are not totally confident with your knots, seek help from your local tackle store. In most cases, the owner will be only too pleased to help out.

NAIL KNOT

This knot is used to attach
backing line or a leader to
a fly line. It is tied with
assistance of a small-diameter
nail or needle. The nail or
needle acts to stiffen the fly
line and help form the knot.

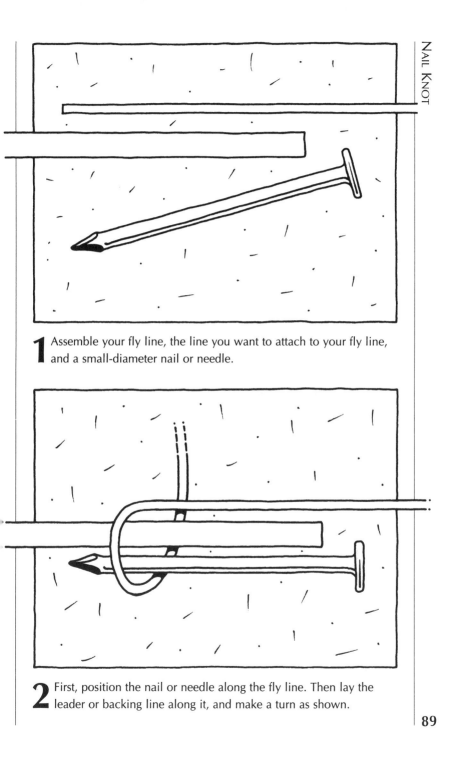

1 Assemble your fly line, the line you want to attach to your fly line, and a small-diameter nail or needle.

2 First, position the nail or needle along the fly line. Then lay the leader or backing line along it, and make a turn as shown.

89

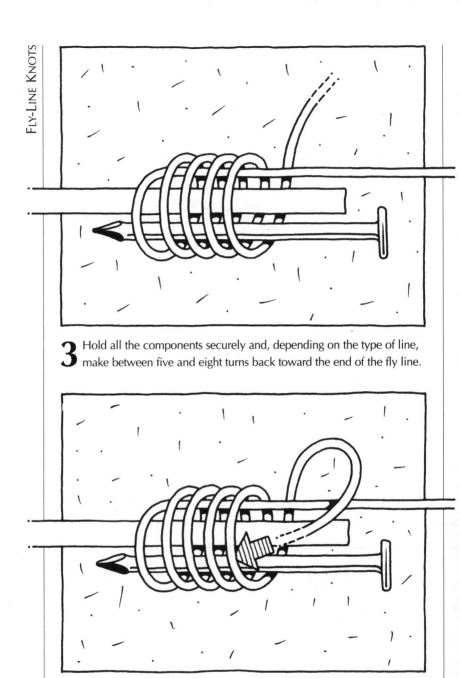

3 Hold all the components securely and, depending on the type of line, make between five and eight turns back toward the end of the fly line.

4 Bring the tag end over, ready to push along the channel created by the nail or needle.

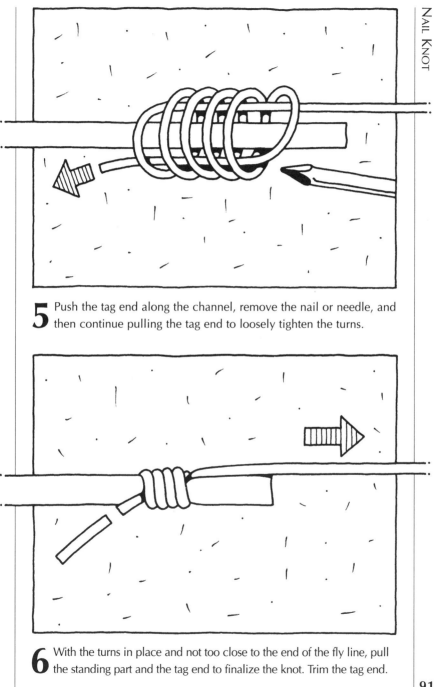

5 Push the tag end along the channel, remove the nail or needle, and then continue pulling the tag end to loosely tighten the turns.

6 With the turns in place and not too close to the end of the fly line, pull the standing part and the tag end to finalize the knot. Trim the tag end.

NEEDLE KNOT

This knot creates the best
solution for joining a
monofilament leader to a fly
line. It is a very neat and
smooth connection that is
extremely strong. It will not
snag on rod guides, or pick
up debris in the water.

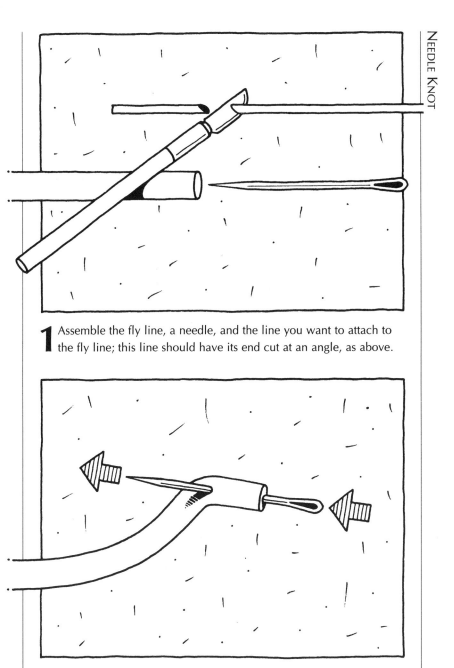

1 Assemble the fly line, a needle, and the line you want to attach to the fly line; this line should have its end cut at an angle, as above.

2 Push the needle along the center of the fly line, and then bend the fly line to allow the needle to exit.

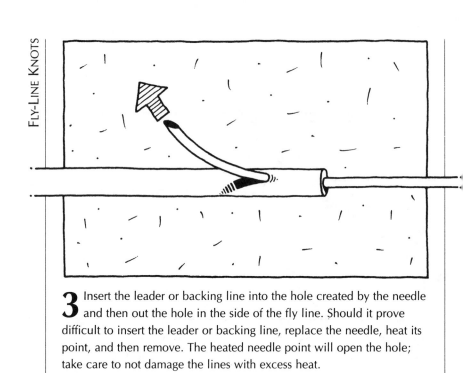

3 Insert the leader or backing line into the hole created by the needle and then out the hole in the side of the fly line. Should it prove difficult to insert the leader or backing line, replace the needle, heat its point, and then remove. The heated needle point will open the hole; take care to not damage the lines with excess heat.

4 Position the needle along the side of the fly line, and make a turn with the tag end of the leader or backing line.

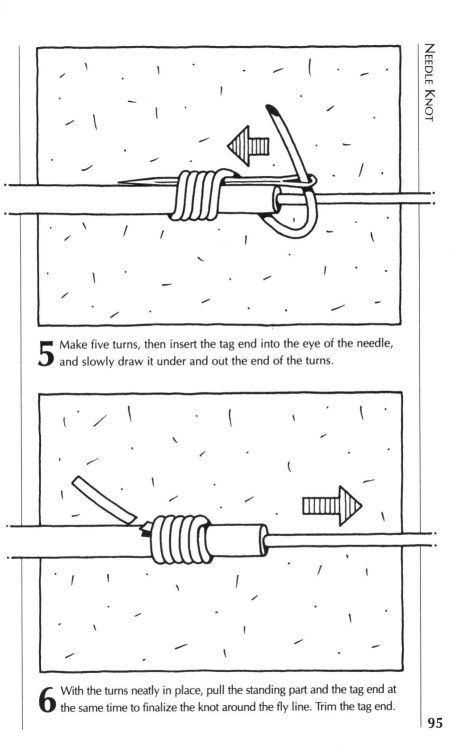

5 Make five turns, then insert the tag end into the eye of the needle, and slowly draw it under and out the end of the turns.

6 With the turns neatly in place, pull the standing part and the tag end at the same time to finalize the knot around the fly line. Trim the tag end.

95

NEEDLE MONO LOOP

This is a good alternative to the needle knot (see page 92) if you prefer a loop at the end of your fly line to make interlocking-loop connections. The tying method is the same as for the needle knot, except you use a doubled monofilament line.

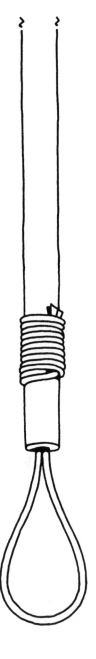

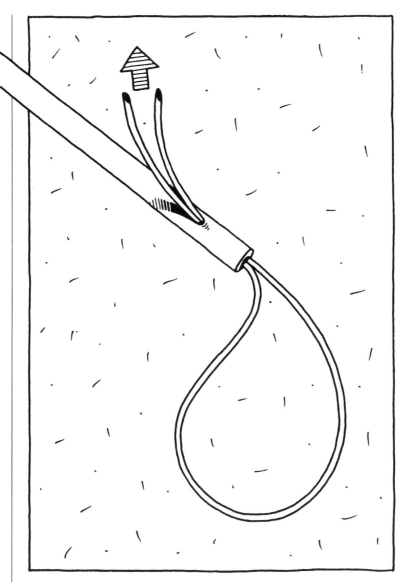

1 Create the hole in the fly line in exactly the same way as the needle knot (see pages 93 and 94). But instead of inserting a single piece of line, insert a piece of line that has been doubled to form a loop at the end of the fly line. Determine the size of loop you require at this stage.

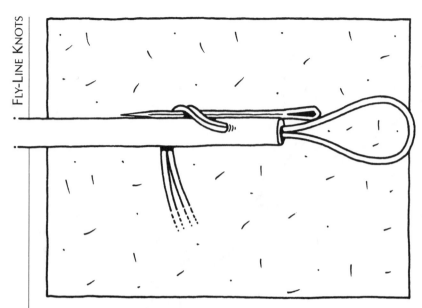

3 With the size of the loop determined, lay the needle along the fly line and start to make the first turn with the two strands of line.

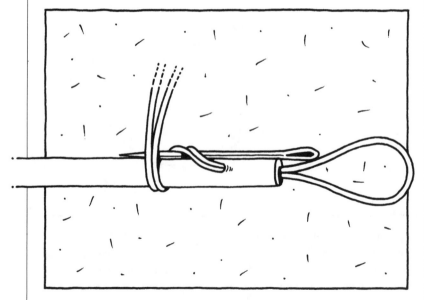

4 Continue the first turn. Because two strands of line are being used, it is important that all the strands seat tightly against each other.

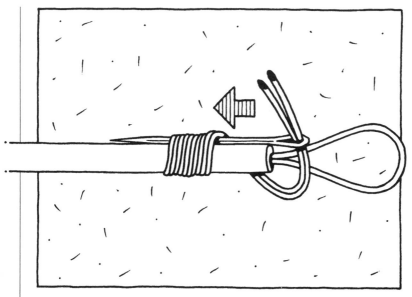

5 Make three to five turns, then insert the tag ends into the eye of the needle, and slowly draw them under and out of the end of the turns.

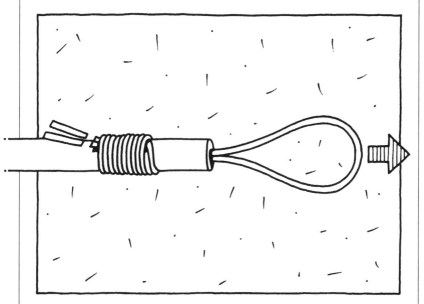

6 With the turns neatly in place, pull the loop and the tag ends at the same time to finalize the knot around the fly line. Trim the tag ends.

99

TUBE NAIL/NEEDLE KNOT

If you find tying the nail knot
(see page 88) or the needle
knot (see page 92) difficult,
substitute a small, hollow tube
for the nail or needle. The
tube will need to be stiff
enough to provide support to
the fly line while you form the
knot, and wide enough to be
able to pass the line through.

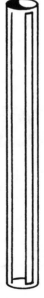

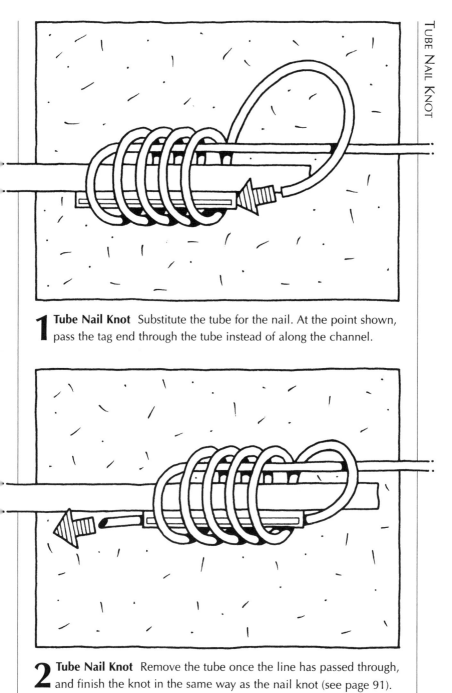

1 **Tube Nail Knot** Substitute the tube for the nail. At the point shown, pass the tag end through the tube instead of along the channel.

2 **Tube Nail Knot** Remove the tube once the line has passed through, and finish the knot in the same way as the nail knot (see page 91).

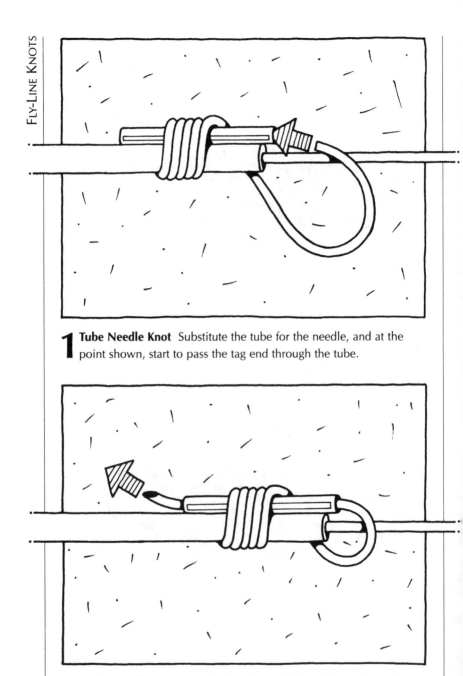

1 **Tube Needle Knot** Substitute the tube for the needle, and at the point shown, start to pass the tag end through the tube.

2 **Tube Needle Knot** Pass the line through the tube. Be sure to keep the the turns tight and in place.

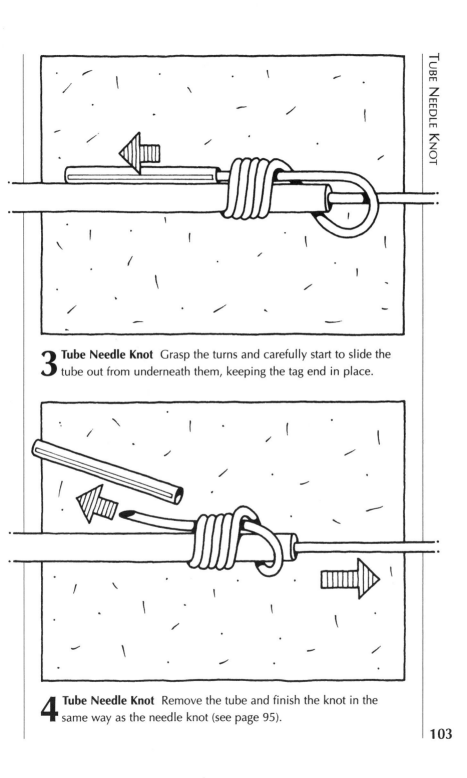

3 **Tube Needle Knot** Grasp the turns and carefully start to slide the
tube out from underneath them, keeping the tag end in place.

4 **Tube Needle Knot** Remove the tube and finish the knot in the
same way as the needle knot (see page 95).

103

EMERGENCY NAIL KNOT

If your nail or needle knot
breaks while you are fishing,
it is possible to solve the
problem by creating an
emergency nail knot
with a strong piece
of monofilament.

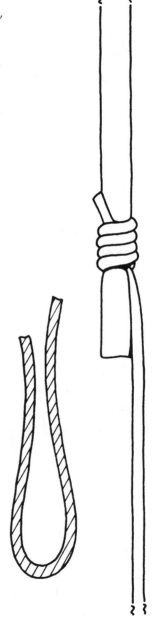

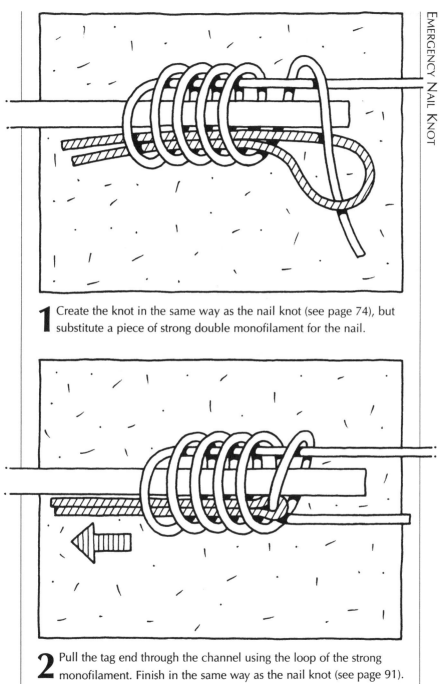

1 Create the knot in the same way as the nail knot (see page 74), but substitute a piece of strong double monofilament for the nail.

2 Pull the tag end through the channel using the loop of the strong monofilament. Finish in the same way as the nail knot (see page 91).

105

5
BOAT KNOTS

And finally, three secure boat knots. Many anglers fish from boats, and it is always useful to know the correct knots for tying up your craft.

Although these knots are referred to as "boat knots," like all knots they can have endless applications. For example, the quick-release knot (see page 114) can be used for any type of temporary fastening—from tying up your boat to tying up your dog!

PILE HITCH

This very neat and practical knot is ideal for a temporary mooring. Its big advantage is that you can tie and untie it very quickly.

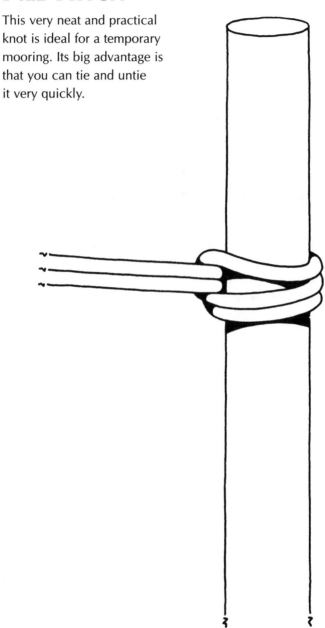

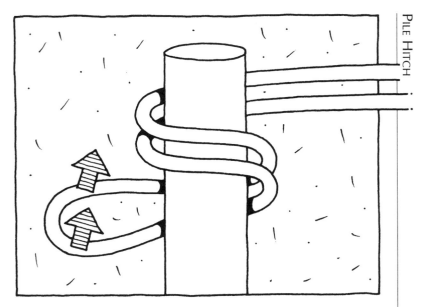

1 Double the end section of a rope and wrap it around a mooring post, leaving a loop big enough to pull back over the post.

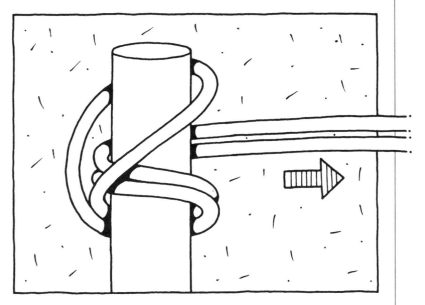

2 Pull the loop over the top of the post, and then pull on the standing part to tighten and secure the knot.

109

ANCHOR BEND

This knot is one of the most secure and widely used hitches for securing a boat to a ring or mooring post. It can also, as its name suggests, be used for tying to an anchor ring. For extra safety, a stopper knot can be added in the form of an additional half hitch.

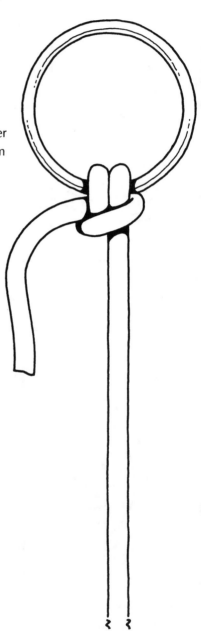

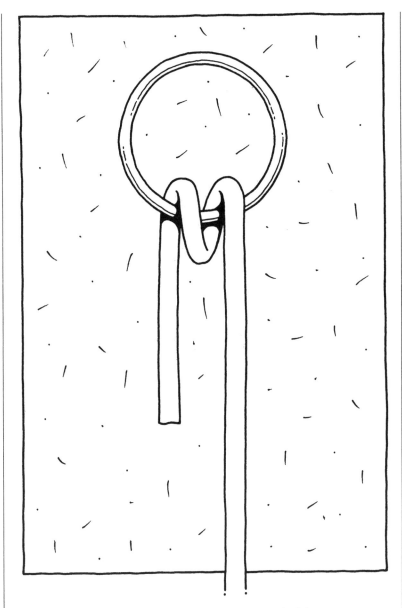

1 Make two turns around the ring with the tag end of the rope, as shown above.

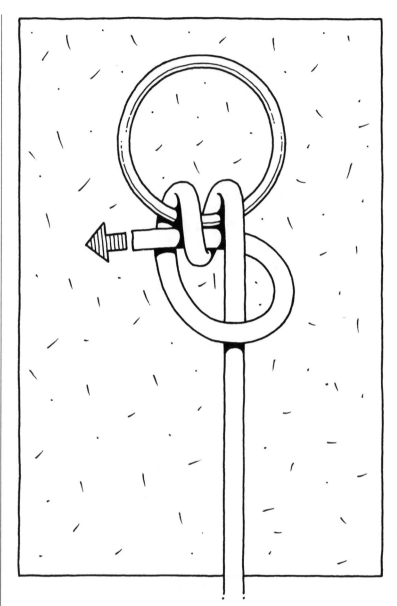

2 Bring the tag end around the standing part and through the lower part of the turn.

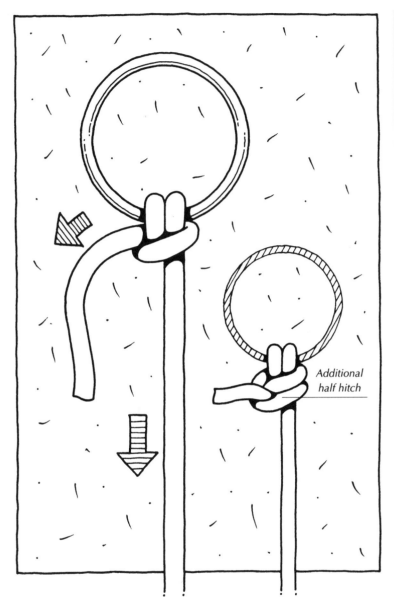

Additional half hitch

3 Pull on the tag end and standing part until the knot is secure. At this point, an additional half hitch can be added for extra security.

QUICK-RELEASE KNOT

This extremely useful knot, also known as the **draw hitch,** can be used in any situation that requires a quick release. The standing part can be put under great tension—but with one pull on the tag end, the knot is undone.

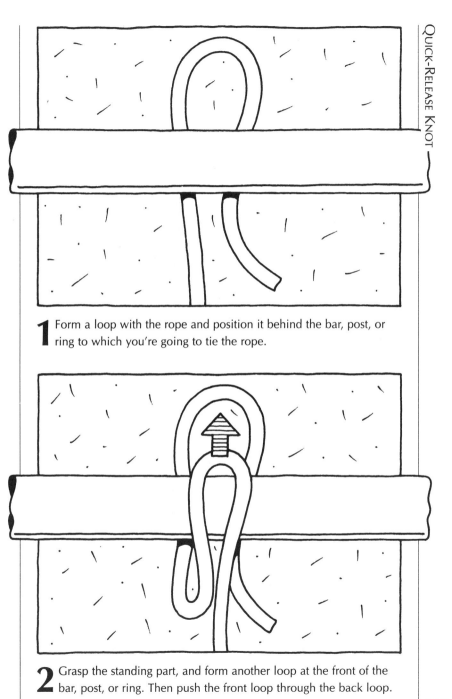

1 Form a loop with the rope and position it behind the bar, post, or ring to which you're going to tie the rope.

2 Grasp the standing part, and form another loop at the front of the bar, post, or ring. Then push the front loop through the back loop.

115

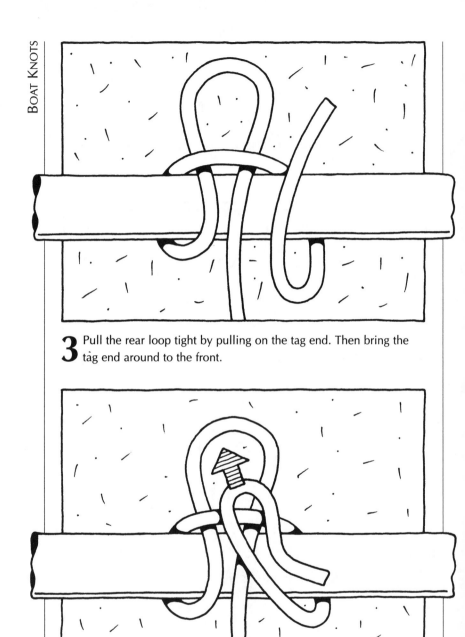

3 Pull the rear loop tight by pulling on the tag end. Then bring the tag end around to the front.

4 Grasp the tag end and form a third loop. This loop is now pushed through the remaining loop.

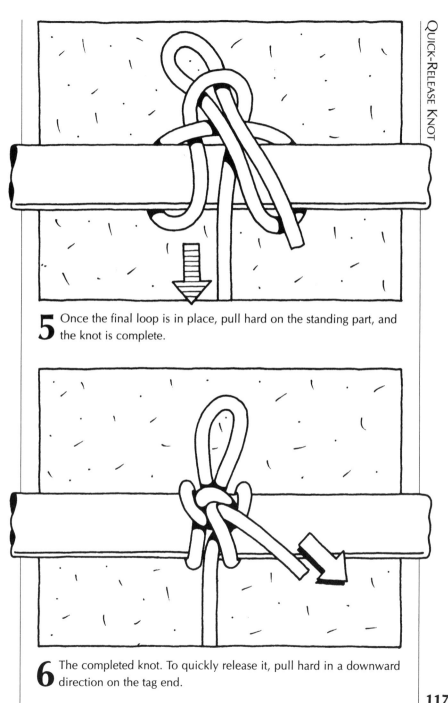

5 Once the final loop is in place, pull hard on the standing part, and the knot is complete.

6 The completed knot. To quickly release it, pull hard in a downward direction on the tag end.

117

CAMPING KNOTS

CONTENTS

INTRODUCTION

Camping, like many outdoor activities, has undergone some revolutionary changes in recent years. Many more people now have the free recreational time and the access to spend time camping, backpacking, and exploring wild areas. But undoubtably one of the biggest changes has been in the equipment that is now available to anyone who wants to venture into the outdoors. The highly developed camping equipment and apparel of today is, in the main, manufactured or constructed from the very latest high-tech, light-weight materials. All ropes and cords are now made from artificial or synthetic materials. There is a vast range of "camping gadgets" available to cope with almost anything that you will need to survive in the outdoors. Arguably the only components that have changed very little over recent years, but are still absolutely essential, are the range of knots that all campers should know.

The Book of Camping Knots gives you the opportunity to master 30 classic camping knots. In focusing solely on the knots, each knot is allocated generous space for clear instructions and meticulous step-by-step illustrations.

The knots are divided into several distinct groups, each of which is used for different purposes. Practice is essential for good knot tying, so select the right knot for the job and practice until you are confident that you can tie it quickly, securely, and literally with your eyes closed. Your survival in the outdoors may depend on it!

Camping Knots

Given the type and range of camping equipment available today, it is quite possible to go on a camping expedition and not have to tie a single knot. On the other hand it is in those difficult moments of having to solve a problem that knowing the right knot to tie can literally be a life saver!

Many of the knots illustrated in this book have several uses and can be adapted to solve different problems. A common problem that campers can face is securing tent guylines on ground that is too hard or rocky to use pegs. The high-tech, self-erecting tent that you have bought may be an excellent tent, but unless you can properly secure it in extreme weather conditions it is not going to be an effective shelter. In this type of situation tie additional guylines from the top of the tent poles to large rocks situated around the tent, the best knots to use for this purpose are hitches (see page 69).

A more serious example of knowing how to tie the correct knots is if you find yourself in an emergency situation and you need to build a shelter to protect you from the wind, rain or sun. Improvised shelters tend to be flimsy so the knots that hold the branches, foliage, or anything else you may use, together, need to be secure. An excellent knot for this purpose is the transom knot (see page 80).

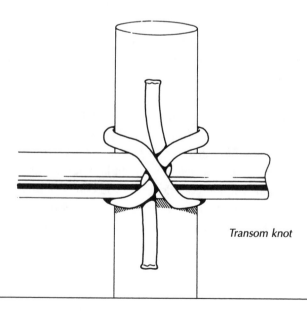

Transom knot

Ropes

Rope is manufactured in either natural or artificial fibers that can be twisted or braided and is available in a wide variety of sizes. Rope size can be measured by circumference or diameter or by a term; for example, "twine," tells you that it is a thin line for various uses.

Traditionally, rope was made by twisting fibers of natural materials together. The most commonly used materials were manila, sisal, coir, hemp, flax, and cotton. The fibers were twisted first into yarn, then into strands, and finally into rope, in a process called laying up. This type of rope is refered to as hawser-laid.

Artificial or synthetic materials have almost completely replaced natural fibers in the manufacture of rope for outdoor use. Man-made filaments can be spun to run the whole length of a line, do not vary in thickness, and do not have to be twisted together to make them cohere. This gives them superior strength.

Nylon, first produced in 1938 for domestic use, was the first man-made material to be used in this way. Since then a range of artificial ropes has been developed to meet different purposes, but they all share certain characteristics. Size for size they are lighter, stronger, and cheaper than their natural counterparts. They do not rot or mildew, are resistant to sunlight, chemicals, oil, gasoline, and most common solvents. They can also be made in a range of colors. Color-coded ropes make for instant recognition of lines of different function and size.

The vast majority of rope in use today, is kernmantle rope (see page 125). It is easy to handle, very flexible and has a good strength-to-weight ratio. Older style hawser-laid nylon rope (see page 124), is still widely used for general camping purposes or where cost is a consideration.

Rope manufactured from artificial fiber, does have some disadvantages, the main one being that they melt when heated. Even the friction generated when one rope rubs against another may be enough to cause damage, so it is vital to check your ropes regularly. It is also possible for heat friction to fuse knotted rope together so that it is impossible to untie the knot. Another disadvantage is that artificial ropes made of continuous filaments are so smooth that knots slip and come undone. Knots may need to be secured with additional knots.

HAWSER-LAID ROPE

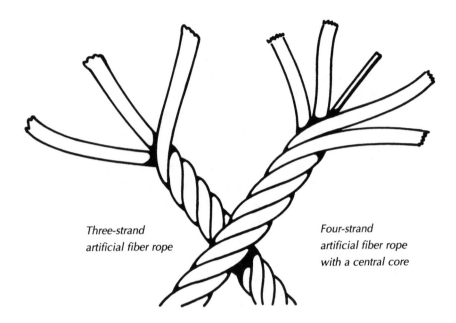

*Three-strand
artificial fiber rope*

*Four-strand
artificial fiber rope
with a central core*

Artificial rope can be laid up or twisted like old-style natural fiber rope. This is known as hawser-laid. Usually three strands of nylon filaments are twisted together to form the rope. There are variations of this available: One very strong variation is four strands of nylon filament twisted around a central nylon core.

The cost of hawser-laid rope is generally about two thirds that of the more widely used kernmantle constructed rope. Laid-up rope, made of thick multifilaments tightly twisted together, may be very resistant to wear, but it may also be difficult to handle because of its stiffness and knots may not hold well. As a general rule, do not buy a rope that is too stiff. Similarly, be wary of twisted rope that is very soft.

This type of rope may be perfectly acceptable for general camping purposes but should be avoided in situations where a rope will be subject to any excesive forms of strain.

KERNMANTLE ROPE

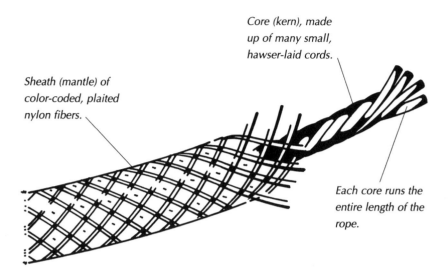

Core (kern), made up of many small, hawser-laid cords.

Sheath (mantle) of color-coded, plaited nylon fibers.

Each core runs the entire length of the rope.

Kernmantle rope is made from synthetic materials, having a core, or "kern," of many small, hawser-laid cords contained in a braided sheath, or "mantle." Kernmantle rope is very strong while being extremely flexible and easy to handle. Its flexibility makes it ideal for knot tying and the smoothness of the outer sheath not only makes the rope easy and comfortable to handle but it also allows for good contact and easy use with a block and pulley or climbing equipment such as karabiners and belay devices.

Some kernmantle ropes are sold featuring various dry treatments. These are highly recommended for use in wet or icy conditions. It means that the rope has been chemically treated to repel water. Kernmantle ropes are likely to absorb upwards of 20 percent of their weight in water when used in wet and icy conditions. The disadvantages of this are first, the rope weighs a lot more, counteracting the light-weight qualities of kernmantle, and second, and most crucial, the rope looses strength, possibly as much as 40 percent. Dry treatment will also prevent dirt particles from working their way into the fibers of the rope and causing damage.

LOOKING AFTER ROPE

Rope is sturdy material, but it is expensive, so it's worth looking after it properly. Caring for rope will help it keep its strength and prolong its life. Avoid dragging it over rough, sharp edges, or dirty, gritty surfaces where particles could get into the rope and damage it. Do not walk on rope or force it into harsh kinks. Inspect it regularly and wash off dirt, grit, and oil. Coil rope carefully and always make sure it is dry before coiling, even if it is artificial fiber rope. If it has been in seawater, rinse thoroughly to remove all salt deposits.

If knots are repeatedly tied in one section of rope, that section will weaken. The tighter the nip or the sharper the curve the greater the chances that the rope will break; if it does, it will part immediately outside the knot.

Finally, never use two ropes of different material together, because only the more rigid of the two will work under strain.

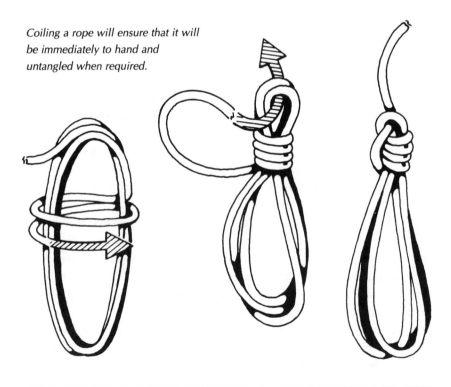

Coiling a rope will ensure that it will be immediately to hand and untangled when required.

TYING FISHING KNOTS

Fishing line is made from strong, flexible monofilament nylon and tying effective knots in this type of material requires a few routine maneuvers to be followed. Instructions for tying the most commonly used fishing knots can be found, starting on page 219.

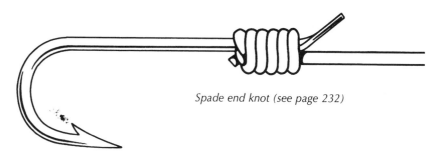

Spade end knot (see page 232)

Tying fishing knots with monofilament nylon:
• Before tying any knot always check the line for any visible signs of damage. If in any doubt, safely discard that section of line.
• To reduce friction and to help the knot seat correctly, lubricate it with saliva or water before drawing it together.
• Draw the knot together slowly and evenly with a minimum of friction to ensure it seats correctly.
• Continue to draw the knot together as tight as possible. A knot will begin to slip just before it breaks—so the tighter it is drawn together, the more force it can withstand before it starts to slip.
• Once the knot has been tightened as much as possible and is seated correctly, trim the knot ends. This will avoid them catching on rod rings, hooks, or weeds.
• Visually check your knot—good knots look good. If you are not fully confident that the knot has been tied and seated correctly—don't gamble! Cut it off and retie it.
• As with all knots, practice tying your fishing knots at home until they become second nature. You will find that you can rely on a small number of knots to cover most types of fishing, but it is important to be able to tie those knots quickly and with full confidence.

How to Use This Book

The diagrams accompanying the descriptions of the knots are intended to be self-explanatory, but for added clarity, sequenced, written instructions and special tying techniques and methods do accompany the knots. There are arrows to show the directions in which you should push or pull the working ends and standing parts of the rope or line. The dotted lines indicate intermediate positions of the rope. When tying a knot you should always have a sufficient working end to complete it. The amount of working end required can often be calculated by looking at the illustration of the finished knot. Always follow the order shown of going over or under a length of line; reversing or changing this order could result in a completely different knot, which might well be unstable, unsafe, and insecure.

Rope Parts

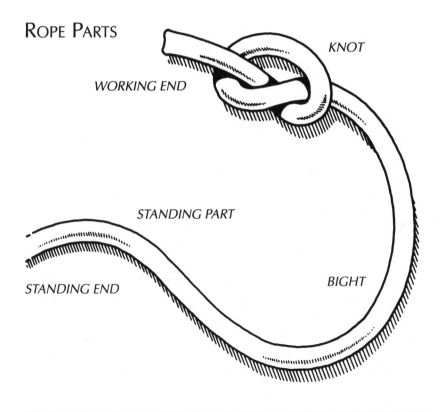

KNOT

WORKING END

STANDING PART

STANDING END

BIGHT

PLEASE...

Respect the great outdoors. When you have left your campsite it should look as if you had never been there. Take all your rubbish away with you—concealing it is not acceptable. The great outdoors must remain unspoiled so that future generations of visitors can enjoy it in the same way that you have.

STOPPER KNOTS

S topper knots, as their name suggests, are used to prevent the end of a rope or line from slipping through an eye, loop, or hole. They can be used to bind the end of a rope so that it will not unravel or weight the end of a rope for throwing purposes and for decoration.

Many camping knots, for example, the bowline (see page 164) can be finished off with a stopper knot tied in the working end for extra security.

OVERHAND KNOT

Also known as the thumb knot, this knot forms the basis for many others. It is used in its own right as a stopper knot and makes a line easier to grip if tied at regular intervals along the line. A tight overhand knot can be difficult to undo if tied in very small-diameter line or if the line becomes wet.

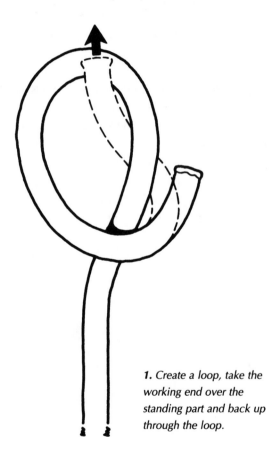

1. Create a loop, take the working end over the standing part and back up through the loop.

2. Pull on the working end and the standing part to form the final knot.

3. A line or rope can be made easier to grip with overhand knots tied at regular intervals.

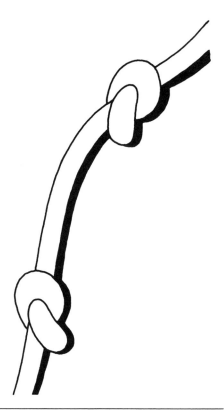

FIGURE-EIGHT KNOT

This is a quick and efficient way of tying a simple and attractive stopper knot at the end a line or rope. The knot's name comes from its characteristic shape. Its interlaced appearance has long been seen as a symbol of interwoven affection. In heraldry it signifies faithful love and appears on various coats of arms—hence its other names, the Flemish or Savoy knot.

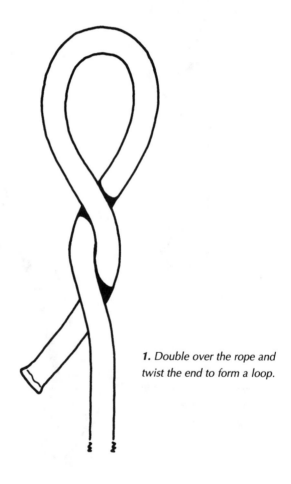

1. Double over the rope and twist the end to form a loop.

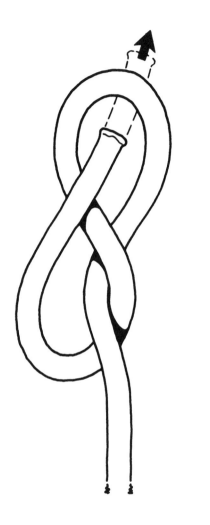

2. Pass the working end over the standing part and then up through the loop.

3. Pull on both the working end and the standing part to form the knot.

HEAVING LINE KNOT

This stopper knot has the advantage of adding considerable weight to the end of the line. This proves particularly useful for throwing the end of a line across a gap or to another person.

The heaving line knot, widely used by sailors, is tied at the end of a lighter line which in turn is attached to a heavier line. The lighter line is thrown first, usually from boat to shore, so the heavier line can then be drawn or heaved behind it.

The knot's other name, the monk's knot, derives from its use by Franciscan monks to weight the ends of the cords they use as belts.

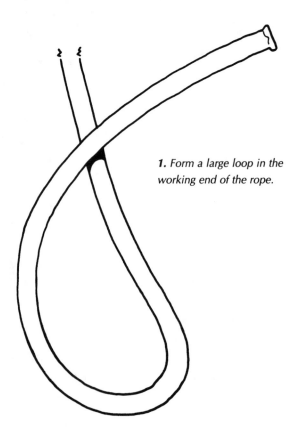

1. Form a large loop in the working end of the rope.

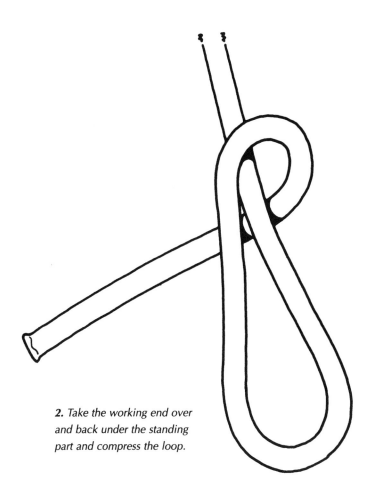

2. Take the working end over and back under the standing part and compress the loop.

continued on page 138

Heaving Line Knot

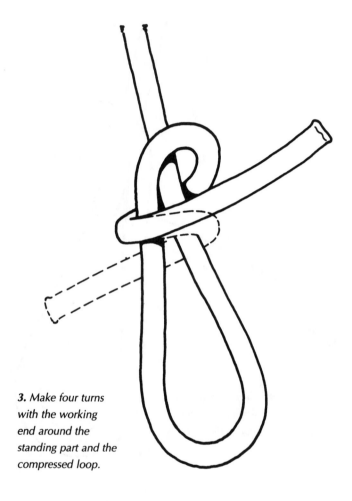

3. Make four turns with the working end around the standing part and the compressed loop.

4. On the fourth turn take the working end down through the loop. Keep the already formed turns as tight as possible.

5. Pull on the working end and the standing part to tighten the knot. As the knot is tightening, form the final knot shape.

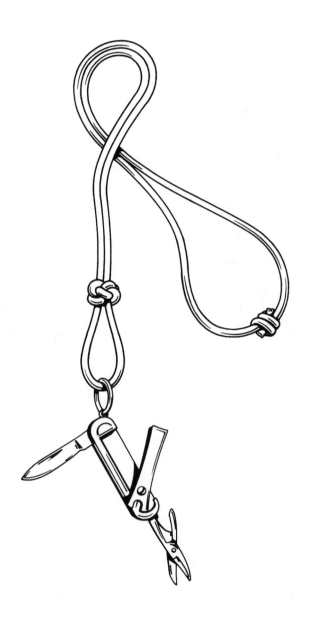

BENDS

$\mathbf{B}$ends are used to join two lengths of rope at their ends to form one longer piece. It is important, if bends are to be secure, for the ropes joined in this way to be of the same kind and the same diameter.

The sheet bend (see page 146) is the exception to this rule. It is very secure, even when it is used to join ropes of different diameters.

REEF KNOT

The reef knot, or square knot, is very often the only knot people know, apart from the granny knot. It gets its name from its nautical use to tie two ends of a rope when reefing or gathering in part of a sail.

The reef knot is not a secure knot and should not be used as one, certainly never with ropes of different diameter. It should only be used to make a temporary join in lines of identical type, weight, and diameter where it will not be put under strain. If the lines have to take strain, stopper knots should be tied in the short ends.

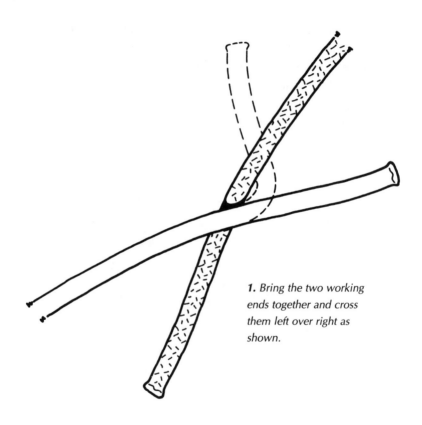

1. Bring the two working ends together and cross them left over right as shown.

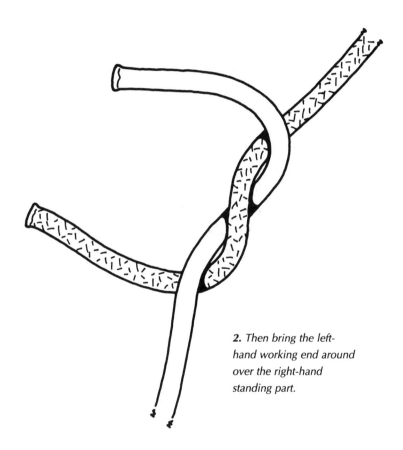

2. Then bring the left-hand working end around over the right-hand standing part.

continued on page 144

Reef Knot

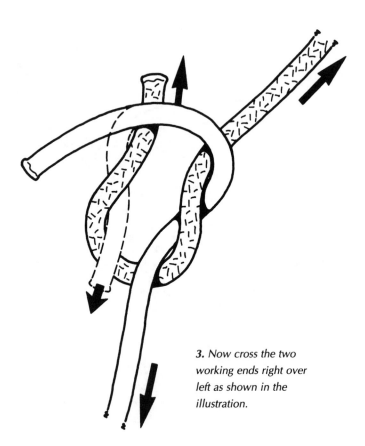

3. Now cross the two working ends right over left as shown in the illustration.

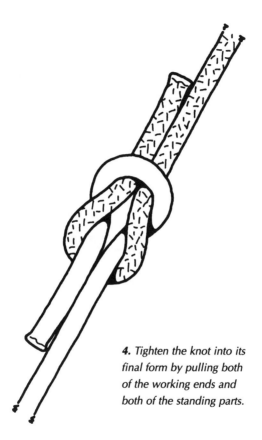

4. *Tighten the knot into its final form by pulling both of the working ends and both of the standing parts.*

Sheet Bend

The sheet bend is probably the most commonly used of all bends and, unlike most bends, it can safely join lines of different diameters. It is not, however, one hundred percent secure and should never be used in circumstances where it will be subject to great strain. Its breaking strength also decreases in direct proportion to the difference in diameter of the lines joined.

A slipped sheet bend is formed by placing a bight between the loop of the heavier rope and the standing part of the lighter one. The slipped knot is more easily untied when the rope is under strain.

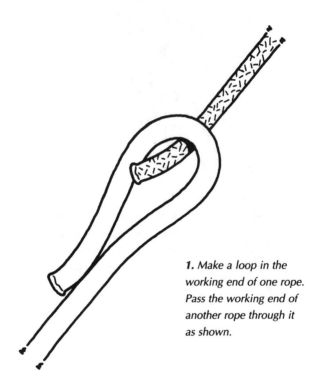

1. Make a loop in the working end of one rope. Pass the working end of another rope through it as shown.

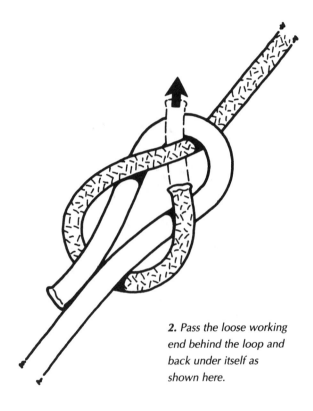

2. Pass the loose working
end behind the loop and
back under itself as
shown here.

continued on page 148

Sheet Bend

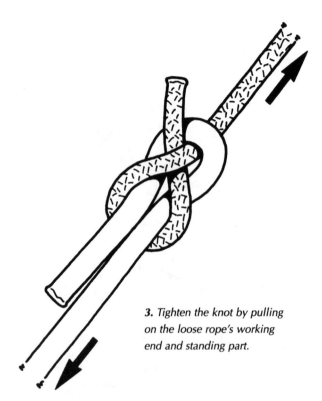

3. Tighten the knot by pulling on the loose rope's working end and standing part.

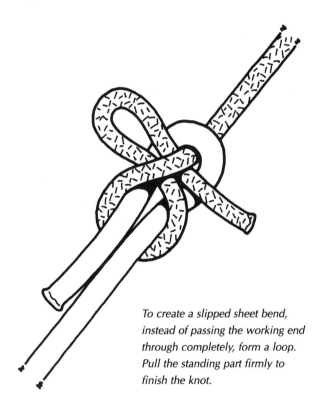

To create a slipped sheet bend,
instead of passing the working end
through completely, form a loop.
Pull the standing part firmly to
finish the knot.

Fisherman's Knot

This knot is said to have been invented in the nineteenth century, but some authorities suggest it was known to the ancient Greeks. It is generally known as the fisherman's knot, but over the years it has picked up many different names (angler's knot, English knot, Englishman's bend, halibut knot, true lover's knot, and waterman's knot). It is formed from two overhand knots that jam against each other; the short ends are on opposite sides and lie almost parallel to their nearest standing part. After use, the two component knots are generally easily separated and undone.

The fisherman's knot is best suited to joining thin lines such as string, cord, twine, or small stuff, and as the name suggests, it is widely used by fishermen for joining the finest of fishing lines.

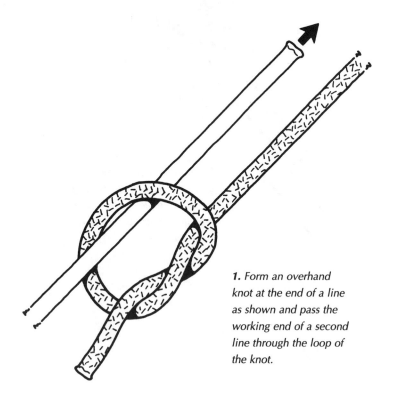

1. Form an overhand knot at the end of a line as shown and pass the working end of a second line through the loop of the knot.

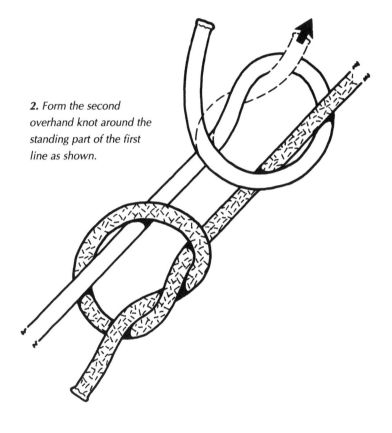

2. Form the second overhand knot around the standing part of the first line as shown.

continued on page 152

Fisherman's Knot

3. Tighten both knots and then pull on the standing parts of both lines.

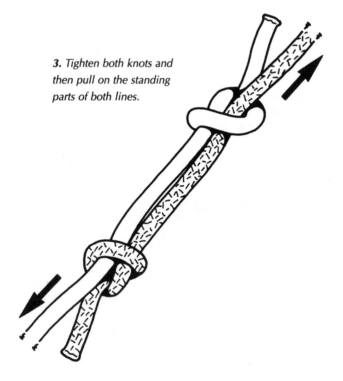

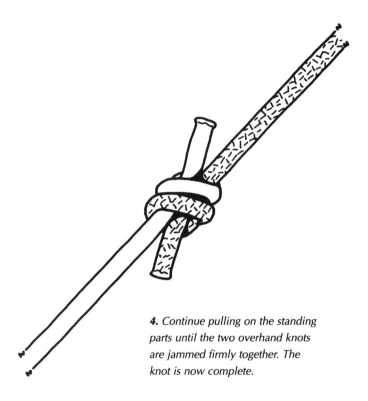

4. *Continue pulling on the standing parts until the two overhand knots are jammed firmly together. The knot is now complete.*

FIGURE-EIGHT BEND

This simple knot (also known as the Flemish bend or knot) is tied by making a figure-eight knot in one end of a line and then following it around with the other working end. It is, despite its simplicity, one of the strongest bends and holds equally well in cord or rope.

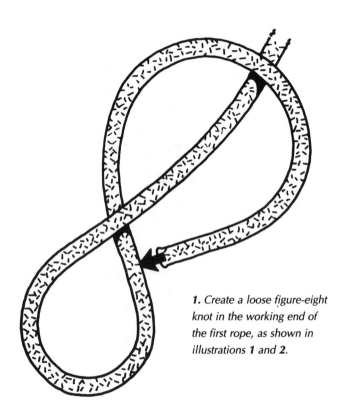

1. Create a loose figure-eight knot in the working end of the first rope, as shown in illustrations 1 and 2.

2. *Do not pull the knot tight at this stage.*

continued on page 156

Figure-Eight Bend

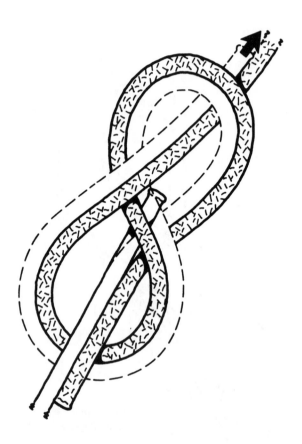

3. Feed the working end of the second rope into the loose figure-eight formed in the first rope and follow the figure-eight pattern around as shown in the illustration.

4. *Tighten the knot into its final form by pulling on the standing part of each rope.*

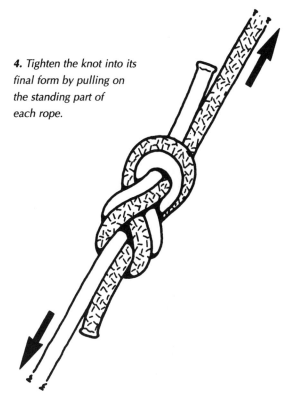

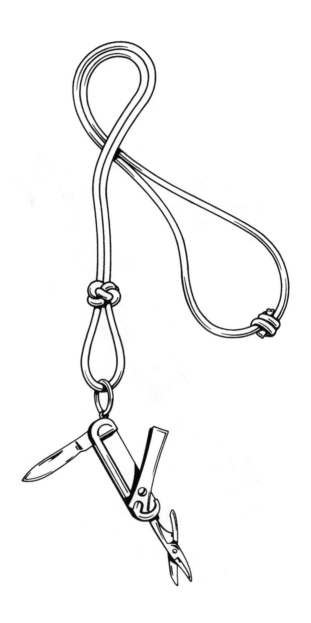

LOOPS

Knots made in the end of a rope by folding it back into an eye or loop and then knotting it to its own standing part are called loops. They are fixed and do not slide.

Loops are particularly important to campers, as they have such a wide variation of use. The figure-eight loop (see page 160), for example, is acknowledged as one of the quickest and most efficient ways to form a secure loop to drop over any object.

FIGURE-EIGHT LOOP

This is one of the best-known and most widely used of all knots. It is probably the safest and quickest way to form a loop at the end of a rope.

It is comparatively easy to tie and it stays tied. Its disadvantages—it is difficult to adjust and cannot easily be untied after loading—tend to be outweighed by its general usefulness.

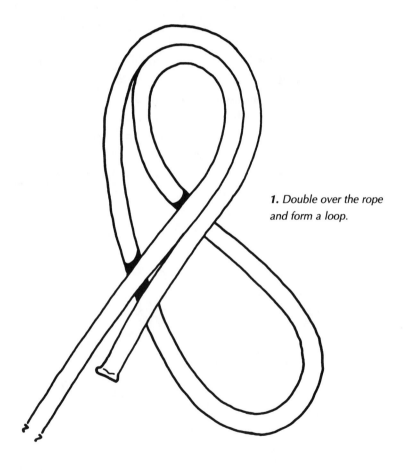

1. Double over the rope and form a loop.

2. Now bring the doubled working end over the doubled standing part and back up through the original loop.

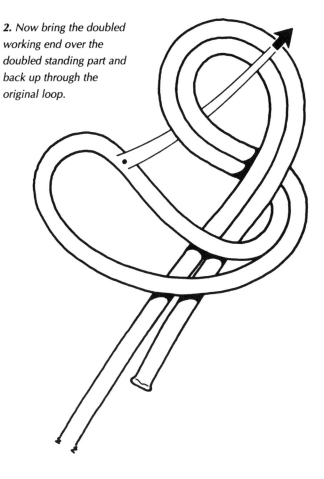

continued on page 162

Figure-Eight Loop

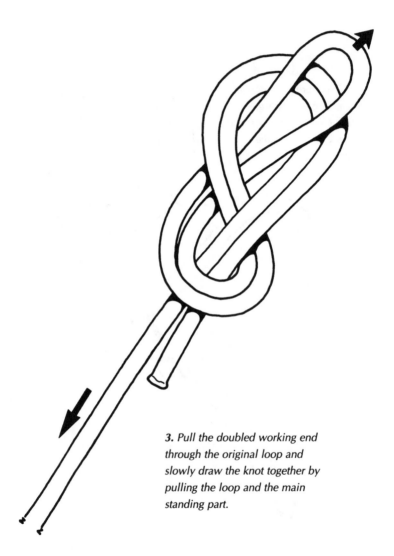

3. Pull the doubled working end through the original loop and slowly draw the knot together by pulling the loop and the main standing part.

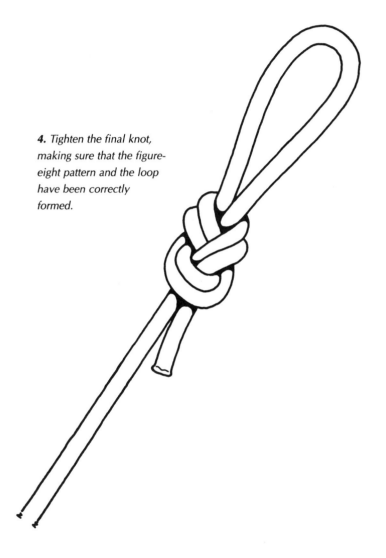

4. Tighten the final knot, making sure that the figure-eight pattern and the loop have been correctly formed.

BOWLINE

The bowline is one of the best-known and most widely used knots. It is tied to form a fixed loop at the end of a line or to attach a rope to an object.

The bowline's main advantages are that it does not slip, come loose, or jam. It is quick and easy to untie, even when a line is under tension, by pushing forward the bight that encircles the standing part of the line. For added security the bowline can be finished with a stopper knot.

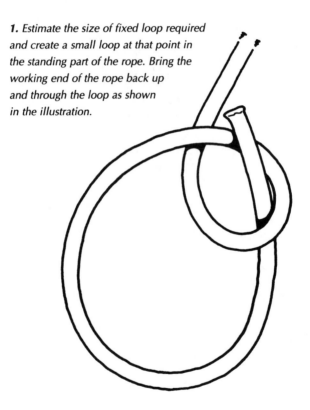

1. Estimate the size of fixed loop required and create a small loop at that point in the standing part of the rope. Bring the working end of the rope back up and through the loop as shown in the illustration.

2. *Take the working end around the back of the standing part and back down through the loop. Then slowly start to pull on the standing part to form the knot.*

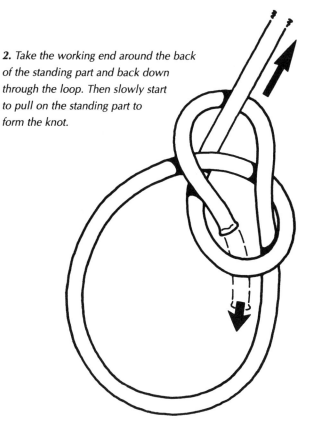

continued on page 166

Bowline

3. Adjust the fixed loop to its required size and then tighten the knot into its final form.

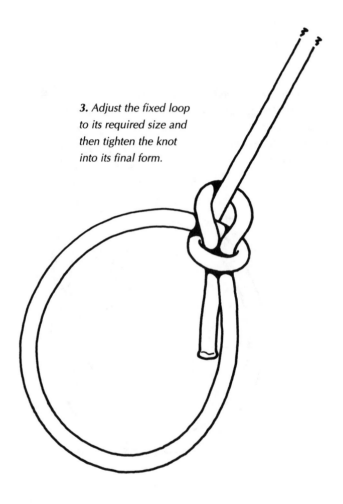

4. *For added security the bowline can be finished with a stopper knot.*

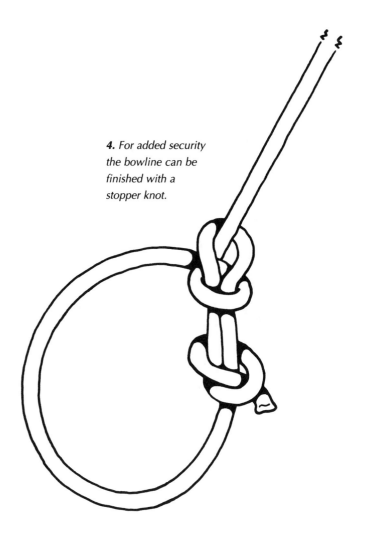

THREE-PART CROWN

This sturdy, secure knot can be used to hang food and gear and it can be used as a decorative knot from which to hang objects. It may become difficult to untie after it has supported a heavy weight.

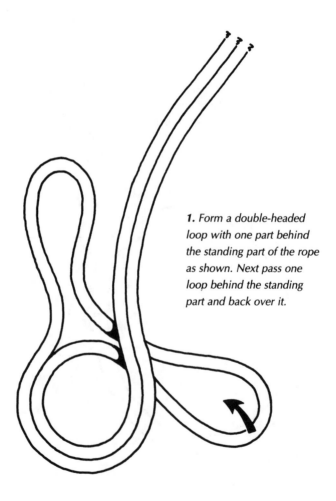

1. Form a double-headed loop with one part behind the standing part of the rope as shown. Next pass one loop behind the standing part and back over it.

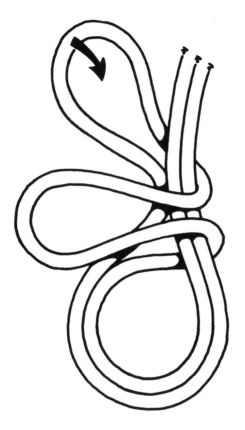

2. _Keeping the first loop held firmly against the standing part, bring the second loop down over it toward the double loop._

continued on page 170

Three-Part Crown

3. Pass the top loop
through the double loop.

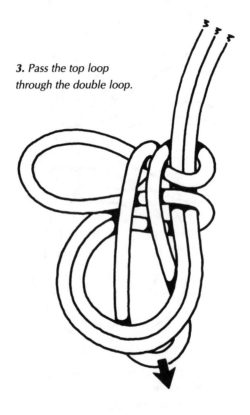

4. Finish the knot by pulling the standing part and the two loops. Take care to keep the two loops equal.

NOOSE

This simple knot is often used by campers and hunters to snare birds and small game such as rabbits. It can also be used in tying a parcel or, on a larger scale, it can be used to put tackle cables under stress.

The noose can be used as a hitch, especially if the hitch is to be formed around a very large object, such as a tree trunk, as a noose can be tied using a fairly short length of line. A constrictor knot, or a clove or cow hitch, would need a much longer length of rope. Also, a noose used as a hitch is very secure.

Another useful feature of the noose is that it can be tied around relatively inaccessible objects. A s long as it is possible to get close enough to pass a rope around, a noose can be tied and tightened.

A stopper knot should be added to the noose to prevent it from slipping.

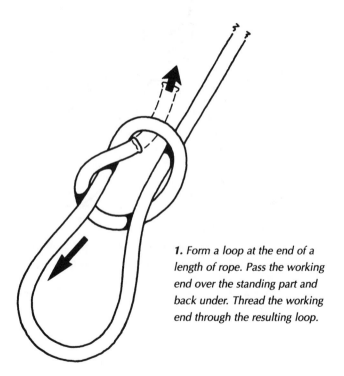

1. Form a loop at the end of a length of rope. Pass the working end over the standing part and back under. Thread the working end through the resulting loop.

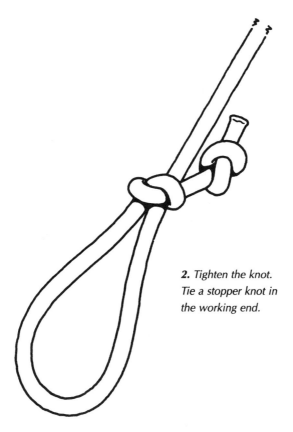

2. Tighten the knot.
Tie a stopper knot in
the working end.

SHORTENINGS

Shortenings are invaluable knots well worth mastering. As their name suggests, they are used to shorten lengths of rope or line without cutting. A rope shortened by means of a knot can always be lengthened later, and a single unbroken line will always be more secure than two lines knotted together.

Shortenings can also be used as an emergency measure to take up damaged lengths of rope. The weakened sections are incorporated into the knot and are not, therefore, subject to strain.

Sheepshank

The sheepshank can be used to shorten any rope to any required length without cutting. It is easy to tie, holds under tension with a good jamming action, does not change its shape, and unties easily.

In an emergency a sheepshank can be used to shorten a damaged line or rope, take care to ensure that the damaged or weakened section of the rope passes through both half hitches.

1. Form three loops at the point in the rope where the shortening will be required. Pull the indicated points of the middle loop through the two outer loops.

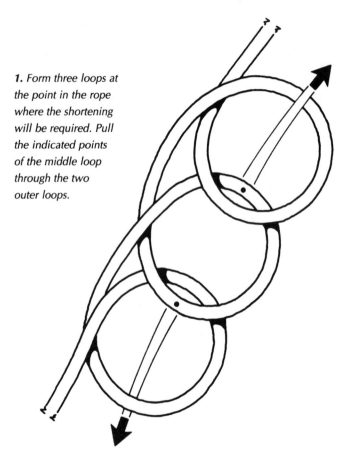

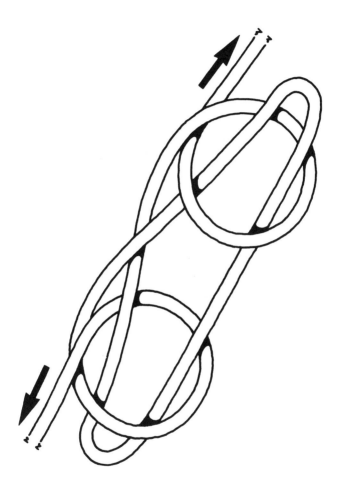

2. Slowly pull on the two main parts of the rope, making sure that the knot retains its shape and form.

continued on page 178

Sheepshank

3. *Tighten the knot into its final form. This knot is very adjustable, but always make sure that the two loops at the end of the knot are of similar proportion.*

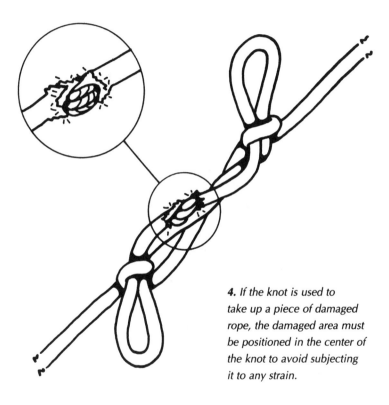

4. If the knot is used to take up a piece of damaged rope, the damaged area must be positioned in the center of the knot to avoid subjecting it to any strain.

LOOP KNOT

This is a very simple knot that can be used to form a quick and simple loop in a rope. More important, it can be used in an emergency to shorten a damaged rope. The weakened or damaged section of the rope is taken up in the center of the knot where it cannot be put under any strain.

The risks involved in using damaged or weakened rope for any outdoor activities are too great!

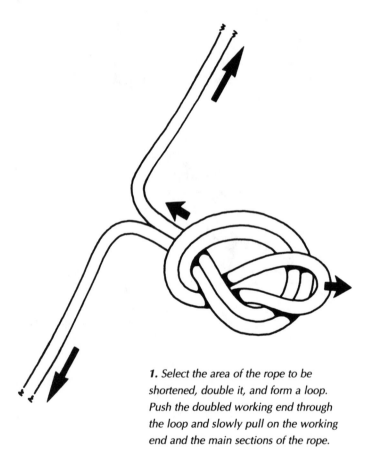

1. Select the area of the rope to be shortened, double it, and form a loop. Push the doubled working end through the loop and slowly pull on the working end and the main sections of the rope.

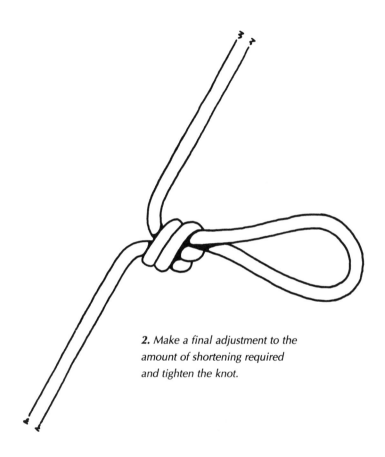

2. Make a final adjustment to the
amount of shortening required
and tighten the knot.

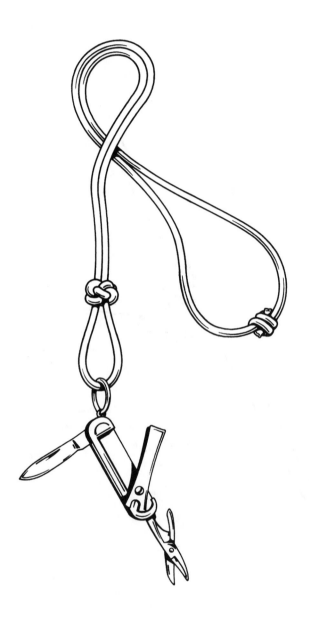

HITCHES

Hitches are knots used to secure a rope to another object (such as a post, peg, ring, luggage rack), or to fix together crossed pieces of rigid material, for example, building a shelter out of branches and foliage.

HALF HITCH

The half hitch is a very widely used fastening. It is, in fact, a single hitch formed around the standing part of another hitch. It is used to complete and strengthen other knots, as in the round turn and two half hitches (see page 202), which can then be used for tying, hanging, hooking objects etc. The slipped half hitch is a useful variation of the simple half hitch; a sharp pull on the working end releases the knot.

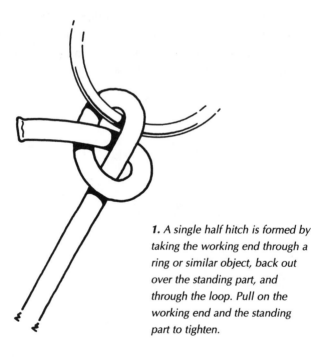

1. A single half hitch is formed by taking the working end through a ring or similar object, back out over the standing part, and through the loop. Pull on the working end and the standing part to tighten.

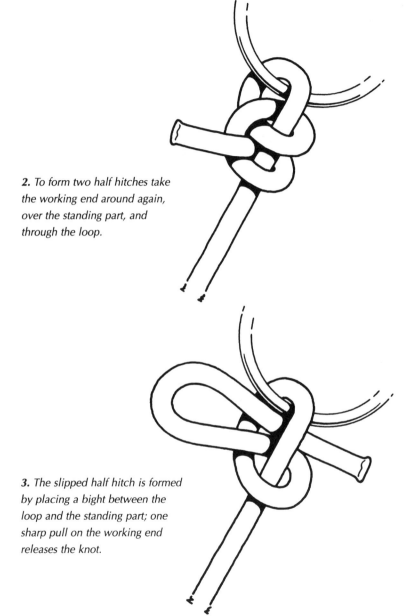

2. To form two half hitches take the working end around again, over the standing part, and through the loop.

3. The slipped half hitch is formed by placing a bight between the loop and the standing part; one sharp pull on the working end releases the knot.

Clove Hitch

The clove hitch is one of the best-known camping knots and probably one of the most valuable hitches. It can be used to fasten a line to a peg, pole, or post or on to another rope that is not part of the knot. It is an easy knot to tie, and can with practice be tied with just one hand. The final knot can be achieved in many different ways.

The clove hitch is not, however, a totally secure knot, as it will work loose if the strain is intermittent and comes from different angles. Under these types of conditions it is best used as a temporary hold, and then replaced by a more stable knot. It can be made more secure by adding a stopper knot to the working end.

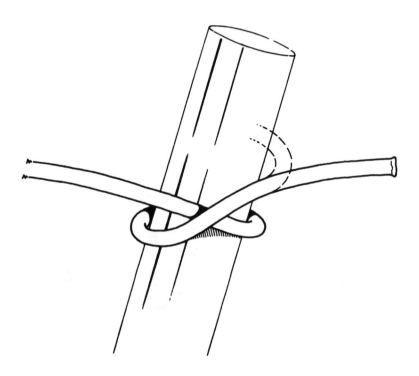

1. Pass the working end around the peg, pole, or post and then cross it over the standing part before starting to pass it around again.

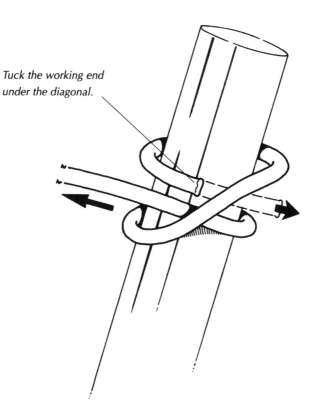

Tuck the working end
under the diagonal.

2. Bring the working end around above the first turn
and tuck it under the diagonal. Slowly start to pull
on the standing part.

continued on page 188

Clove Hitch

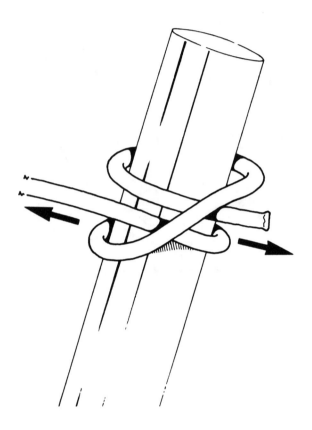

3. Slowly pull the working end and the standing part, making sure that the knot keeps its pattern and shape.

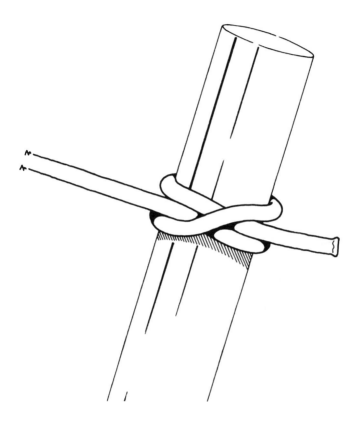

4. *Tighten the knot into its final form.*

CONSTRICTOR KNOT

This is a popular all-purpose knot because it is firm and does not slip. It can be used as a permanent or temporary fastening. As a permanent fastening, the constrictor knot grips so firmly that if there is a need to untie it, usually the only way is to cut it free. To be sure of being able to untie it if used as a temporary fastening, the last tuck should be made with a bight to make a slip knot.

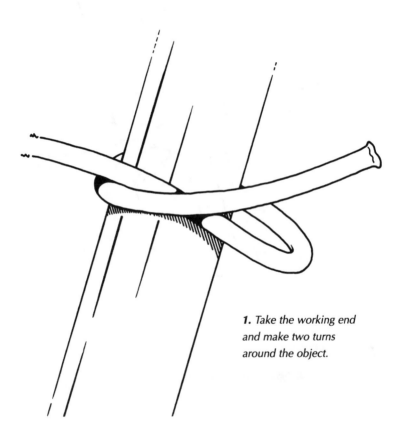

1. Take the working end and make two turns around the object.

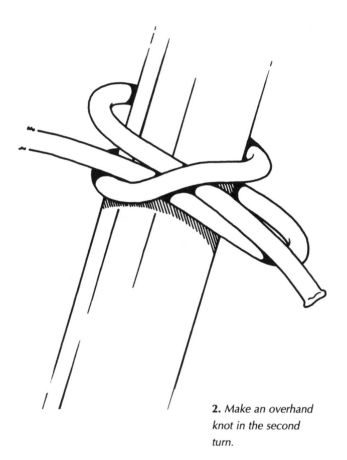

2. Make an overhand
knot in the second
turn.

continued on page 192

Constrictor Knot

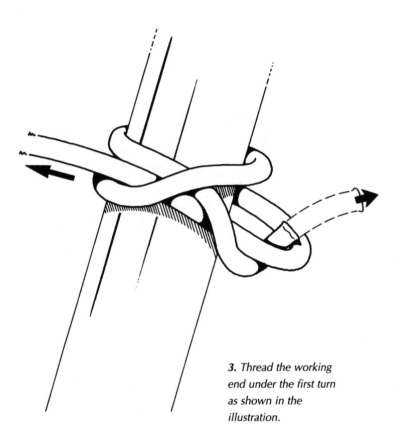

3. Thread the working end under the first turn as shown in the illustration.

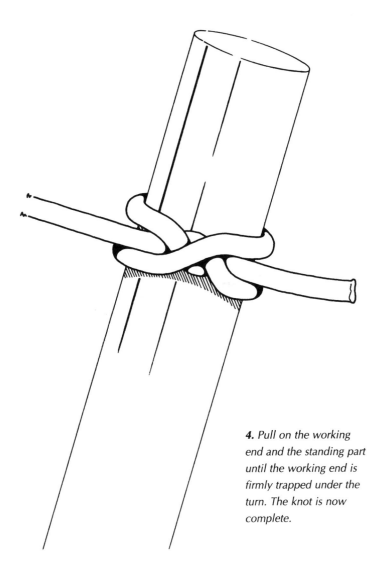

4. Pull on the working end and the standing part until the working end is firmly trapped under the turn. The knot is now complete.

TRANSOM KNOT

This is similar to a constrictor knot (see page 76). It is used to fix together crossed pieces of rigid material and has a wide range of camping and outdoor uses, for example, to fasten tent poles together and kit to luggage racks. If used as a permanent knot, the ends may be trimmed off for neatness.

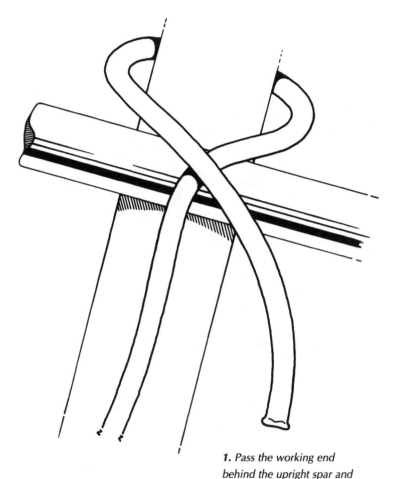

1. Pass the working end behind the upright spar and back across the rope.

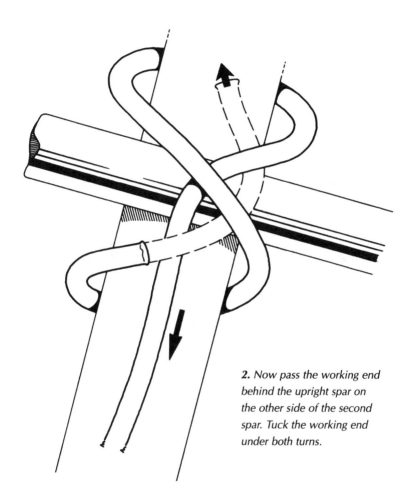

2. Now pass the working end behind the upright spar on the other side of the second spar. Tuck the working end under both turns.

continued on page 196

Transom Knot

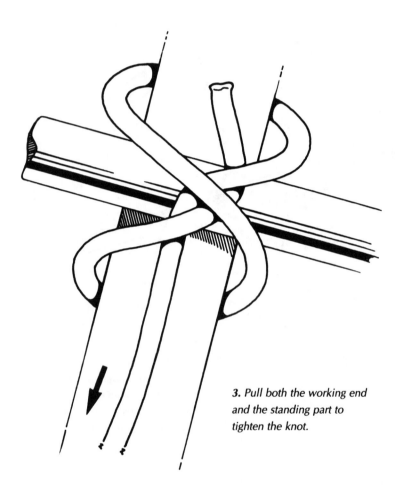

3. Pull both the working end and the standing part to tighten the knot.

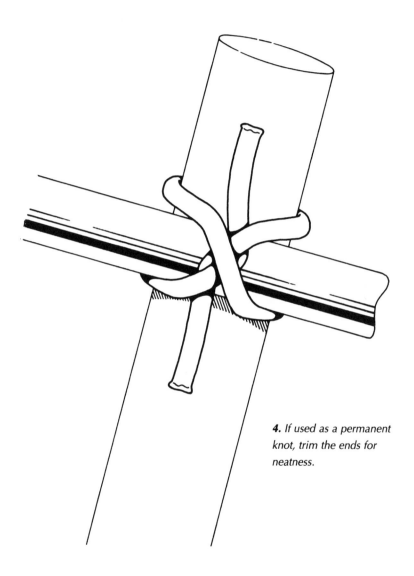

4. If used as a permanent
knot, trim the ends for
neatness.

PILE HITCH

The pile hitch is a very neat and practical hitch for securing objects to a post. It is ideal as a temporary fixing. The big advantage of this hitch is that it is very easy to tie and release quickly.

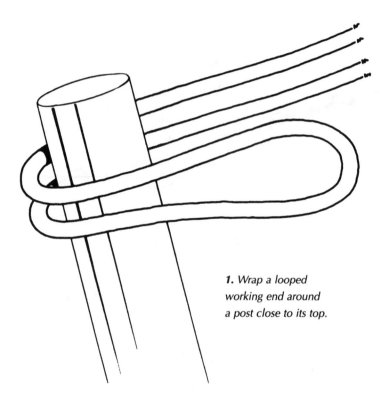

1. Wrap a looped working end around a post close to its top.

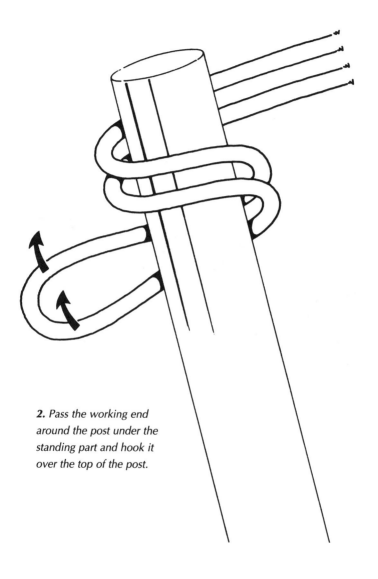

2. Pass the working end around the post under the standing part and hook it over the top of the post.

continued on page 200

Pile Hitch

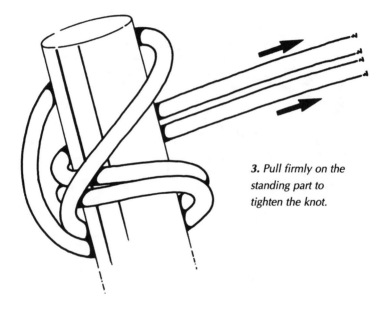

3. Pull firmly on the standing part to tighten the knot.

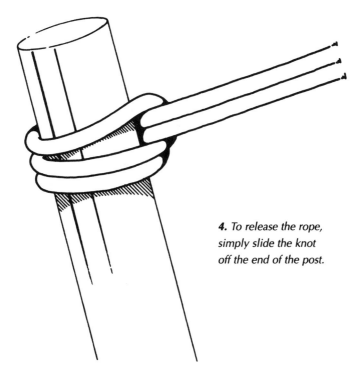

4. To release the rope, simply slide the knot off the end of the post.

ROUND TURN AND TWO HALF HITCHES

This knot is strong, dependable, and when correctly tied, it never jams. This makes it very versatile; you can use it whenever you want to fasten a line to a ring, hook, stake, post, pole, handle, or rail. Once one end of a rope has been secured with a round turn and two half hitches, the other end can be tied with a second knot. This is especially useful for fastening down unwieldy, bulky objects.

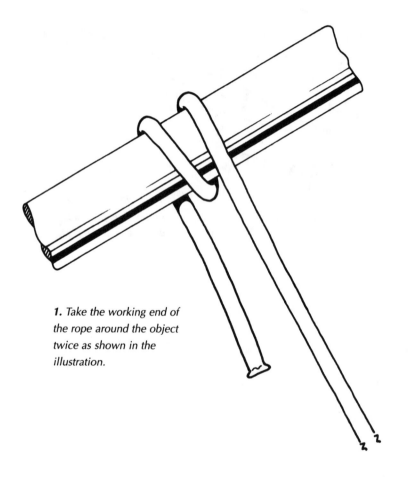

1. Take the working end of the rope around the object twice as shown in the illustration.

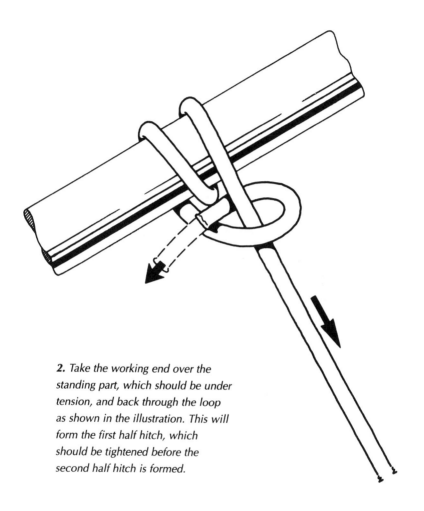

2. Take the working end over the standing part, which should be under tension, and back through the loop as shown in the illustration. This will form the first half hitch, which should be tightened before the second half hitch is formed.

continued on page 204

Round Turn and Two Half Hitches

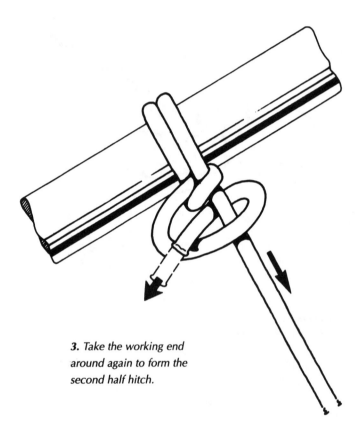

3. Take the working end around again to form the second half hitch.

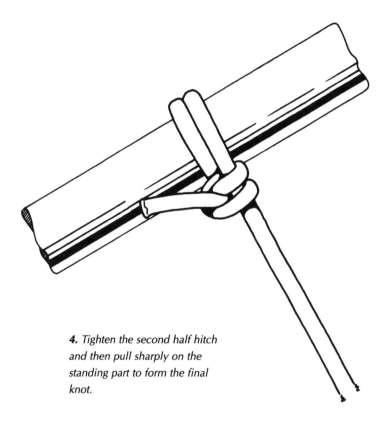

4. *Tighten the second half hitch and then pull sharply on the standing part to form the final knot.*

HIGHWAYMAN'S HITCH

The name of this knot comes from its legendary use by highwaymen and robbers to give them quick release of their horses' reins and so ensure a fast getaway. It is also called the draw hitch.

One pull on the working end and the knot is undone, but the standing end can be put under tension. It is useful for tethering animals, lowering loads, and as a temporary fastening.

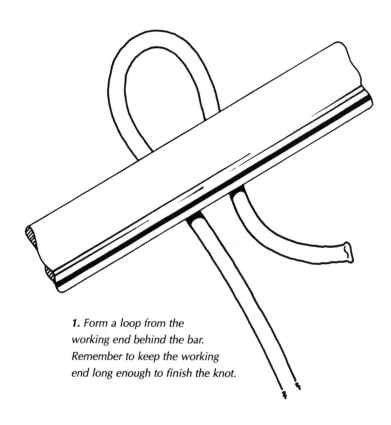

1. Form a loop from the working end behind the bar. Remember to keep the working end long enough to finish the knot.

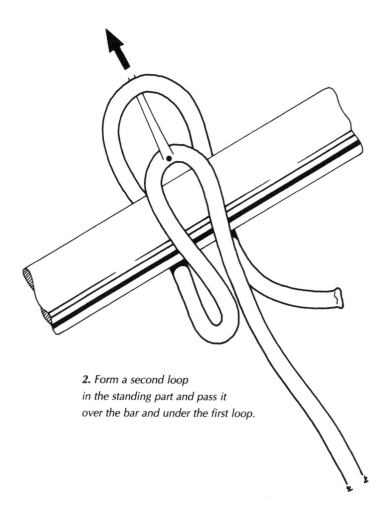

2. Form a second loop
in the standing part and pass it
over the bar and under the first loop.

continued on page 208

Highwayman's Hitch

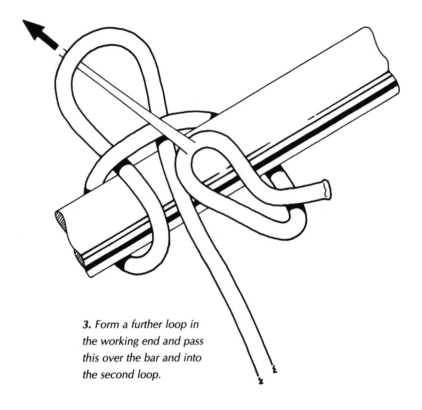

3. Form a further loop in the working end and pass this over the bar and into the second loop.

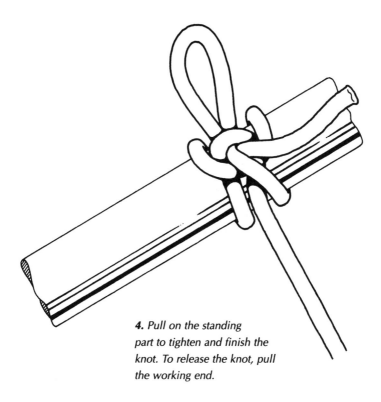

4. Pull on the standing part to tighten and finish the knot. To release the knot, pull the working end.

WAGONER'S HITCH

The wagoner's hitch is a very useful, practical knot that makes it possible to pull tight a line or rope yet leave it ready for immediate release. This makes it an ideal knot for securing loads or deck gear.

Once the line has been heaved tight, it should be secured with at least two half hitches.

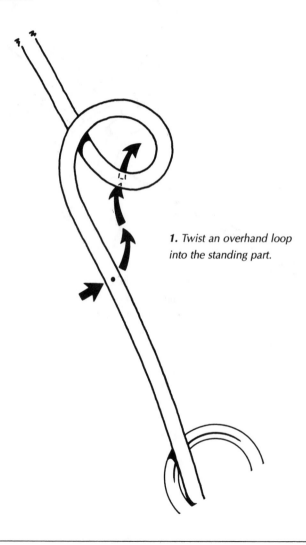

1. *Twist an overhand loop into the standing part.*

2. Take hold of the line close to the loop and pass a new loop through it from underneath the line.

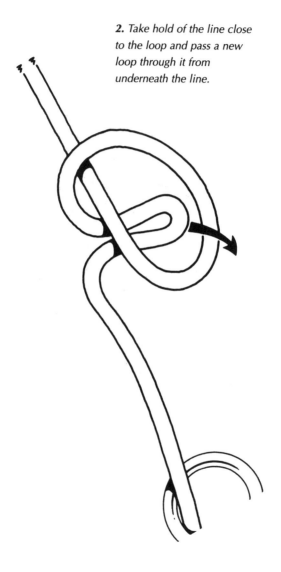

continued on page 212

Wagoner's Hitch

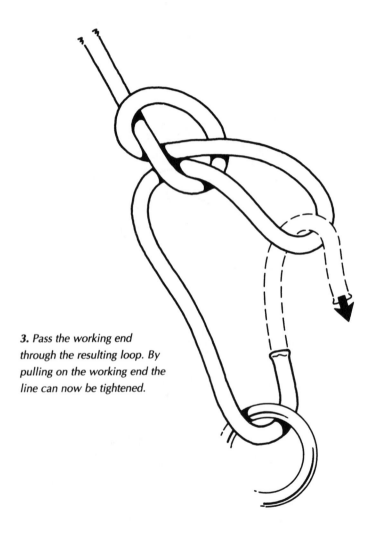

3. Pass the working end through the resulting loop. By pulling on the working end the line can now be tightened.

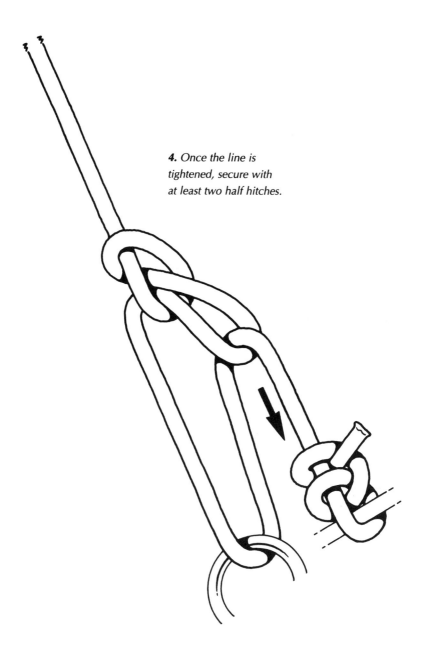

4. Once the line is tightened, secure with at least two half hitches.

TIMBER HITCH

The timber hitch is a temporary noose formed around such objects as tree trunks, planks, and poles so that they can be dragged, pulled, raised, or lowered.

It is made by doubling the working end on itself and twisting it around its own part (not the standing part of the hitch) several times. If the object is very thick, more twists are added. It is a very useful hitch in that it can be quickly put on, is very secure, and does not jam. Unfortunately, it is easy for beginners to tie it incorrectly.

1. Pass the working end around the object to be moved. Take it behind the standing part and then through the resulting loop.

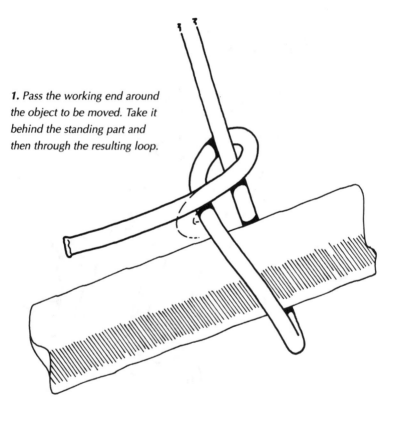

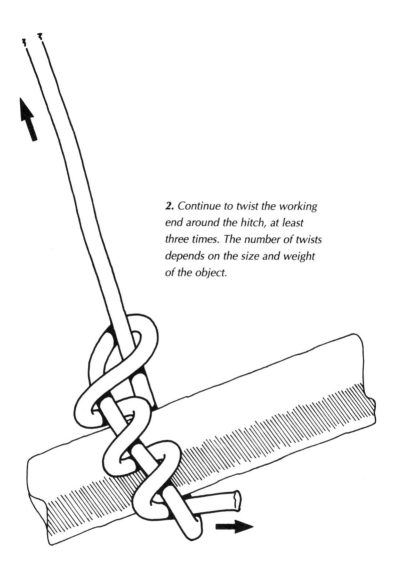

2. Continue to twist the working end around the hitch, at least three times. The number of twists depends on the size and weight of the object.

continued on page 216

Timber Hitch

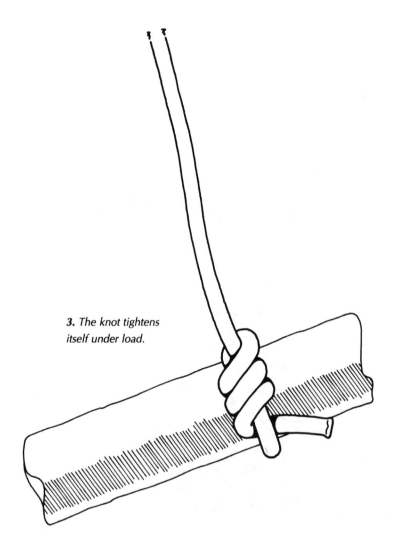

3. The knot tightens
itself under load.

The **killick hitch** is a variation of the timber hitch specifically used for dragging and towing. It is created by first tying a timber hitch and then, some distance down the line, adding a half hitch.

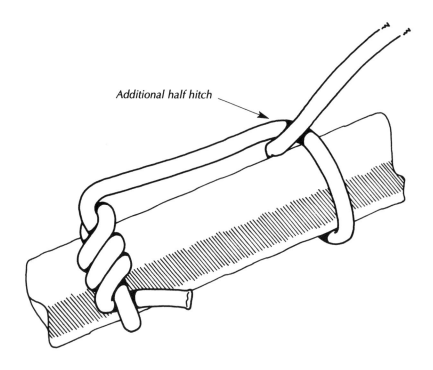

Additional half hitch

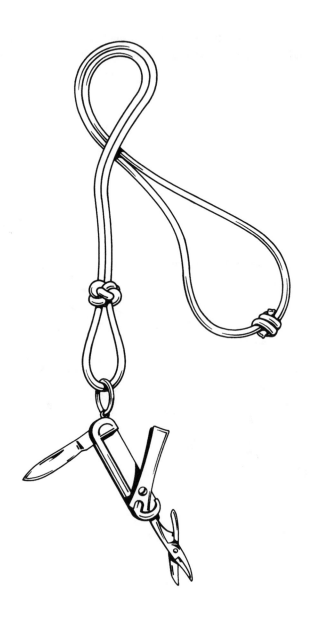

FISHING KNOTS

Camping and fishing have always been closely connected. Camping sites are invariably near streams, rivers, or lakes, so the opportunity to relax with a lazy day's fishing or to catch your supper is never far away. This section contains a collection of the most commonly used fishing knots. Don't forget: An incorrectly tied fishing knot could lose you that fish of a lifetime!

BLOOD KNOT

This knot is a firm favorite with many fishermen and one of the most widely used fishing knots in the world.

It has a relatively high knot strength, with the turns (a minimum of five with each line) helping it absorb strain and shock. It is most effective for joining monofilament lines of the same or similar diameters, but can also be used in many other fishing situations.

1. Lay the two lines alongside each other.

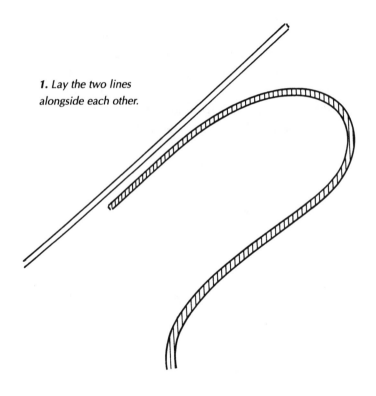

2. Make four or five turns around one line and then pass the working end under the standing part of the same line.

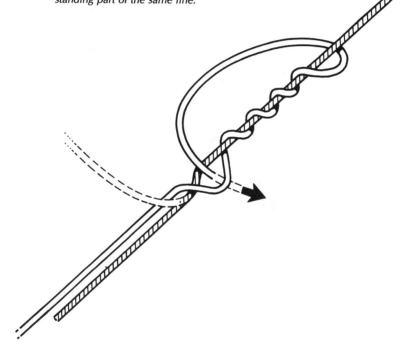

continued on page 222

Blood Knot

3. Repeat the process with
the second line.

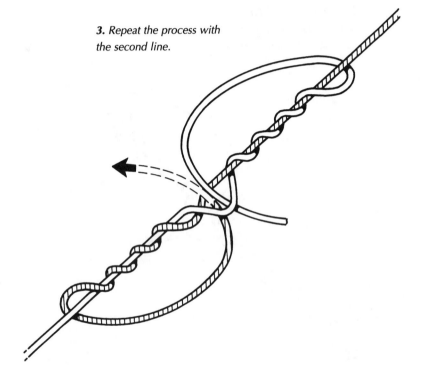

4. *Carefully pull the standing parts to seat and tighten the knot.*

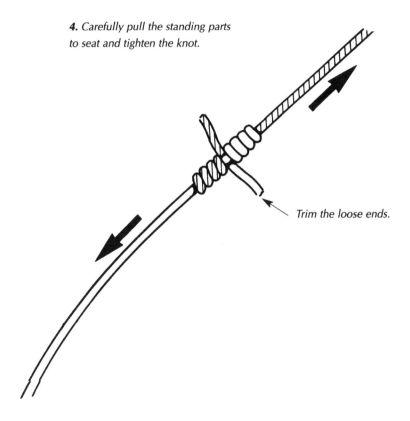

Trim the loose ends.

Tucked Half Blood Knot

Also known as the improved clinch knot, this old, tried, and tested knot is a firm favorite with many fishermen. It is very successfully tied with fine monofilament, but when heavier monofilament is used it can prove difficult to draw the knot up tightly.

1. Thread the working end through the eye of the hook and make four or five turns around the standing part.

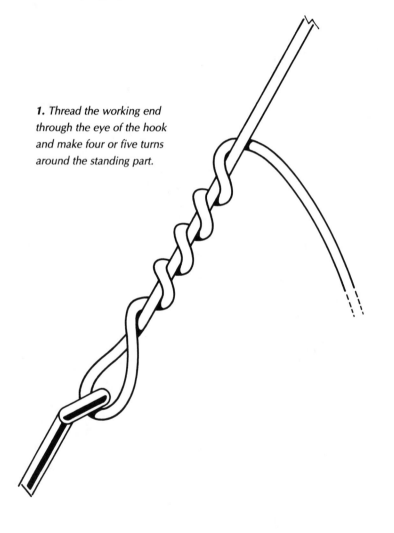

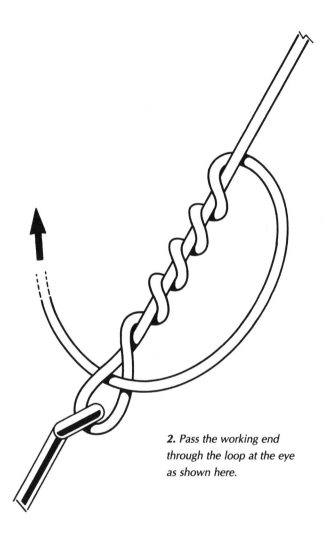

2. Pass the working end
through the loop at the eye
as shown here.

continued on page 226

Tucked Half Blood Knot

3. Pass the working end back through itself. Seat the knot correctly by pulling the standing part and the working end.

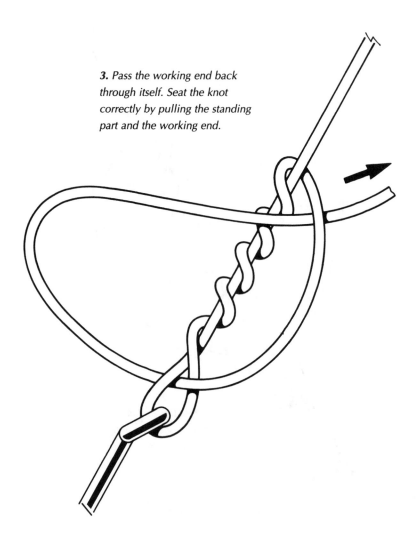

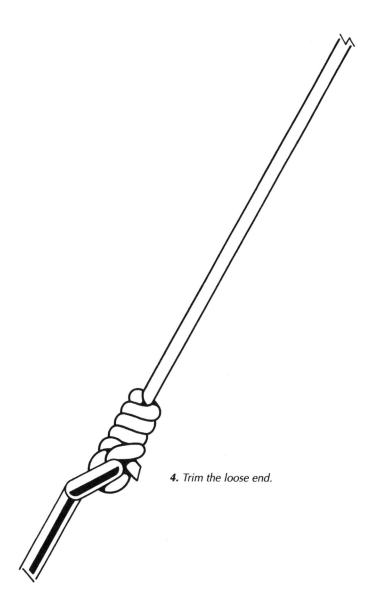

4. Trim the loose end.

DOUBLE LOOP KNOT

The double loop knot, or surgeon's loop, will not slip and can be tied very quickly. It is tied with a single length of line.

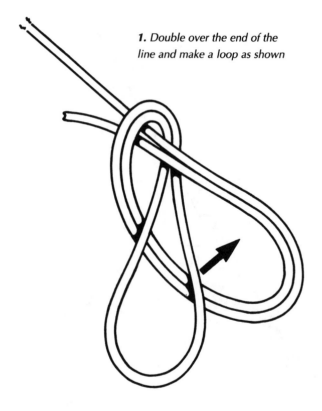

1. Double over the end of the line and make a loop as shown

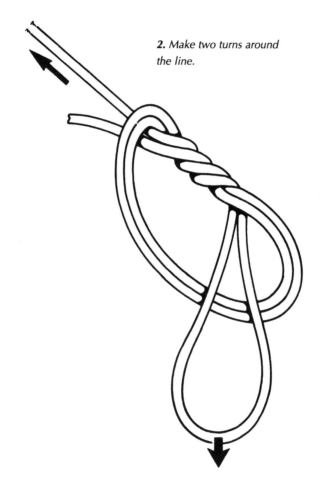

2. Make two turns around the line.

continued on page 230

Double Loop Knot

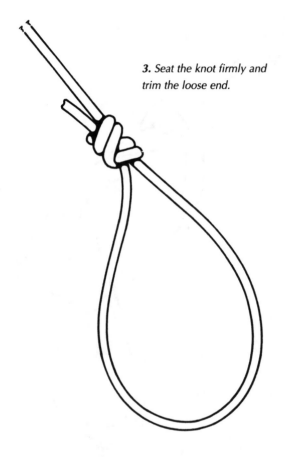

3. Seat the knot firmly and trim the loose end.

Interlocking loops are a quick
and easy method of putting
tackle together.

Spade End Knot

Use this knot to attach hooks with a spade end as opposed to an eyed end. It is important to seat the knot correctly around the hook shank.

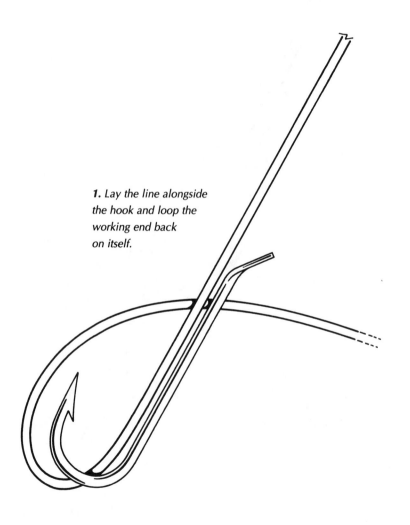

1. Lay the line alongside the hook and loop the working end back on itself.

2. *Make a turn just below the spade.*

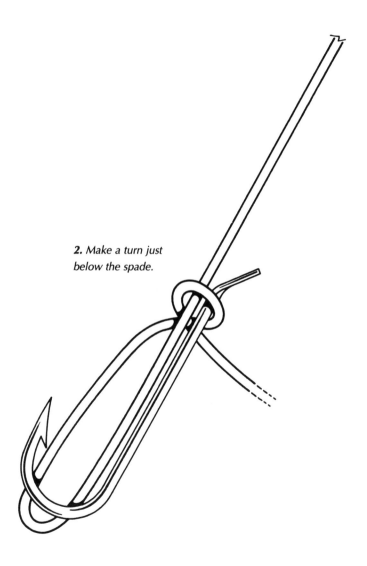

continued on page 234

Spade End Knot

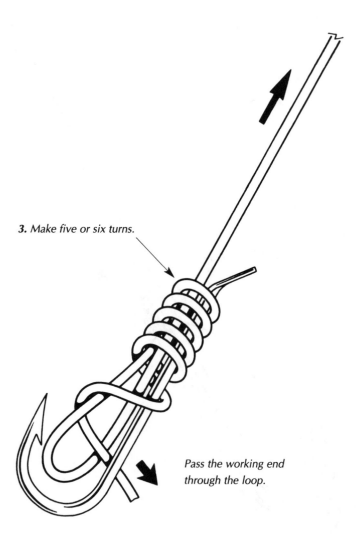

3. Make five or six turns.

Pass the working end
through the loop.

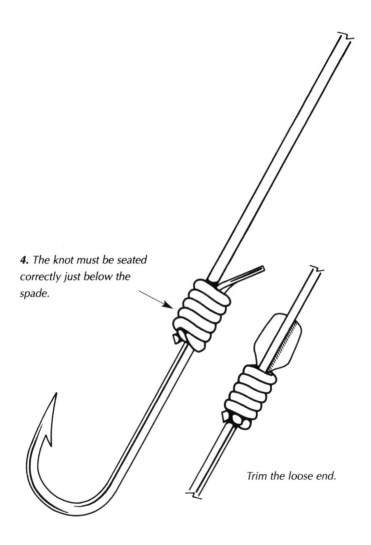

4. The knot must be seated correctly just below the spade.

Trim the loose end.

Applied Knots

Applied knots are knots that are tied to be used for a specific purpose. Often combinations of knots are used to create the required solution. This section contains three very useful examples of applied knots for camping. But remember, with the information contained in this book and a little imagination you can apply many of these camping knots to your next camping trip.

ROPE LADDER

A rope ladder is a great example of how a piece of rope and some knots can create an extremely useful piece of equipment. To tie a ladder of any substantial length is going to require a long piece of rope, so provision for this should be made before starting. A worthwhile exercise is to tie up just one ladder rung as a test to help you estimate the amount of rope that will be required.

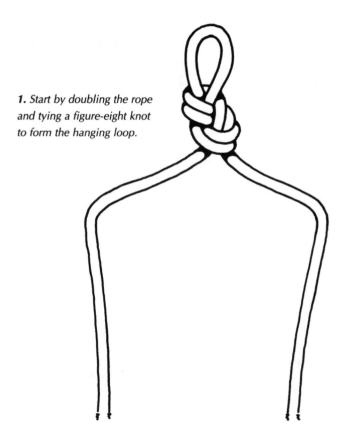

1. Start by doubling the rope and tying a figure-eight knot to form the hanging loop.

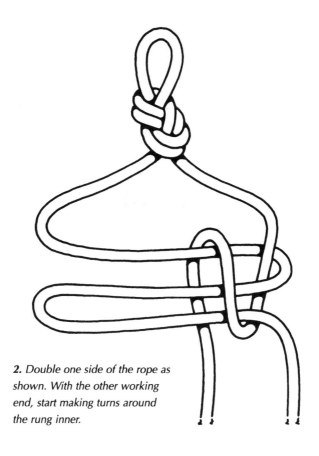

2. Double one side of the rope as shown. With the other working end, start making turns around the rung inner.

continued on page 240

Rope Ladder

3. Make twelve turns, or as many as necessary depending on the width of ladder. Tighten the rung by pulling the standing part and the working end as you finish each one.

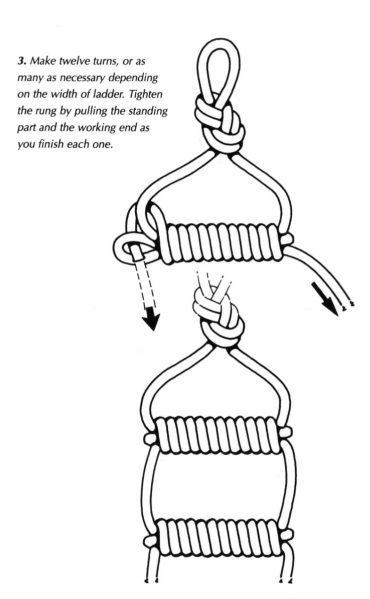

Repeat for as many rungs required. Finish the ladder at the bottom with whichever decorative knot you prefer.

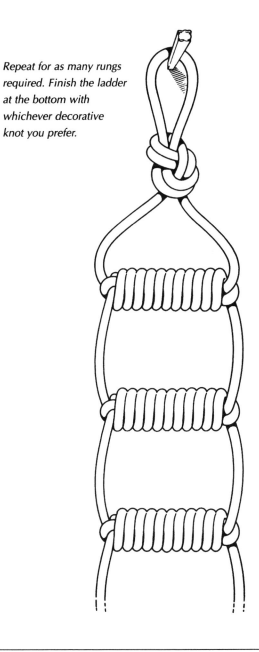

KNIFE LANYARD

A lanyard is usually worn around the neck or attached to a belt for the purpose of holding a wide variety of objects. Even though its technical name is the knife lanyard knot, it is also regularly used for holding whistles, watches, and binoculars. Because the knot is left in view, its very decorative appearance is a great asset.

It may help to create the first two steps around your hand, as shown in the illustration.

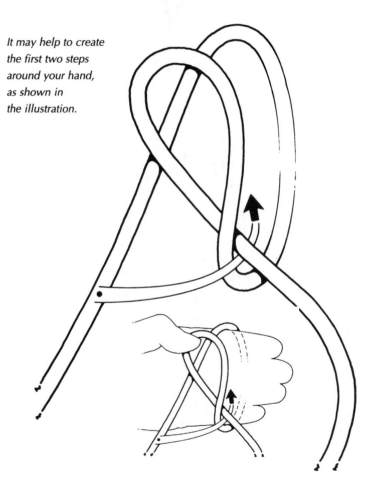

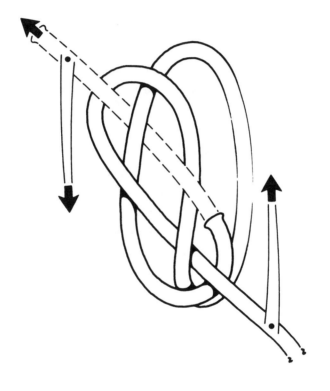

continued on page 244

Knife Lanyard

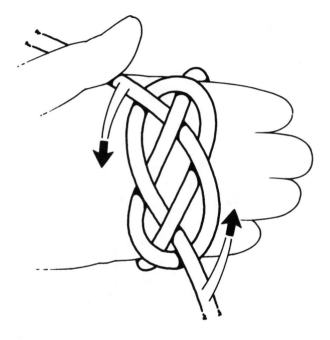

At this point, the knot should look like this, with the pattern on the front and the main loop running behind your hand.

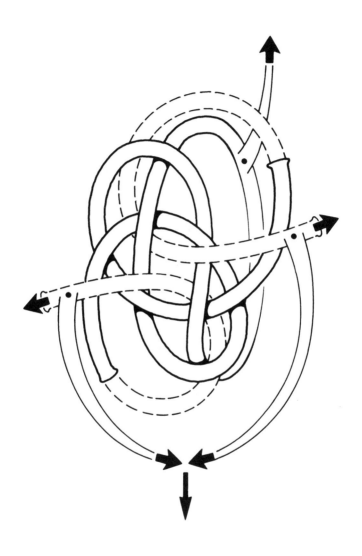

continued on page 246

Knife Lanyard

Slowly draw the knot together, working it into its final shape.

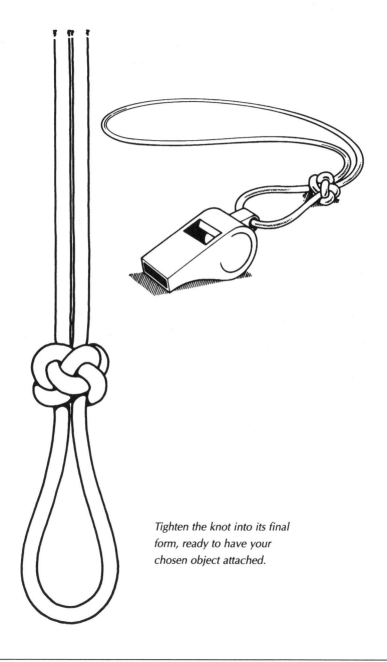

Tighten the knot into its final form, ready to have your chosen object attached.

Barrel Sling

This applied knot is specifically designed to hold a cylindrical container or object. It is particularly useful for suspending open containers off the ground. It can be used for cooking purposes as long as it is tied with thin wire and not rope.

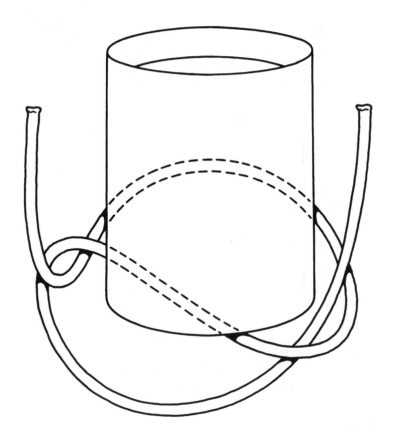

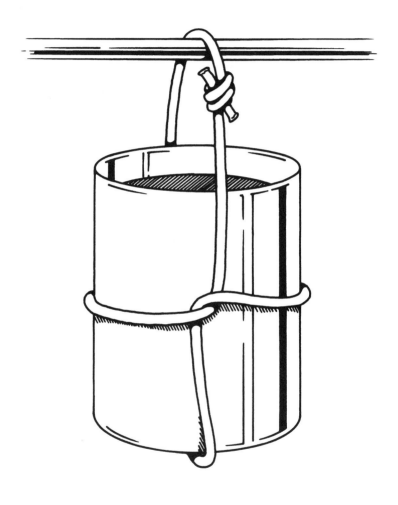

CLIMBING KNOTS

CONTENTS

INTRODUCTION

Climbing and mountaineering, like many activities, have undergone some revolutionary changes in recent years. Long gone are the tweed jackets, leather boots, and natural fiber ropes. The highly developed climbing equipment and apparel of today is, in the main, manufactured or constructed from the very latest "high-tech" materials. Apparel is now lightweight, breathable, and totally water- and windproof. Ropes and equipment are now made from artificial or synthetic materials. Arguably the only components, apart from the rocks and mountains, that have changed very little over recent years are the absolutely essential climbing knots.

The Book of Climbing Knots gives you the opportunity to master 30 classic climbing and mountaineering knots. In focusing solely on the knots and not the techniques and skills of climbing, each knot is allocated generous space for clear instructions and meticulous step-by-step illustrations.

The knots are divided into several distinct groups, each of which is used for different purposes. Practice is essential for good knot tying, so select the right knot for the job and practice until you are confident that you can tie it quickly, securely, and literally, with your eyes closed. Your life may depend on it!

ROPES

Rope is the most important piece of equipment that a climber will possess. It must be rope that is specifically designed and manufactured for climbing. Such rope is often referred to as "dynamic"; this means that it will stretch slightly when under load, helping to absorb the shock of a fall, which effectively increases the breaking strain.

Artificial or synthetic materials have almost completely replaced natural fibers in the manufacture of climbing rope. Man-made filaments can be spun to run the whole length of a line, do not vary in thickness, and do not have to be twisted together to make them cohere. This gives them superior strength.

Nylon, first produced in 1938 for domestic use, was the first man-made material to be used in this way. Since then a range of artificial ropes have been developed to meet different purposes, but they all share certain characteristics. Size for size they are lighter, stronger, and cheaper than their natural counterparts. They do not rot or mildew, are resistant to sunlight, chemicals, oil, gasoline, and most common solvents. They can also be made in a range of colors. Color-coded ropes for climbing make for instant recognition of lines of different function and size.

The vast majority of climbing rope in use today is kernmantle rope (see page 258). It is easy to handle, very flexible, and has a good strength-to-weight ratio. Older-style hawser-laid nylon rope (see page 257), is still widely used for training purposes or where cost is a consideration.

Rope manufactured from artificial fiber does have some disadvantages, the main one being that it melts when heated. Even the friction generated when one rope rubs against another may be enough to cause damage, so it is vital to check your ropes regularly. It is also possible for heat friction to fuse knotted rope together so that it is impossible to untie the knot. Another disadvantage is that artificial ropes made of continuous filaments are so smooth that knots slip and come undone. Knots may need to be secured with additional knots.

Choosing a modern climbing rope is no easy task! There is a vast array of designs, sizes, lengths, colors, and prices. The aim of the next few pages is to explain the main differences and how to look after rope. If in doubt about what rope to purchase, always consult an experienced climber or someone at your local climbing equipment store, who in most cases will be very willing to help you.

HAWSER-LAID ROPE

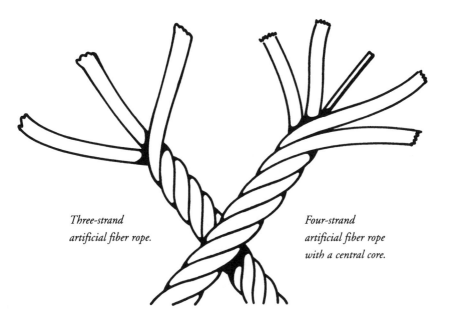

*Three-strand
artificial fiber rope.*

*Four-strand
artificial fiber rope
with a central core.*

Artificial rope laid up or twisted like old-style natural fiber rope is known as hawser-laid. Usually three strands of nylon filaments are twisted together to form the rope. There are variations of this available. One very strong variation is four strands of nylon filament twisted around a central nylon core.

The cost of hawser-laid rope is generally about two thirds that of the more widely used kernmantle constructed climbing rope. Laid-up rope, made of thick multifilaments tightly twisted together, may be very resistant to wear, but it may also be difficult to handle because of its stiffness and knots may not hold well. As a general rule, do not buy a rope that is too stiff. Similarly, be wary of twisted rope that is very soft.

This type of rope may be perfectly acceptable for instructional purposes and novice climbing but should be avoided for any serious forms of climbing and should never be used with mechanical rope ascending and belay devices.

KERNMANTLE

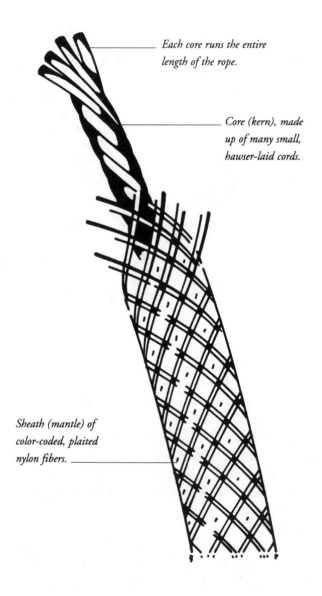

Each core runs the entire
length of the rope.

Core (kern), made
up of many small,
hawser-laid cords.

Sheath (mantle) of
color-coded, plaited
nylon fibers.

Kernmantle rope is made from synthetic materials having a core, or "kern," of many small, hawser-laid cords contained in a braided sheath, or "mantle." It is this structure that gives the rope all the qualities required for climbing. Kernmantle rope is very strong while being extremely flexible and easy to handle. Its flexibility makes it ideal for knot tying. It has the big climbing advantage of the correct amount of elasticity, helping to absorb the shock of a fall; too much elasticity will increase the the distance fallen by a climber. Good-quality kernmantle climbing rope will give low initial stretch under light loads. The object of this is to minimize wasted effort in rope climbing where, for example, prusiking (see page 344) is involved. This can occur on very big climbs where one person will climb the rock first and the remaining climbers will climb the rope. The smoothness of the outer sheath of kernmantle rope not only makes the rope easy and comfortable to handle but it also allows for good contact and easy use with climbing equipment such as karabiners, descendeurs, and belay devices.

Some climbing ropes are sold featuring various dry treatments. These are highly recommended if climbing in wet or icy conditions. It means that the rope has been chemically treated to repel water. Kernmantle ropes are likely to absorb upwards of 20 percent of their weight in water when used in wet and icy conditions. The disadvantages of this are first, the rope weighs a lot more, counteracting the lightweight qualities of kernmantle; and second, and most crucial, the rope loses strength, possibly as much as 40 percent. Dry treatment will also prevent dirt particles from working their way into the fibers of the rope and causing damage. It is recommended that for all-weather climbing, dry-treated rope, which will generally cost more than untreated rope, is used.

Always buy climbing rope from an approved or recognized dealer. It is now compulsory for all climbing rope to carry descriptive tape tags and labels that clearly state the rope has met all of the standards set by the Union Internationale des Associations d'Alpinisme (UIAA). The UIAA is the governing international body that sets all safety standards adhered to in climbing and mountaineering. With so many variations and types of rope for sale it can be all too easy to confuse, for example, a rope designed for sailing use with a climbing rope. The danger lies in that the sailing rope will not have met any of the stringent tests set by the UIAA. Your approved or recognized dealer will, in most cases, always be willing to help you select and buy the correct climbing rope.

ROPE SIZES AND LENGTHS

Climbing rope is manufactured in a range of sizes, determined by the diameter of the rope, and a range of rope lengths. Different manufactures may produce rope of slightly varying diameters but as a general guide four thicknesses are used in climbing: 5mm (¹/₄ in), 7mm (¹/₃ in), 9mm (³/₈ in), and 11mm (¹/₂ in). The equivalent thicknesses in hawser-laid rope are 1, 2, 3, and 4.

Standard rope lengths are 45m (150ft), 50m (165ft), and 60m (195ft). Check with your approved or recognized dealer for any different rope sizes. They will, in most cases, be keen to offer advice without prejudice on all climbing equipment.

All synthetic rope ends can be sealed using heat. When you buy standard lengths of rope the ends will be factory sealed. If you should need to cut synthetic rope yourself, use a sharp knife and then melt the end with a cigarette lighter or on an electric ring.

5mm (¹/₄ in) rope
These light, flexible ropes are used for threading through climbing protection devices and for creating prusik loops.

7mm (¹/₃ in) rope
These ropes are used for threading through medium-size climbing protection devices.

9mm (³/₈ in) double or half rope

Many climbing techniques use a pair of ropes. This rope is specifically designed to be used in pairs and is best suited for mountaineering, alpine climbing, and long rock climbs.

9mm (³/₈ in) single rope

This lightweight rope is designed to be used singly and is favored by sport climbers where weight is a priority. It is also used for threading through large climbing protection devices.

11mm (¹/₂ in) rope

This rope is the main climbing rope, used for general rock climbing. It is an all-around rope and works well on everything from sports to long free routes. It has a good strength-to-weight ratio and it can also be used for slings.

LOOKING AFTER ROPE

Climbing rope is sturdy material, but it is expensive, so it's worth looking after it properly. Caring for rope and using it correctly will help it keep its strength and prolong its life. Here are some guidelines for good rope care.

* Avoid dragging rope over rough, sharp edges, or dirty, gritty surfaces where particles could get into the rope and damage it.

* Do not walk on rope.

* Do not force rope into harsh kinks.

* Do not use as a tow rope or for anything else other than climbing purposes.

* Inspect rope regularly and wash off any dirt or grit with a mild detergent.

* If rope has been in salt water, rinse thoroughly to remove all salt deposits.

* Always store rope in a dry place, out of sunlight, and away from such things as car battery acid.

* If rope has been damaged in any way or has sustained a severe fall it should be discarded in the interests of safety.

* If knots are repeatedly tied in one section of rope, that section will weaken.

* Always use your own ropes for climbing, preferably ones that you have bought. If you borrow a rope, make sure you know its history.

* The life of a climbing rope obviously depends on the amout of use, but as a general rule rope should be dicarded and replaced after two to three years.

* Finally, never use two ropes of different material together, because only the more rigid of the two will work under strain.

ROPE DAMAGE

Core damage can be detected by lumps or bulges in the rope. The sheath can be unaffected by this and show no external damage. As the main strength of the rope is in the core, this is extremely dangerous and the rope should be discarded immediately.

Sheath damage is usually the result of the rope rubbing across a sharp edge, or a sharp stone or rock dropping onto the rope. The core will often be unaffected by this damage but the rope is now unsafe and should be discarded immediately.

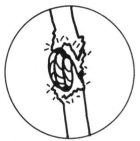

COILING ROPE

Coiling a rope will ensure that it will be immediately at hand and untangled when required.

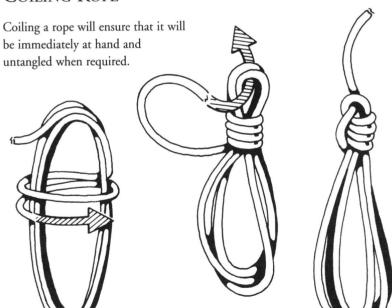

HOW TO USE THIS BOOK

The diagrams accompanying the descriptions of the knots are intended to be self-explanatory, but for added clarity, sequenced, written instructions and special tying techniques and methods do accompany the knots. There are arrows to show the directions in which you should push or pull the working ends and standing parts of the rope or line. The dotted lines indicate intermediate positions of the rope. When tying the knot you should always have a sufficient working end to complete the knot. The amount of working end required can often be calculated by looking at the illustration of the finished knot. Always follow the order shown of going over or under a length of line; reversing or changing this order could result in a completely different knot, which might well be unstable, unsafe, and insecure.

ROPE PARTS

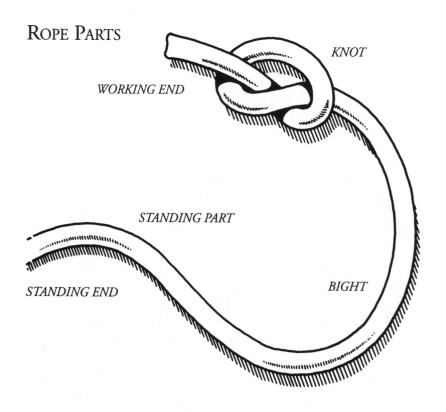

KNOT

WORKING END

STANDING PART

STANDING END

BIGHT

WARNING

Friction-generated heat may cause synthetic rope to weaken and break without warning (see page 256). Rock climbers and mountaineers should exercise extreme caution when using synthetic rope in situations that may cause friction damage. **The result could be fatal.**

STOPPER KNOTS

Stopper knots, as their name suggests, are used to prevent the end of a rope or line from slipping through an eye, loop, or hole. They can be used to bind the end of a rope so that it will not unravel, weight the end of a rope for throwing purposes, and for decoration.

Many climbing knots, for example, the climber's bowline (see page 310) can be finished off with a stopper knot tied in the working end for extra security.

FIGURE-EIGHT KNOT

This is a quick and efficient way of tying a simple and attractive stopper knot at the end of a line or rope. The knot's name comes from its characteristic shape. Its interlaced appearance has long been seen as a symbol of interwoven affection. In heraldry it signifies faithful love and appears on various coats of arms—hence its other names, the Flemish or Savoy knot.

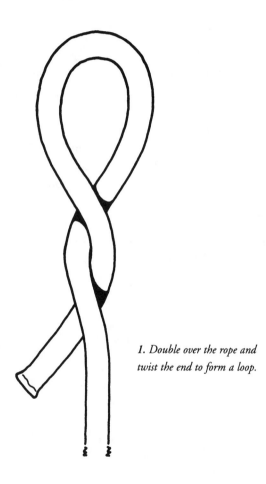

1. Double over the rope and twist the end to form a loop.

2. Pass the working end over the standing part and then up through the loop.

3. Pull on both the working end and the standing part to form the knot.

HEAVING LINE KNOT

This stopper knot has the advantage of adding considerable weight to the end of the line. This proves particularly useful for throwing the end of a line across a gap or to another climber.

The heaving line knot is widely used by sailors, who tie it at the end of a lighter line, which in turn is attached to a heavier line. The lighter line is thrown first, usually from boat to shore, so the heavier line can then be drawn or heaved behind it.

The knot's other name, the monk's knot, derives from its use by Franciscan monks to weight the ends of the cords they use as belts.

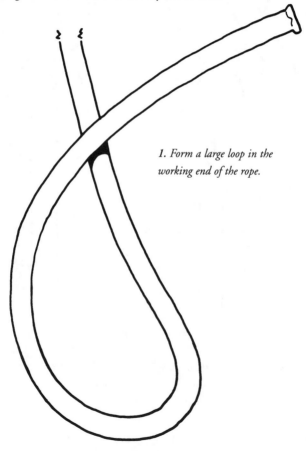

1. Form a large loop in the working end of the rope.

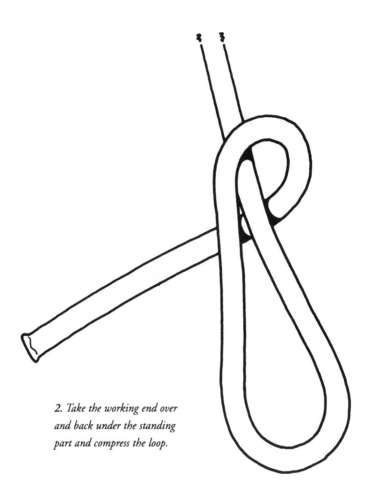

2. Take the working end over and back under the standing part and compress the loop.

continued on page 272

Heaving Line Knot

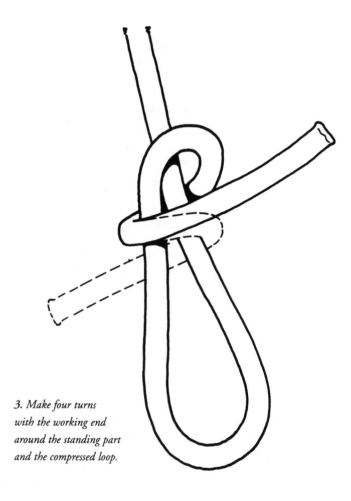

3. Make four turns
with the working end
around the standing part
and the compressed loop.

4. On the fourth turn take the working end down through the loop. Keep the already formed turns as tight as possible.

5. Pull on the working end and the standing part to tighten the knot. As the knot is tightening, form the final knot shape.

BENDS

Bends are used to join two lengths of rope at their ends to form one longer piece. It is important, if bends are to be secure, for the ropes joined in this way to be of the same kind and the same diameter.

The sheet bend (see "Essential Outdoor Knots," page 366) is the exception to this rule. It is very secure, even when it is used to join ropes of different diameters.

FISHERMAN'S KNOT

It is known that this classic knot was used by the ancient Greeks. It is generally known as the fisherman's knot, but over the years it has picked up many different names (including English knot, halibut knot, and waterman's knot).

It is formed from two overhand knots (see page 362) that jam against each other. After use, the two component knots are generally easily separated and undone. The fisherman's knot should be used to join lines of equal thickness and is not suitable for large-diameter rope.

NOTE: The fisherman's knot and the fisherman's bend (see page 382) are quite different and should not be confused with each other.

1. Take the first line and form an overhand knot at the working end.

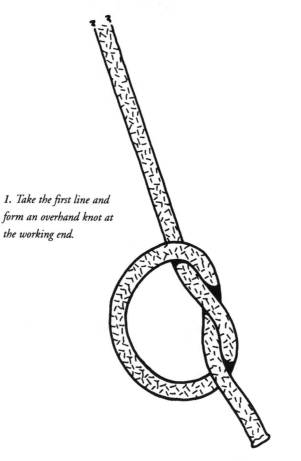

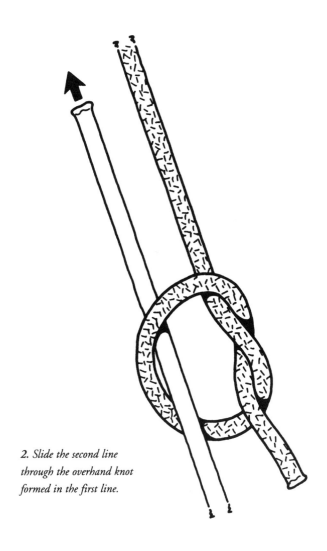

2. Slide the second line through the overhand knot formed in the first line.

continued on page 278

Fisherman's Knot

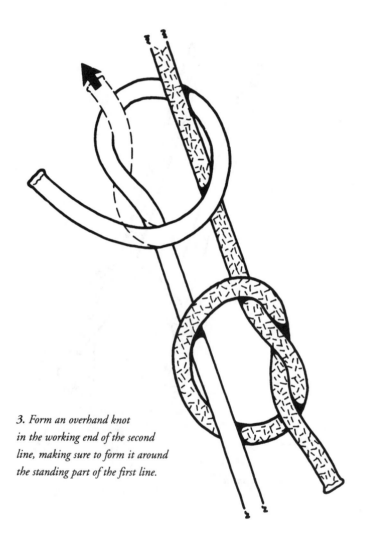

3. Form an overhand knot
in the working end of the second
line, making sure to form it around
the standing part of the first line.

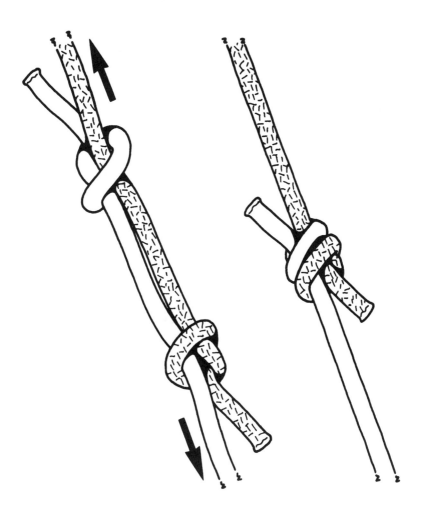

4. *Tighten both of the overhand knots and slowly draw them together by pulling on the standing part of each line.*

5. *Continue pulling on the standing parts until the two overhand knots are jammed firmly together. The knot is now complete.*

DOUBLE FISHERMAN'S KNOT

This extension of the fisherman's knot is one of the most widely used climbing knots and is one of the safest ways to join rope or cord. It is probably the best way to create a sling (loop) from a single piece of rope or cord.

It is good practice to seize the ends of the knot with sticky tape to keep them from catching on the rock face and to minimize the risk of the knot's working loose.

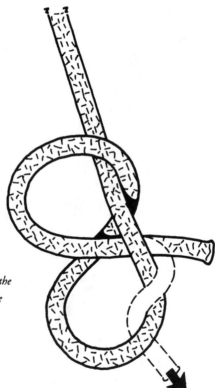

1. Form a double overhand knot in the working end of the first line.

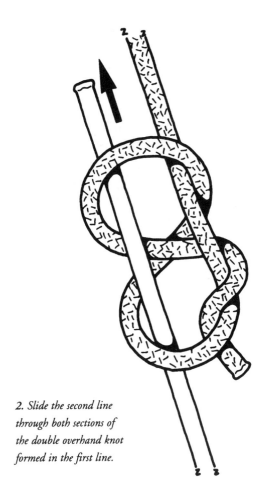

2. Slide the second line
through both sections of
the double overhand knot
formed in the first line.

continued on page 282

Double Fisherman's Knot

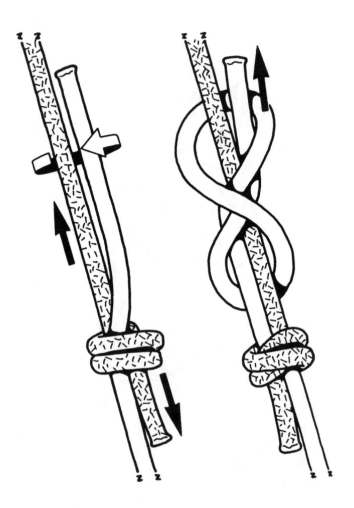

3. Tighten the double overhand knot
in the first line. It helps at this point
to turn the knot assembly over.

4. Form a double overhand knot
in the working end of the second
line, making sure to form it around
the standing part of the first line.

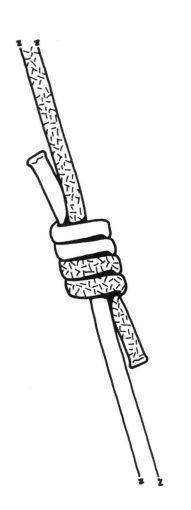

5. Tighten the second double overhand knot and pull on both standing parts until the two knots are jammed firmly together. The knot is now complete.

6. Seize the ends of the knot with sticky tape to keep them from catching on the rock face and to minimize the risk of the knot's working loose.

CARRICK BEND

This knot is formed from two overhand knots crossing each other. It is a very stable knot, does not slip, and is a very secure way of joining two ropes of similar diameter but different type. It can be used to tie heavy ropes together, but this does form a bulky knot that is unsuitable, for example, for passing through a karabiner.

In its flat form before it is fully drawn together it is valued for its distinctive symmetric appearance and can often be seen in various forms of design.

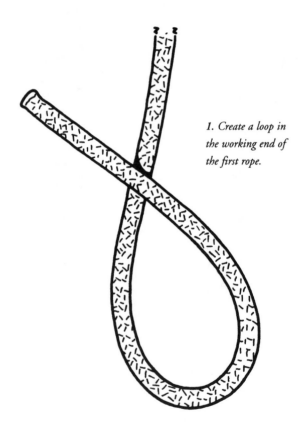

1. Create a loop in the working end of the first rope.

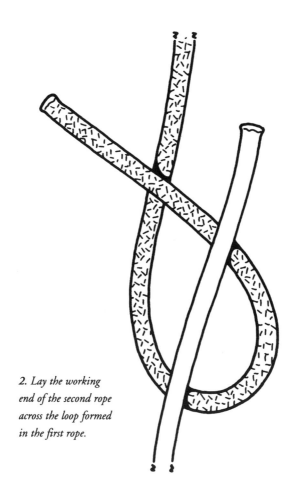

2. *Lay the working end of the second rope across the loop formed in the first rope.*

continued on page 286

Carrick Bend

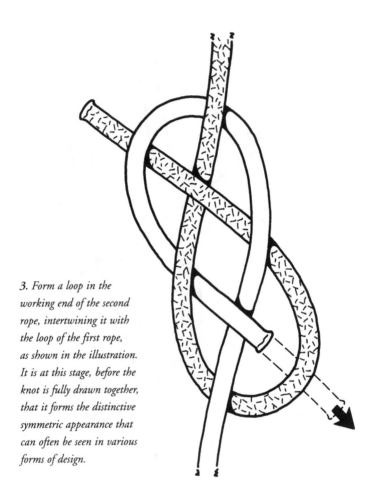

3. *Form a loop in the working end of the second rope, intertwining it with the loop of the first rope, as shown in the illustration. It is at this stage, before the knot is fully drawn together, that it forms the distinctive symmetric appearance that can often be seen in various forms of design.*

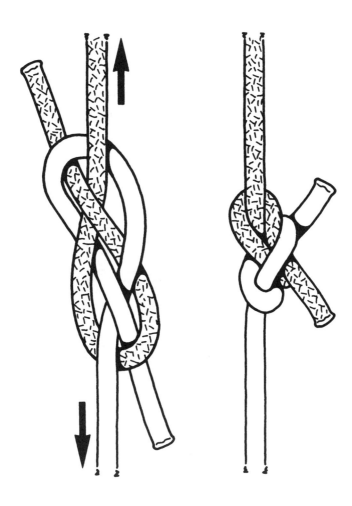

4. *Slowly draw the knot together by pulling on both standing parts.*

5. *Continue to draw the knot tight until the two loops lock together.*

HUNTER'S BEND

The Hunter's, or rigger's, bend is based on two overhand knots. It is strong, stable, and has a good grip and the advantage of being easy to untie.

It is named after Dr. Edward Hunter, a retired physician, who was reported to have invented it in 1968. Subsequent research, however, revealed that the same knot had been described nearly twenty years earlier by Phil D. Smith, in an American publication called *Knots for Mountaineers*. He had devised the knot while working on the waterfront in San Francisco and called it the rigger's bend. Whoever first invented it, the Hunter's, or rigger's, bend remains a good knot with many useful qualities.

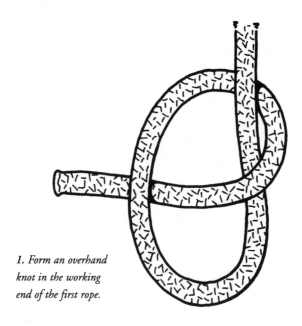

1. Form an overhand knot in the working end of the first rope.

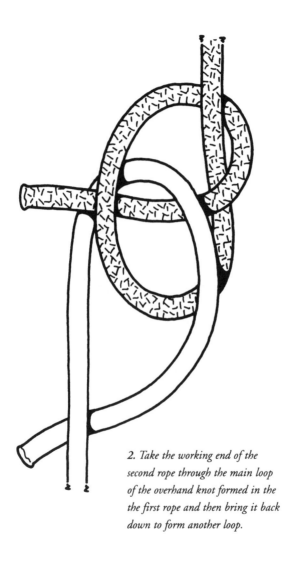

2. *Take the working end of the*
second rope through the main loop
of the overhand knot formed in the
the first rope and then bring it back
down to form another loop.

continued on page 290

Hunter's Bend

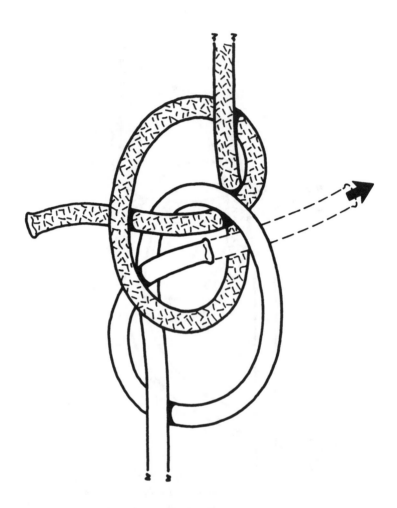

*3. Form an overhand knot in the working end of
the second rope, intertwining it with the overhand
knot of the first rope, as shown in the illustration.*

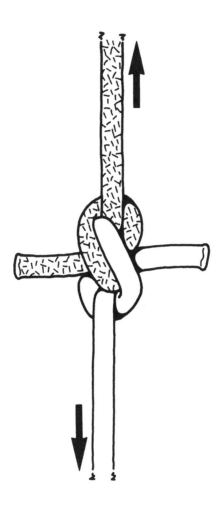

4. Tighten the knot by pulling on both standing parts until the two overhand knots lock together. The knot is now complete.

TAPE KNOT

Most "tapes" are sewn into slings at the manufacturing stage. Should you ever need to tie two tape ends together, use the tape knot.

It is a relatively simple knot to tie and after you have drawn the knot tight it is advisable to seize the ends with sticky tape to minimize the possibility of the knot's working loose. As with all climbing knots, you should check the knot regularly to ensure it is still tied firmly.

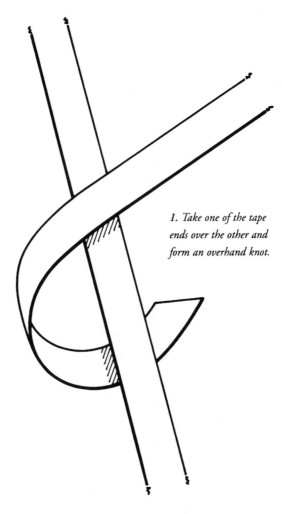

1. Take one of the tape ends over the other and form an overhand knot.

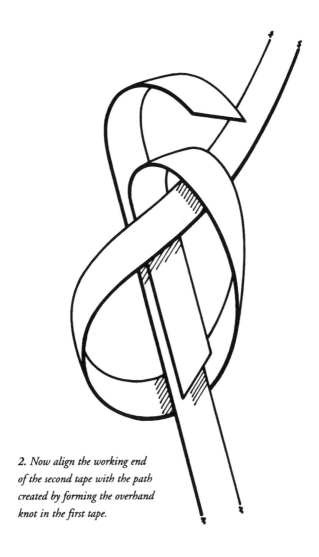

*2. Now align the working end
of the second tape with the path
created by forming the overhand
knot in the first tape.*

continued on page 294

Tape Knot

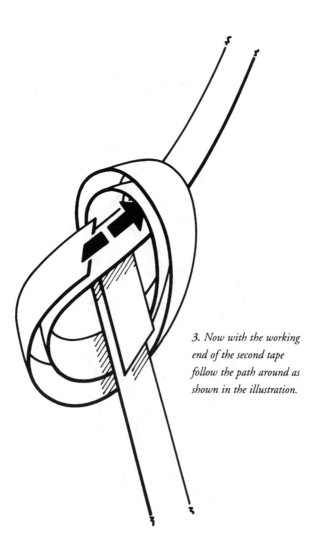

3. Now with the working
end of the second tape
follow the path around as
shown in the illustration.

4. Tighten the knot by pulling on both the standing parts until the two overhand knots mesh together. Seize the tape ends with sticky tape to keep them from catching on the rock face and to minimize the risk of the knot's working loose.

LOOPS

K nots made in the end of a rope by folding it back into an eye or loop and then knotting it to its own standing part are called loops. They are fixed and do not slide.

Loops are particularly important to climbers who find these knots indispensable for tying on and when using anchors.

FIGURE-EIGHT LOOP

This is one of the best known and most widely used of all climbing knots. It is probably the safest way to form a loop in the main climbing rope and is regularly used for tying on and attaching to anchors.

It is comparatively easy to tie and stays tied. Its disadvantages—it is difficult to adjust and cannot easily be untied after loading—tend to be outweighed by its general usefulness.

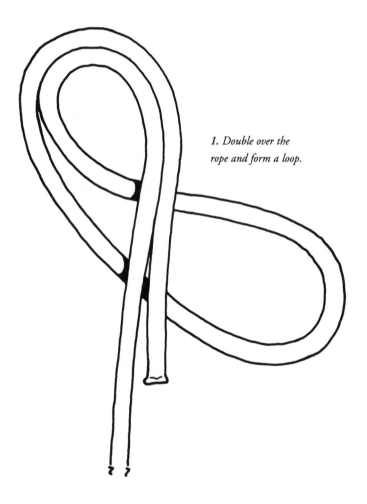

1. Double over the rope and form a loop.

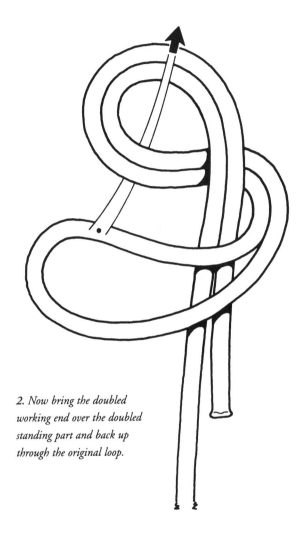

2. Now bring the doubled
working end over the doubled
standing part and back up
through the original loop.

continued on page 300

Figure-Eight Loop

3. Pull the doubled working end through the original loop and slowly draw the knot together by pulling the loop and the main standing part.

*4. Tighten the final knot,
making sure that the figure-
eight pattern and the loop
have been correctly formed.*

THREADED FIGURE-EIGHT

This variation of the figure-eight loop is used when you want to tie a loop around something rather than drop it over or onto something. This knot is most widely used for "tying on"—securely connecting a rope to a harness. For added security, a stopper knot should be added.

Tying on using a correctly tied threaded figure-eight knot is a maneuver that all climbers should be able to do with their eyes closed!

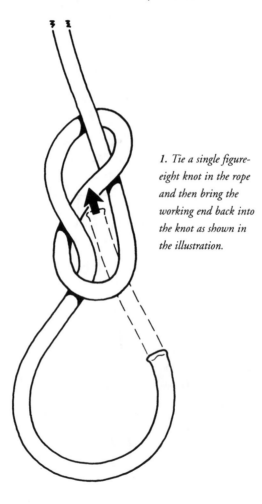

1. Tie a single figure-eight knot in the rope and then bring the working end back into the knot as shown in the illustration.

2. Now begin to follow the path of the first figure-eight knot with the working end.

continued on page 304

Threaded Figure-Eight

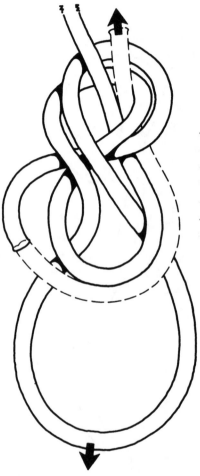

3. *Continue to follow the path of the original knot and bring the working end out in line with the standing part.*

4. *Tighten and form the final knot. A stopper knot can be added at this stage for extra security.*

ALPINE BUTTERFLY KNOT

This knot is used to create a secure loop in a line or rope. It can be a difficult knot to tie, so practice is required. But on the plus side, it unties easily, does not slip, and the loop does not shrink when the knot is tightened.

Once a very popular climbing knot, the alpine butterfly knot has now lost some of its popularity due to other emerging climbing knots and newly designed equipment, but it still remains a very secure and effective loop.

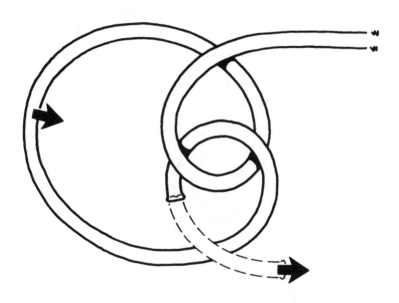

1. Form a loop in the rope, bring the working end around through the loop, and form another loop.

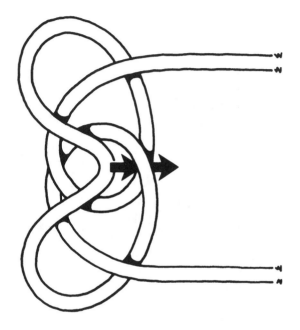

2. Create the rope pattern shown in the illustration and push the bight of the rope through in the direction of the arrows.

continued on page 308

Alpine Butterfly Knot

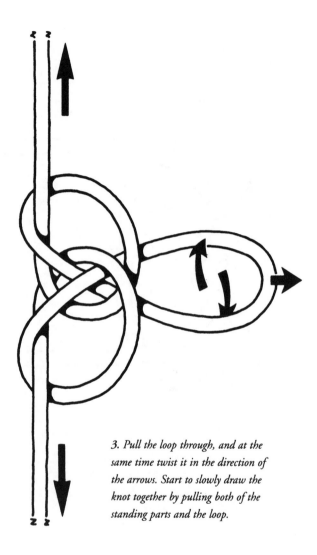

3. *Pull the loop through, and at the same time twist it in the direction of the arrows. Start to slowly draw the knot together by pulling both of the standing parts and the loop.*

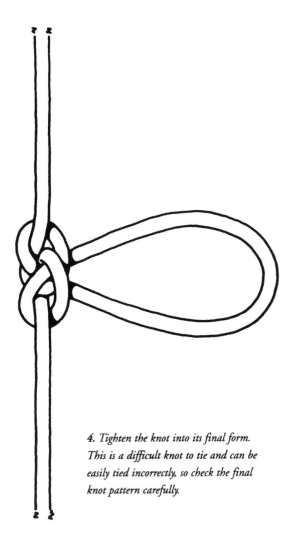

4. *Tighten the knot into its final form. This is a difficult knot to tie and can be easily tied incorrectly, so check the final knot pattern carefully.*

CLIMBER'S BOWLINE

A climber's bowline is also known as a bulin knot. It is a classic knot for tying on and has the advantage of being easy to adjust. It can be used either when tying on around the waist or to a harness.

A note of caution: Although the climber's bowline is fast to tie and easily untied, it does have a tendency to work loose, especially if the rope is new or stiff. It should always, therefore, be used in conjunction with a stopper knot.

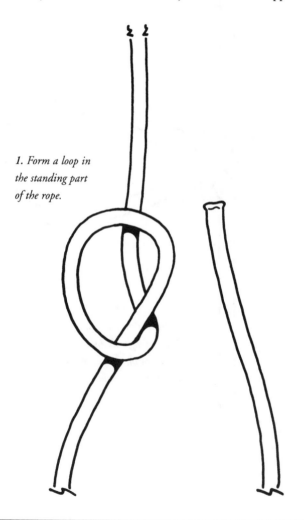

1. Form a loop in the standing part of the rope.

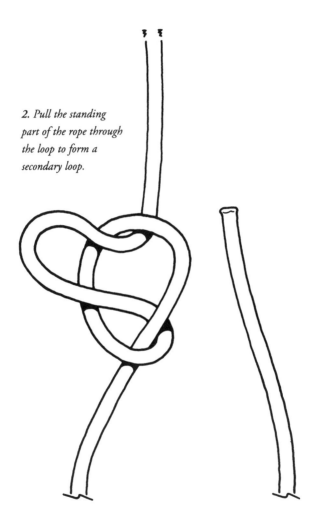

2. Pull the standing part of the rope through the loop to form a secondary loop.

continued on page 312

Climber's Bowline

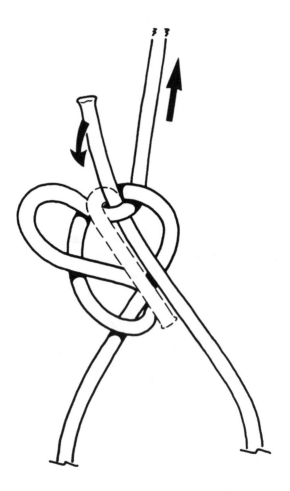

3. Push the working end through the secondary
loop and pull it straight back over as shown in
the illustration. Pull the standing part and the
knot will form.

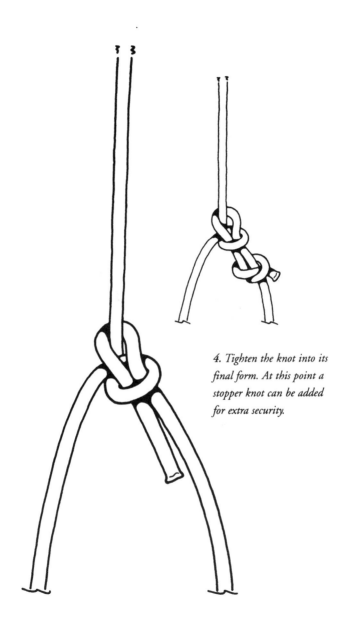

4. Tighten the knot into its final form. At this point a stopper knot can be added for extra security.

SPANISH BOWLINE

This is a very strong knot that has been widely used in mountain rescue work and is also known as the chair knot. It is formed by two separate and independent loops that will hold securely and are very safe, even under considerable strain.

To effect a rescue, one loop is slipped over the casualty's head, around the back, and under the armpits; the other loop goes around the legs behind the knees. It is vitally important that each loop is tightened to the individual's size and locked into position, otherwise an unconscious casualty could easily fall through the loops.

The Spanish bowline is also a very useful for hoisting large objects and pieces of equipment.

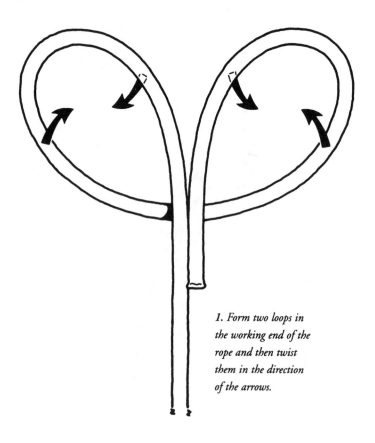

1. Form two loops in the working end of the rope and then twist them in the direction of the arrows.

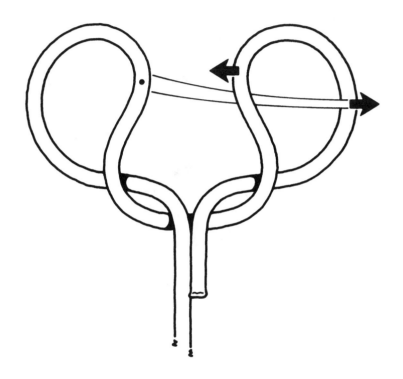

*2. Pull the left-hand twisted loop
through the right-hand twisted loop.*

continued on page 316

Spanish Bowline

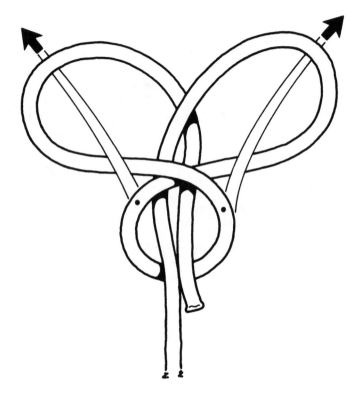

*3. Pull the two indicated points of
the newly formed lower loop through
the upper loops.*

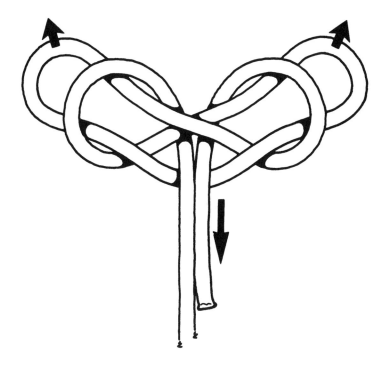

4. Slowly pull on the three points indicated by the arrows, making sure that the knot keeps its pattern and shape.

continued on page 318

Spanish Bowline

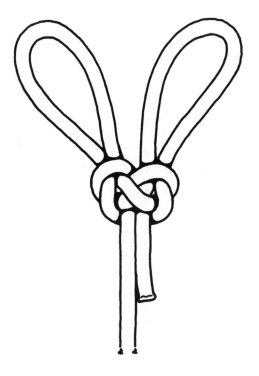

5. *Before tightening the knot into its final form, adjust the loops to the required sizes.*

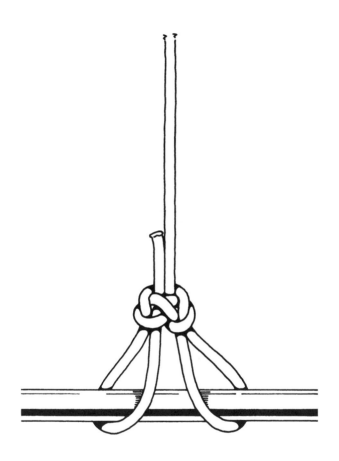

6. The Spanish bowline is very useful for hoisting large objects and pieces of equipment.

SHORTENINGS

Shortenings are invaluable knots, well worth mastering. As their name suggests, they are used to shorten lengths of rope or line without cutting. A rope shortened by means of a knot can always be lengthened later, and a single unbroken line will always be more secure than two lines knotted together.

Shortenings can be used as an emergency measure to take up damaged lengths of climbing rope. The weakened sections are incorporated into the knot and are not, therefore, subject to strain.

SHEEPSHANK

The sheepshank can be used to shorten any rope to any required length without cutting. It is easy to tie, holds under tension with a good jamming action, does not change its shape, and unties easily.

In a climbing emergency a sheepshank can be used to shorten a damaged line or rope, but take care to ensure that the damaged or weakened section of the rope passes through both half hitches.

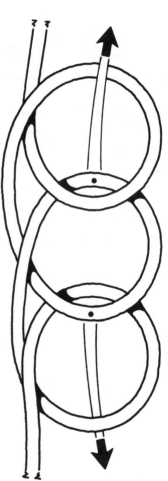

1. Form three loops at the point in the rope where the shortening will be required. Pull the indicated points of the middle loop through the two outer loops.

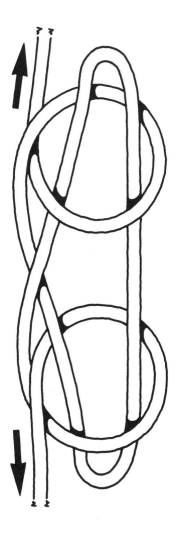

2. *Slowly pull on the two main parts of the rope, making sure that the knot retains it, shape and form.*

continued on page 324

Sheepshank

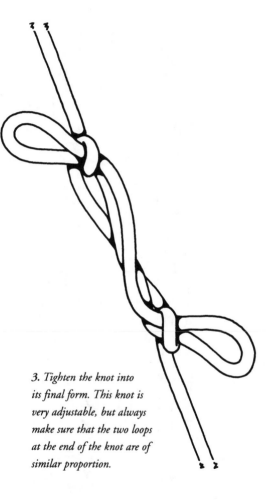

3. *Tighten the knot into its final form. This knot is very adjustable, but always make sure that the two loops at the end of the knot are of similar proportion.*

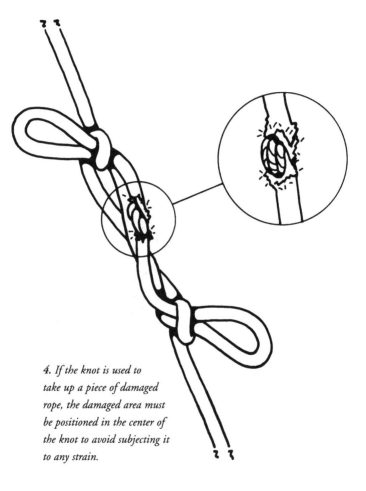

4. If the knot is used to take up a piece of damaged rope, the damaged area must be positioned in the center of the knot to avoid subjecting it to any strain.

LOOP KNOT

This knot can be used to form a quick and simple loop in a rope or, more important, it can be used in an emergency to shorten a damaged rope. The weakened or damaged section of the rope is taken up in the center of the knot, where it cannot be put under any strain.

Should your climbing ropes become weakened or damage, dispose of them at the first opportunity. The risks involved in using damaged or weakened rope for any climbing activities are too great!

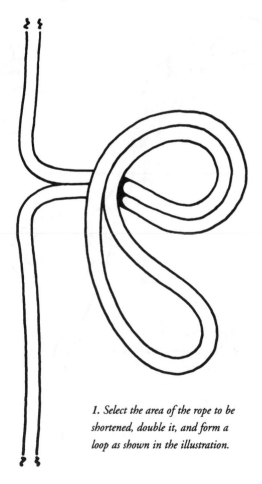

1. Select the area of the rope to be shortened, double it, and form a loop as shown in the illustration.

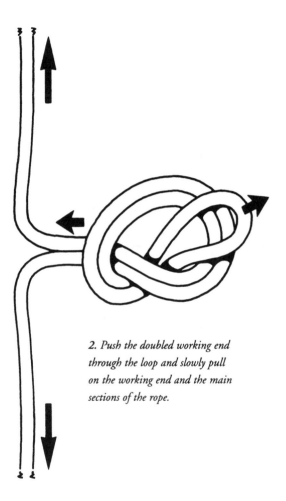

2. Push the doubled working end through the loop and slowly pull on the working end and the main sections of the rope.

continued on page 328

Loop Knot

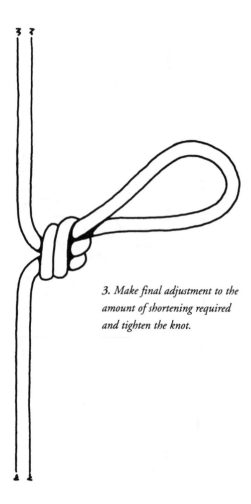

3. Make final adjustment to the amount of shortening required and tighten the knot.

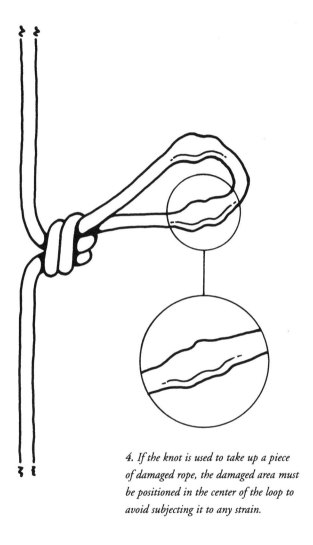

4. *If the knot is used to take up a piece of damaged rope, the damaged area must be positioned in the center of the loop to avoid subjecting it to any strain.*

Hitches

Hitches are knots used to secure a rope to another object (such as a karabiner, protection device, stake), or to another rope that does not play any part in the actual tying, for example, attaching a sling to the main climbing rope.

CLOVE HITCH

The clove hitch is one of the best known and most valuable of general hitches. Its main climbing use is to attach line or rope to metal pegs or stakes. It is a relatively easy knot to tie and can, with practice, be tied with just one hand, which is essential because its normal use is in situations where speed is essential.

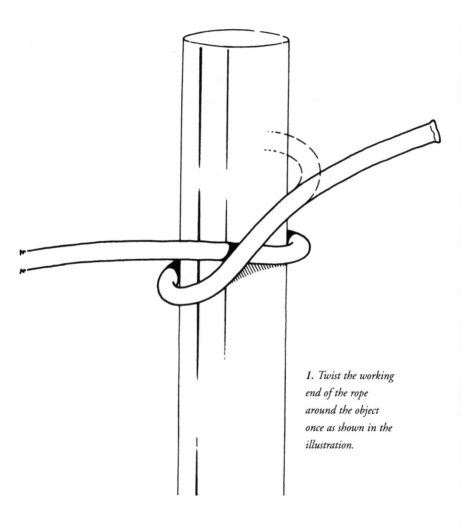

1. Twist the working end of the rope around the object once as shown in the illustration.

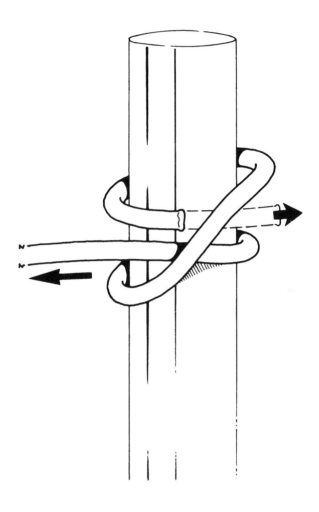

2. Twist the working end a second time, directing it out underneath the crossed-over section of the first twist.

continued on page 334

Clove Hitch

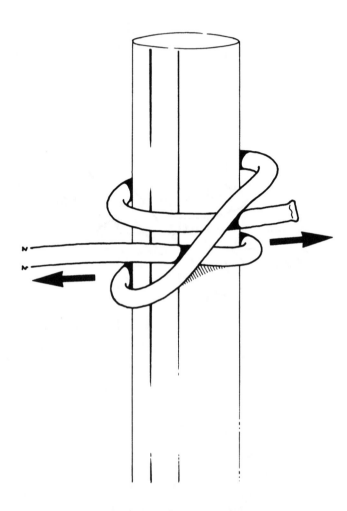

3. Slowly pull the working end and
the standing part, making sure that
the knot keeps its pattern and shape.

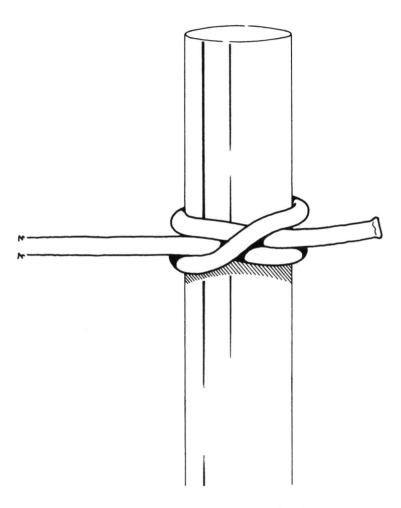

4. Tighten the knot into its final form.

Clove Hitch—Over a Stake

This variation of the clove hitch is dropped over a peg or stake rather than tied around the object. It is formed by two overlapping half hitches and with practice can be tied very quickly. It is specifically used to attach a tape sling to a peg or stake.

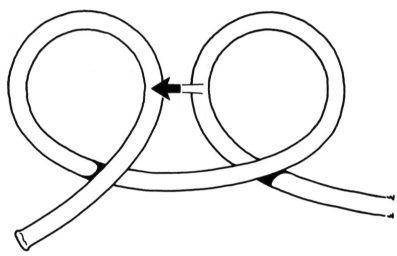

1. Form two loops in the working end of the rope and pull the right-hand loop over the top of the left-hand loop.

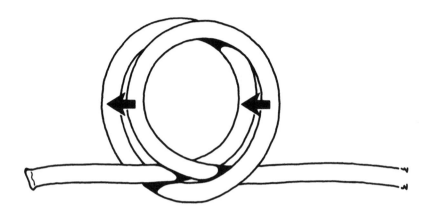

2. Position the two loops on top of each other.

3. Adjust the size of the loops to fit the object.

continued on page 338

Clove Hitch—Over a Stake

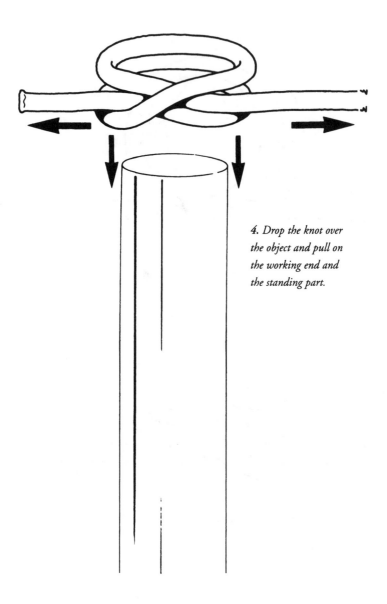

4. Drop the knot over the object and pull on the working end and the standing part.

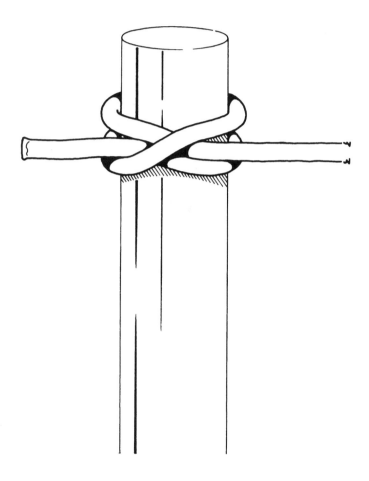

5. Tighten the knot into its final form.

CLOVE HITCH—MADE ON A RING

This further variation of the clove hitch is specifically used to attach a line or rope to a ring or similar construction. It is possible to quickly loosen and re-tighten this knot to control or regulate the length of line leading to the ring or similar construction.

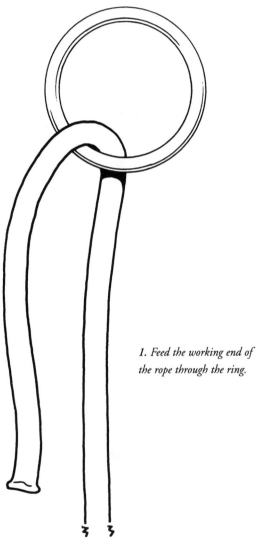

1. Feed the working end of the rope through the ring.

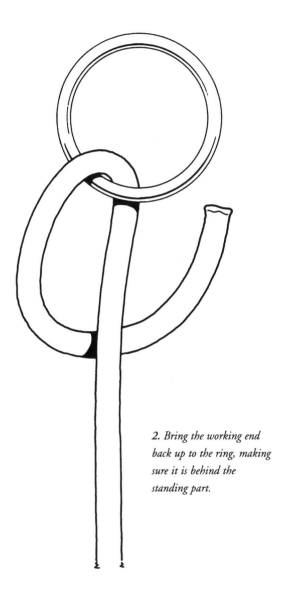

2. Bring the working end
back up to the ring, making
sure it is behind the
standing part.

continued on page 342

Clove Hitch—Made on a Ring

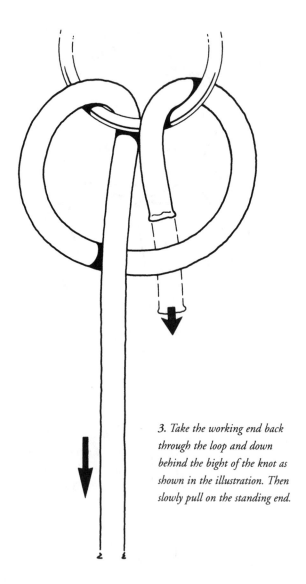

3. Take the working end back
through the loop and down
behind the bight of the knot as
shown in the illustration. Then
slowly pull on the standing end.

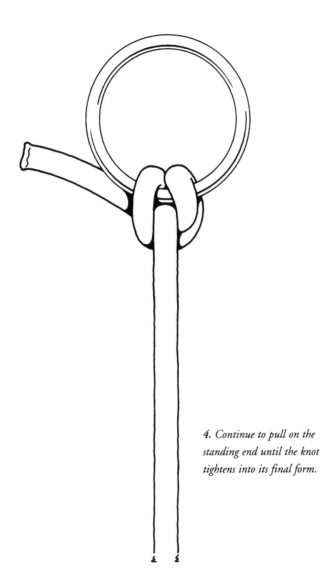

4. Continue to pull on the standing end until the knot tightens into its final form.

PRUSIK KNOT

This knot was devised by Dr. Carl Prusik in 1931. It is used to attach slings to the main climbing rope in such a way that they slide freely when the knot is loose but hold firm under a sideways load.

The Prusik knot does not always slide easily and, once the load is in place, it can only be released by removing the weight and freeing the turns of the rope. The knot must be tied with rope that is considerably thinner than the main climbing rope, and it is important to remember that the knot can slip if the rope is wet or icy.

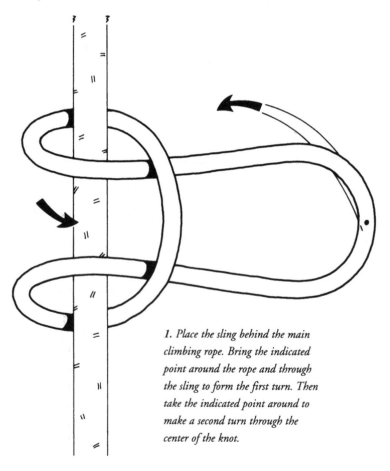

1. Place the sling behind the main climbing rope. Bring the indicated point around the rope and through the sling to form the first turn. Then take the indicated point around to make a second turn through the center of the knot.

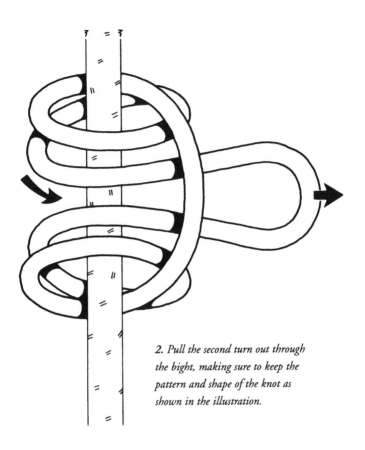

2. Pull the second turn out through the bight, making sure to keep the pattern and shape of the knot as shown in the illustration.

continued on page 346

Prusik Knot

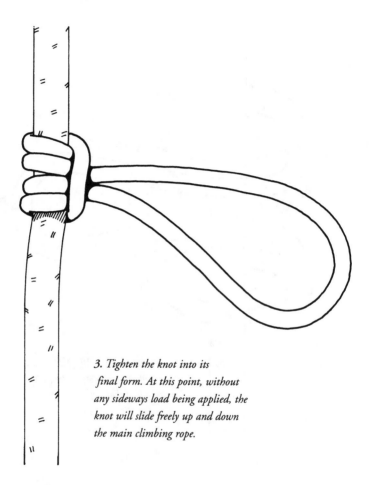

3. Tighten the knot into its
final form. At this point, without
any sideways load being applied, the
knot will slide freely up and down
the main climbing rope.

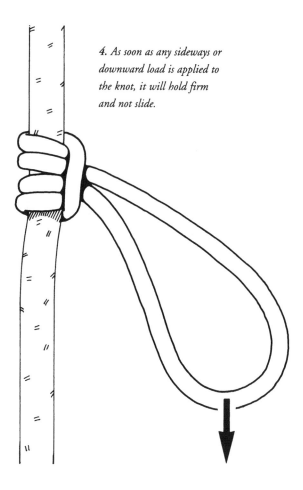

4. As soon as any sideways or downward load is applied to the knot, it will hold firm and not slide.

BACHMANN HITCH

This knot is a very useful alternative to the Prusik knot. It moves more easily, is less likely to jam, and works better on wet and icy ropes. It is tied in combination with a screwgate karabiner, which in turn provides a good handhold.

It is essential that the Bachmann knot is tied with rope much thinner than the main climbing rope. Practice tying this knot with one hand.

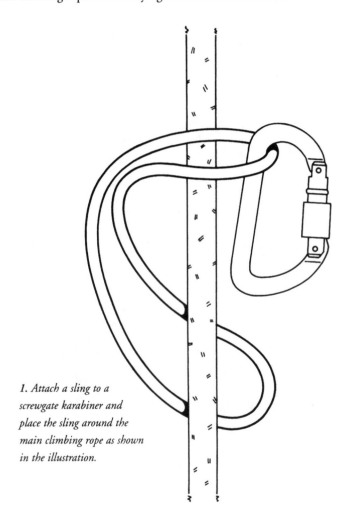

1. Attach a sling to a screwgate karabiner and place the sling around the main climbing rope as shown in the illustration.

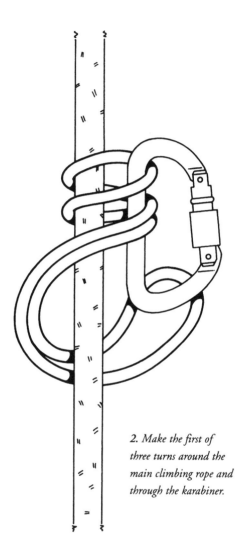

2. Make the first of three turns around the main climbing rope and through the karabiner.

continued on page 350

Bachmann Hitch

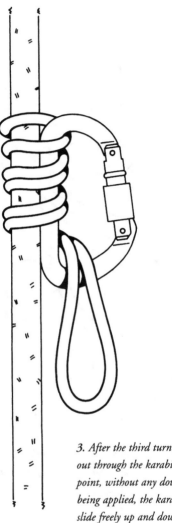

3. *After the third turn pull the loop out through the karabiner. At this point, without any downward load being applied, the karabiner will slide freely up and down the main climbing rope.*

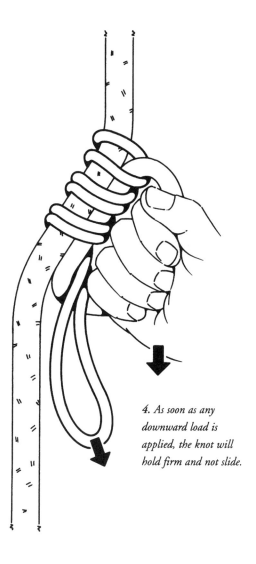

4. As soon as any downward load is applied, the knot will hold firm and not slide.

ITALIAN HITCH

The Italian hitch is an innovative climbing knot used for belaying, and was introduced into the mountaineers' lexicon of knots in 1974. Its chief advantage lies in its means of absorbing the energy of a fall.

The climbing rope is attached to a karabiner with an Italian hitch and this will check a climber's fall by locking up. The knot also allows the climbing rope to be paid out or pulled in to provide slack or tension when required.

It is the official means of belaying (that is, fixing a running rope around a rock or cleat) of the Union Internationale des Associations d'Alpinisme. The major disadvantage of this knot, also called the munter friction hitch or sliding ring hitch, is that it is easy to tie incorrectly.

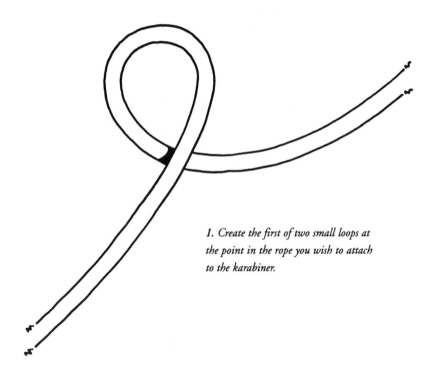

1. Create the first of two small loops at the point in the rope you wish to attach to the karabiner.

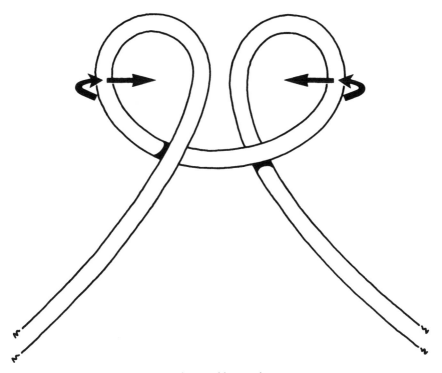

2. Create the second loop in the opposite way to the first, as shown above. Pull the two loops together in the direction of the arrows.

continued on page 354

Italian Hitch

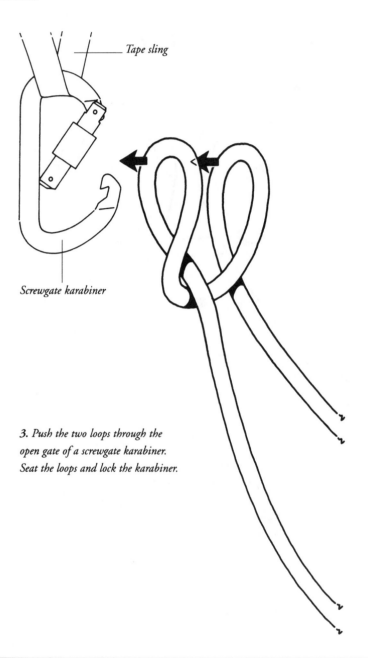

Tape sling

Screwgate karabiner

3. Push the two loops through the open gate of a screwgate karabiner. Seat the loops and lock the karabiner.

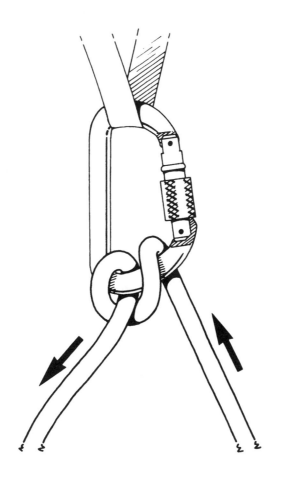

*4. Tighten the knot. The climbing rope
can now be paid out or pulled in to
provide slack or tension when required.*

ROLLING HITCH

This knot, also known as the manger's, or magnus, hitch, is basically a clove hitch with the first turn repeated. It is used in climbing as a way of securing a smaller rope to a larger one that is under strain. When the lighter rope is perpendicular to the heavier rope the knot can be easily slid along, but it will tighten as soon as lateral strain is put on the lighter rope.

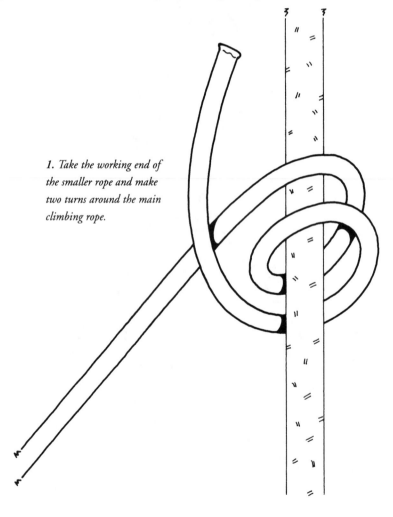

1. Take the working end of the smaller rope and make two turns around the main climbing rope.

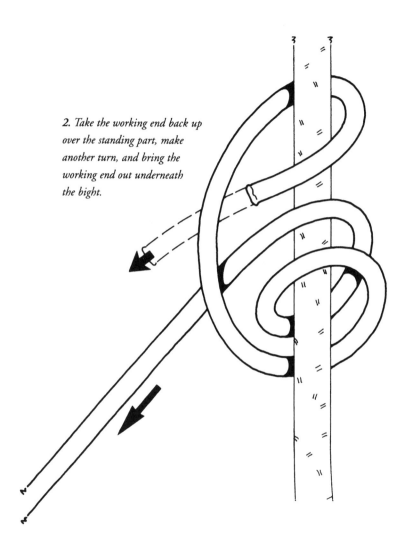

2. Take the working end back up over the standing part, make another turn, and bring the working end out underneath the bight.

continued on page 358

Rolling Hitch

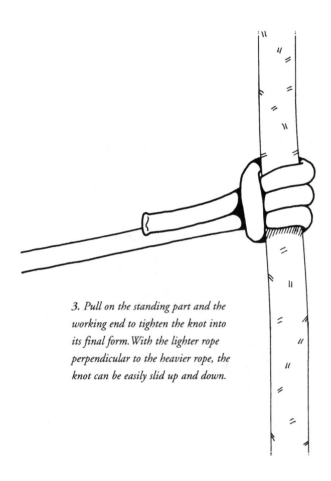

3. *Pull on the standing part and the working end to tighten the knot into its final form. With the lighter rope perpendicular to the heavier rope, the knot can be easily slid up and down.*

*4. As soon as lateral strain is put
on the lighter rope the knot will
tighten and hold firm.*

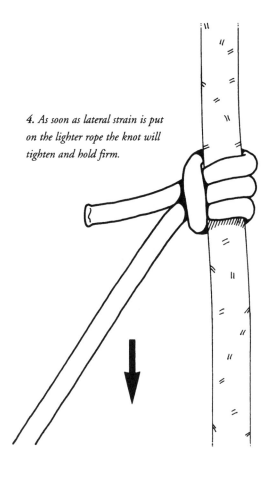

ESSENTIAL
OUTDOOR KNOTS

This section describes a selection of knots that are essential for general outdoor use. Climbers, like many people who venture into the outdoors, require a basic knowledge of knots that can be used in all situations and not just the knots that are required for their particular chosen activity.

Overhand Knot

Also known as the thumb knot, this knot forms the basis for many others. It is used in its own right as a stopper knot and makes a line easier to grip if tied at regular intervals along the line. A tight overhand knot can be difficult to undo if tied in very-small-diameter line or if the line becomes wet.

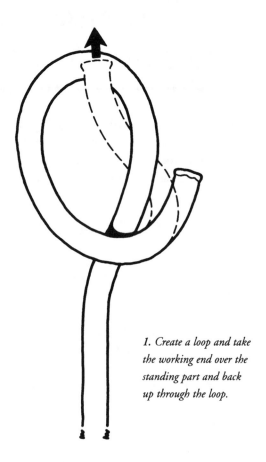

1. Create a loop and take the working end over the standing part and back up through the loop.

2. Pull on the working end and the standing part to form the final knot.

3. A line or rope can be made easier to grip with overhand knots tied at regular intervals.

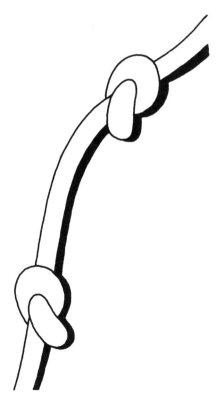

REEF KNOT

The reef knot, or square knot, is very often the only knot people know how to tie, apart from the granny knot. It gets its name from its nautical use in which two ends of a rope are tied when reefing or gathering in part of a sail.

The reef knot is not a secure knot and should not be used as one, certainly never with ropes of different diameter. It should only be used to make a temporary join in lines if identical type, weight, and diameter where it will not be put under strain. If the lines have to take strain, stopper knots should be tied in the short ends.

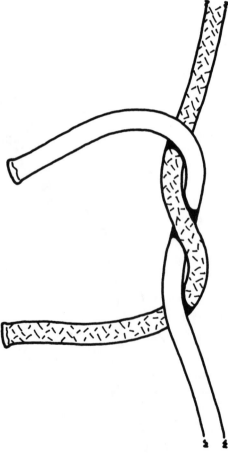

1. Bring the two working ends together and cross them left over right as shown in the illustration.

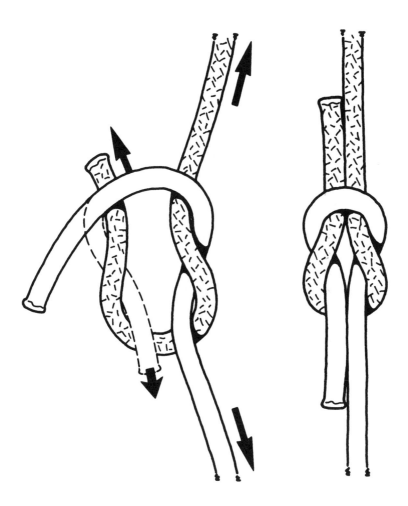

2. Now cross the two working ends right over left as shown in the illustration.

3. Tighten the knot into its final form by pulling both of the working ends and both of the standing parts.

SHEET BEND

The sheet bend is probably the most commonly used of all bends and, unlike most bends, it can safely join lines of different diameters. It is not, however, 100 percent secure and should never be used in circumstances where it will be subject to great strain. Its breaking strength also decreases in direct proportion to the difference in diameter of the lines joined.

A slipped sheet bend is formed by placing a bight between the loop of the heavier rope and the standing part of the lighter one. The slipped knot is more easily untied when the rope is under strain.

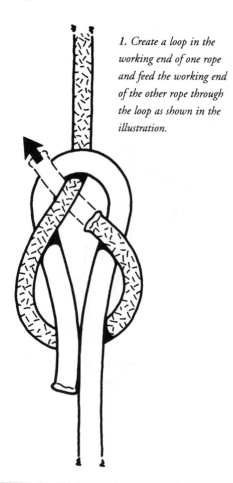

1. Create a loop in the working end of one rope and feed the working end of the other rope through the loop as shown in the illustration.

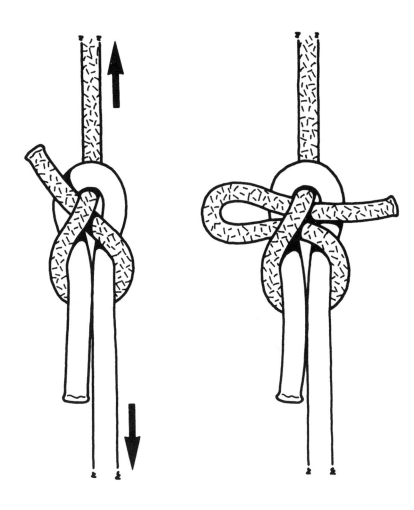

2. Pull on the standing part of both ropes to tighten the knot into its final form.

3. The slipped sheet bend is formed by placing a bight between the loop and the standing part; one sharp pull on the working end releases the knot.

FIGURE-EIGHT BEND

This simple knot (also known as the Flemish bend or knot) is tied by making a figure-eight knot in one end of a line and then following it around with the other working end. It is, despite its simplicity, one of the strongest bends and holds equally well in cord or rope.

1. Create a loose figure-eight knot in the working end of the first rope as shown in the illustration.

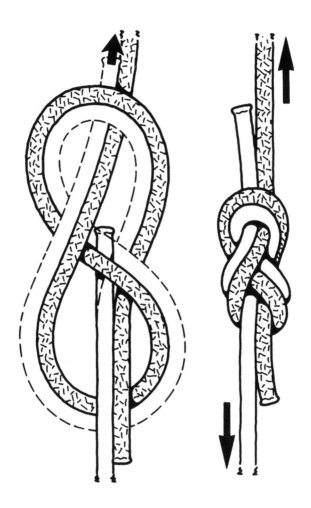

2. Feed the working end of the second rope into the loose figure-eight formed in the first rope and follow the figure-eight pattern around as shown in the illustration.

3. Tighten the knot into its final form by pulling on the standing part of each rope.

BOWLINE

The bowline is one of the best known and most widely used knots. It is tied to form a fixed loop at the end of a line or to attach a rope to an object.

The bowline's main advantages are that it does not slip, come loose, or jam. It is quick and easy to untie, even when a line is under tension, by pushing forward the bight that encircles the standing part of the line. For added security the bowline can be finished with a stopper knot.

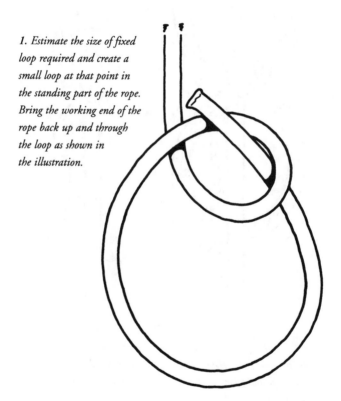

1. Estimate the size of fixed loop required and create a small loop at that point in the standing part of the rope. Bring the working end of the rope back up and through the loop as shown in the illustration.

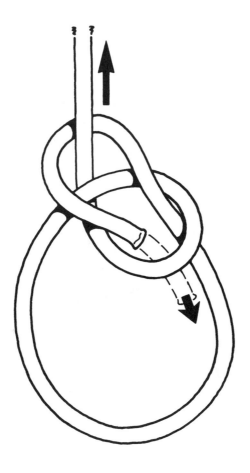

2. Take the working end around the back of the standing part and back down through the loop. Then slowly start to pull on the standing part to form the knot.

continued on page 372

Bowline

3. Adjust the fixed loop to its required size and then tighten the knot into its final form.

4. For added security the bowline can be finished with a stopper knot.

HALF HITCH

The half hitch is a very widely used fastening. It is, in fact, a single hitch formed around the standing part of another hitch. It is used to complete and strengthen other knots, as in the round turn and two half hitches (see page 376), which can then be used for tying, hanging, hooking objects, etc. The slipped half hitch is a useful variation of the simple half hitch; a sharp pull on the working end releases the knot.

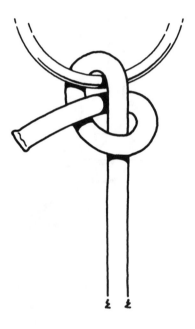

1. A single half hitch is formed by taking the working end through a ring, or similar object, back out over the standing part and through the loop. Pull on the working end and the standing part to tighten.

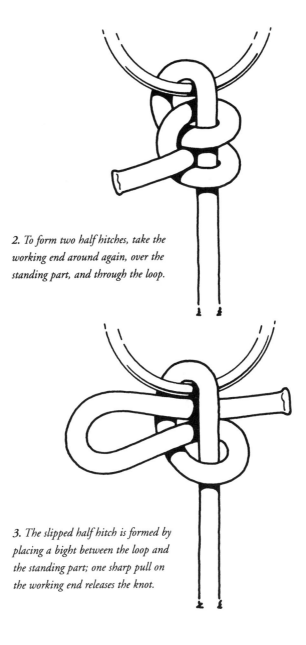

2. To form two half hitches, take the working end around again, over the standing part, and through the loop.

3. The slipped half hitch is formed by placing a bight between the loop and the standing part; one sharp pull on the working end releases the knot.

ROUND TURN AND TWO HALF HITCHES

This knot is strong, dependable, and when correctly tied, it never jams. This makes it very versatile; you can use it whenever you want to fasten a line to a ring, hook, stake, post, pole, handle, or rail. Once one end of a rope has been secured with a round turn and two half hitches, the other end can be tied with a second knot. This is especially useful for fastening down unwieldy, bulky objects.

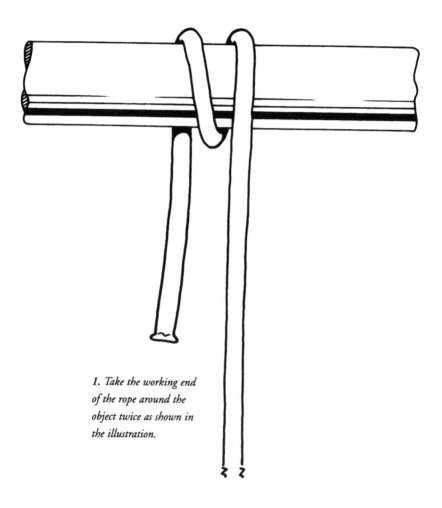

1. Take the working end of the rope around the object twice as shown in the illustration.

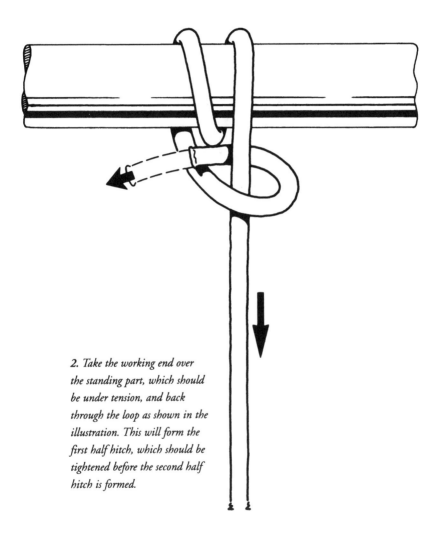

2. Take the working end over the standing part, which should be under tension, and back through the loop as shown in the illustration. This will form the first half hitch, which should be tightened before the second half hitch is formed.

continued on page 378

Round Turn and Two Half Hitches

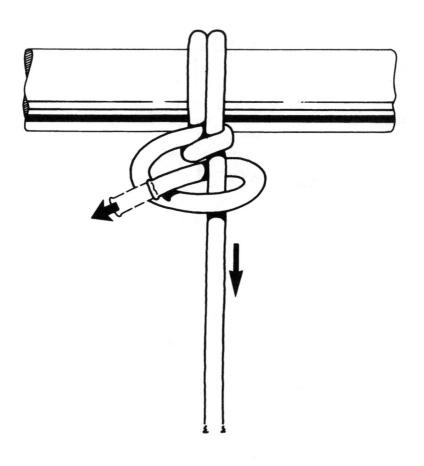

3. Take the working end around again to form the second half hitch.

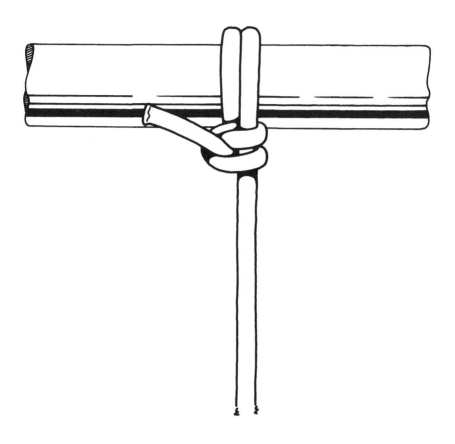

4. Tighten the second half hitch and then pull sharply on the standing part to form the final knot.

CONSTRICTOR KNOT

This is a popular all-purpose knot because it is firm and does not slip. It can be used as a permanent or temporary fastening. As a permanent fastening, the constrictor knot grips so firmly that if there is a need to untie it, usually the only way is to cut it free. To be sure of being able to untie it if used as a temporary fastening, the last tuck should be made with a bight to make a slip knot.

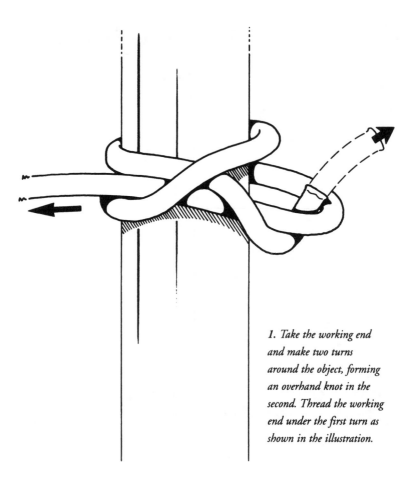

1. Take the working end and make two turns around the object, forming an overhand knot in the second. Thread the working end under the first turn as shown in the illustration.

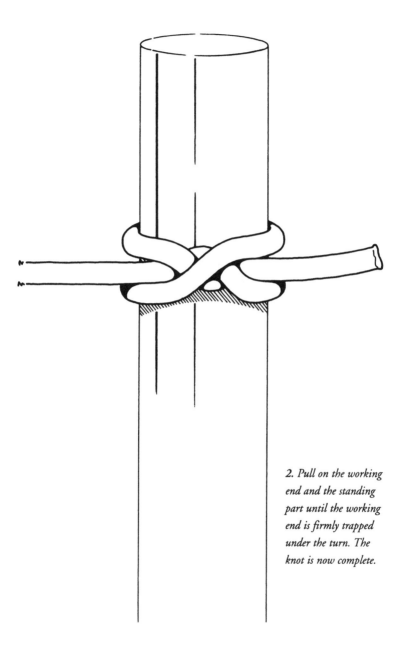

2. Pull on the working end and the standing part until the working end is firmly trapped under the turn. The knot is now complete.

FISHERMAN'S BEND

The fisherman's bend is one of the most secure and widely used hitches. It can be tied around an object or through a ring or similar device. It is a very quick knot to tie, and for additional security an additional half hitch can be added.

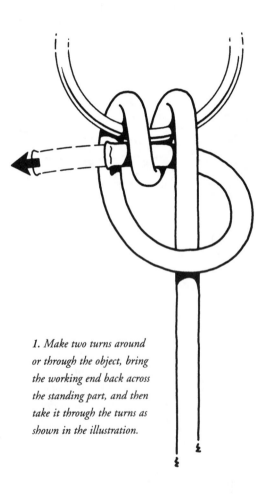

1. Make two turns around or through the object, bring the working end back across the standing part, and then take it through the turns as shown in the illustration.

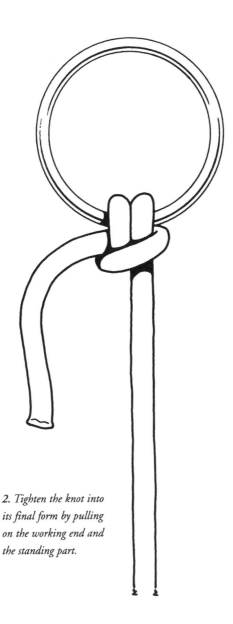

2. Tighten the knot into its final form by pulling on the working end and the standing part.

SAILING KNOTS

CONTENTS

INTRODUCTION

Sailing has undergone some revolutionary changes in recent years. It is now possible to navigate a craft using satellites and autopilots. Hulls are constructed from a variety of artificial materials, masts are made from aluminum, and rigging on modern-day yachts is almost entirely made of stainless steel. But the one component that has changed very little over time and is still totally necessary for any form of sailing or boating is the knot.

Sailing, like many other pursuits, has seen natural fiber ropes almost totally replaced by artificial fiber and wire ropes, but natural fiber ropes are still favored by some sailors and have distinct advantages, especially when it comes to decorative knotting.

The Book of Sailing Knots gives you the opportunity to master 50 classic sailing knots tied in rope. The knots have been restricted to those tied only in natural and artificial rope to devote each the space for clear instructions and meticulous step-by-step illustrations. Securing rope ends is also fully discussed.

The knots are divided into several distinct groups, each of which is used for different purposes. Practice is essential for good knot tying, so select the right knot for the job and practice until you are confident that you can tie it quickly and securely, in a flat calm or a storm force wind!

HISTORY

The art of knotting is as ancient as humankind. Stone Age people used knots to secure and fasten their traps, clothing, and housing; coiled and braided rope was found in the tomb of Tutankhamen; the Inca people of Peru used knotted string instead of written figures; and the Greeks, Romans, and other civilizations probably knew as much about knots as we do today.

It was, however, seamen and sailors, particularly those who served aboard the great sailing vessels of the eighteenth and nineteenth centuries, who exploited the full potential of knot tying both practically and decoratively.

The length of the voyages undertaken by sailing ships left sailors with little to do for much of the time; this was particularly true on whalers, which were at sea longer than other ships and were heavily overmanned. Isolated on board, unable for the most part to read and write, sailors had to find some way to fill their idle hours, and knotting was an ideal way of passing the time.

There was no shortage of raw materials. Sailing ships carried miles of rigging, and there was always a plentiful supply of spoiled rope (known as "junk") available for knotting. Sailors used their leisure hours to develop ways of tying knots that were both decorative and highly functional.

Knotting on board ship was often competitive, with secrets and intricacies of particular knots jealously guarded. Sailors were also responsible for many of the colorful descriptive names still given to particular sailing knots: the Turk's head (see page 504) and monkey's fist (see page 500), for example.

ROPES

Rope is manufactured in either natural or artificial fibers that can be twisted or braided and is available in a wide variety of sizes. Rope size can be measured by circumference or diameter or by a term; for example, twine, that tells you that it is a thin line for various uses.

Traditionally, rope was made by twisting fibers of natural materials together. The most commonly used materials were manila, sisal, coir, hemp, flax, and cotton. The fibers were twisted first into yarn, then into strands, and finally into rope, in a process called laying up. If you examine a piece of ordinary three-strand rope you will notice the strands go up and to the right, like a corkscrew. It has been "laid" right-handed. When the rope was made the fibers were twisted together to form right-hand yarn, the yarn was then twisted in the opposite direction to form left-hand strands, and these were twisted to form right-laid rope. If you uncoil one strand you can clearly see it is laid up left-handed, or twisted the opposite way to the whole rope. This is a vital principle of traditional rope making. Even with one strand removed, the other two strands cling together, leaving a groove where the missing strand should be. It is the alternate twisting that creates the tension that holds the rope together and gives it strength.

Three-strand natural fiber rope.

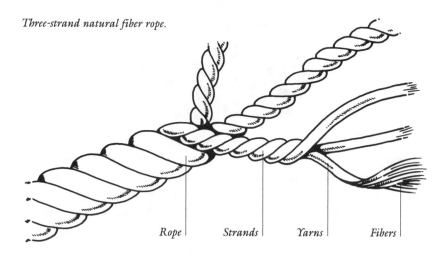

Rope | Strands | Yarns | Fibers |

NATURAL FIBER ROPE

For thousands of years, until shortages during World War II led to the development of man-made fibers, rope was made from natural materials— cotton and flax for manageability, coir and sisal for cheapness, manila and hemp for strength.

Natural fiber rope is normally three-strand and right laid. Four-strand, left-laid rope is much rarer and ten percent weaker—adding further strands does not increase strength. Cable-laid line (a nine-strand cable laid up left-handed from three-strand ropes) is 40 percent weaker than hawser-laid (three-strand) rope of the same diameter.

Natural fibers are only as long as the plant from which they were derived allows; the ends of these individual fibers (known as staples) are what gives natural rope its hairy, rough appearance. This gives them better traction and resistance than smooth man-made fibers. However, natural fibers have many disadvantages. They lack elasticity, and swell and become heavy when wet, making knots difficult to untie. They attract mildew and will rot if not stored properly, and they can be weakened and made brittle by strong sunlight, chemicals, and salt.

Nowadays, natural fiber rope is becoming less used in the sailing world, but for decorative purposes many still prefer vegetable fibers for their traditional appearance and the beauty of their natural colors and textures.

ARTIFICIAL FIBER ROPE

Artificial or synthetic materials have almost completely replaced natural fibers in the manufacture of rope. Man-made filaments can be spun to run the whole length of a line, do not vary in thickness, and do not have to be twisted together to make them cohere. This gives them superior strength.

Nylon, first produced in 1938 for domestic use, was the first man-made material to be used in this way. Since then a range of artificial ropes has been developed to meet different purposes, but they all share certain characteristics. Size for size they are lighter, stronger, and cheaper than their natural counterparts. They do not rot or mildew and are not affected by sea water. They are resistant to sunlight, chemicals, oil, gasoline, and most common solvents. They absorb less water than natural fiber ropes, and so their wet breaking strain remains constant. They can also be made in a range of colors.

Color-coded ropes for sailing make for instant recognition of lines of different function. In addition, artificial ropes have high tensile strength, are capable of absorbing shocks, and have excellent load-bearing qualities.

Nylon (Polyamide) fibers make ropes that are both strong and elastic, giving them outstanding capacity for absorbing shock loads. They are good for towing and, because they do not rot or float, they are particularly useful in sailing. One big advantage that sailors have found with this type of rope is that it is far more comfortable to hold and use than natural fiber rope.

Polyester (Dacron) ropes are nearly as strong as nylon and give very little stretch. They do not float and are highly resistant to wear and weathering. They are widely used in sailing for sheets and halyards. Polyester is also used in small sizes for twine.

Polypropylene (Polyethylene) is not as strong as nylon or polyester but it does make a good, inexpensive, all-purpose rope. Its one main advantage is that it is the only fiber that floats, thus making it particularly suitable for water-ski tow ropes and rescue lines. Floating does mean, however, that it may be caught in or cut by a propeller.

Because of their very nature, artificial ropes are constantly being developed and improved for a variety of different pursuits. It is always worth checking with your local chandler or specialist rope supplier about any new products that come onto the market for sailing and boating.

Braided artificial fiber rope

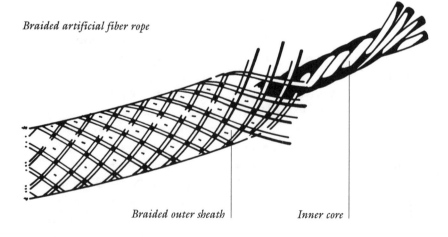

Braided outer sheath   *Inner core*

Twisted artificial fiber rope

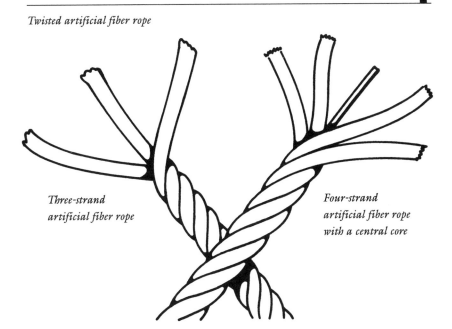

*Three-strand
artificial fiber rope*

*Four-strand
artificial fiber rope
with a central core*

Artificial fiber ropes do have some disadvantages, the main one being that they melt when heated. Even the friction generated when one rope rubs against another may be enough to cause damage, so it is vital to check your ropes regularly. Use plastic tubing to protect sections of artificial rope that you know will be subject to friction. It is also possible for heat friction to fuse knotted rope together so that it is impossible to untie the knot. Another disadvantage is that artificial ropes made of continuous filaments are so smooth that knots slip and come undone. Knots may need to be secured with additional knots or seized.

Artificial rope can be laid up or twisted like natural fiber rope or it can be formed into braided rope with an outer sheath of sixteen or more strands surrounding a central core that is either braided and hollow or made up of solid parallel, or slightly twisted, filaments. Braided rope is softer, more flexible, and quite a lot stronger.

Laid-up rope, made of thick multifilaments tightly twisted together, may be very resistant to wear but it may also be difficult to tie, and knots may not hold well. Do not buy a rope that is too stiff. Similarly, be wary of twisted rope that is very soft.

Shortening a Rope or Line

The most successful and secure way to shorten a rope or line without cutting it is to use the **sheepshank**. The sheepshank is very much a sailor's knot and shares the special characteristics of other nautical knots in that it does not chafe, has a good jamming action, holds under tension, and unties easily.

Another important use of the sheepshank is the emergency repair of a damaged line. To remove the strain from the damaged section, tie a sheepshank, incorporating the weakened section in the middle of the knot. This will provide you with valuable time to make an effective repair or to replace the line.

The sheepshank

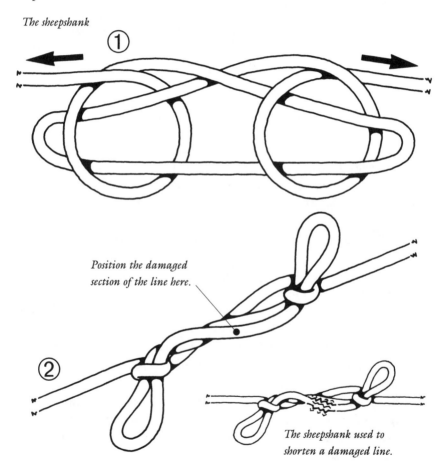

Position the damaged section of the line here.

The sheepshank used to shorten a damaged line.

LOOKING AFTER ROPE

Rope is sturdy material, but it is expensive, so it's worth looking after it properly. Caring for rope will help it keep its strength and prolong its life. Avoid dragging it over rough, sharp edges, or dirty, gritty surfaces where particles could get into the rope and damage it. Do not walk on rope or force it into harsh kinks. Inspect it regularly and wash off dirt, grit, and oil. Coil rope carefully and always make sure it is dry before coiling, even if it is artificial fiber rope. If it has been in sea water, rinse thoroughly to remove all salt deposits. At the end of the season, wash all ropes in a mild detergent, removing oil or tar stains with gasoline or trichloroethylene.

If knots are repeatedly tied in one section of rope, that section will weaken. The tighter the nip or the sharper the curve the greater the chances that the rope will break; if it does, it will part immediately outside the knot.

Finally, never use two ropes of different material together, because only the more rigid of the two will work under strain.

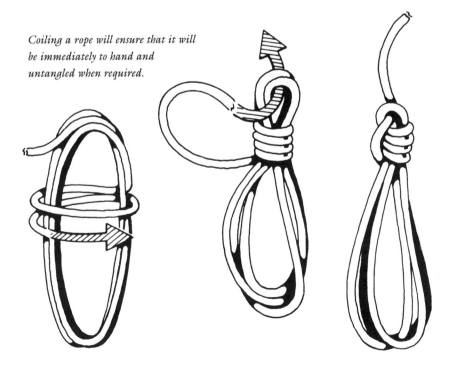

Coiling a rope will ensure that it will be immediately to hand and untangled when required.

CLEATING A LINE

A cleat is a deck fitting that is used to tie lines to on a temporary basis. The line is made fast to the cleat with a hitch. This particular hitch is often the first knot that prospective sailors come into contact with.

It is a simple but effective hitch, but it is also a hitch that many people tie incorrectly. It is easy to think that the more turns you put around a cleat the stronger the connection is going to be. This is not correct. If tied correctly, this hitch only requires a couple of turns to grip firmly and this also then makes it quicker to release.

Because lines have to be alternately made fast and quickly released as a matter of course in sailing, this is an important knot to learn.

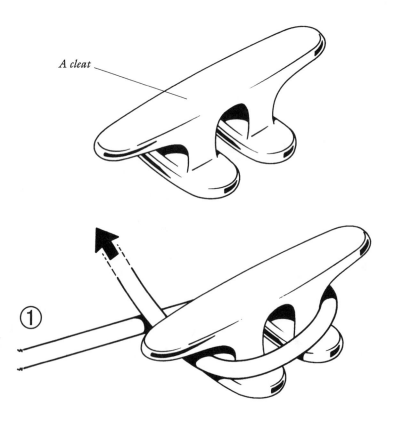

A cleat

①

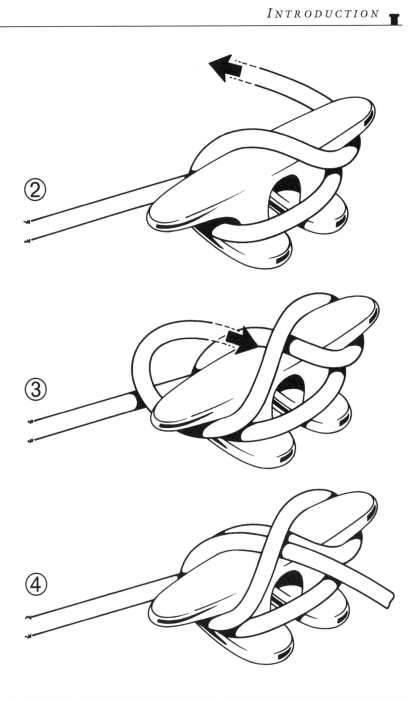

TOOLS

For the majority of sailing knots the only tool that will be required is a sharp implement to cut the rope or line. But the tying of a few knots can be made considerably easier by using some specialized tools. Because certain knot-tying tools are very specialized, they can only be obtained from chandlers or specialist sailing equipment suppliers.

A selection of the most useful tools and implements are featured here. If you have a particular knot-tying problem, contact your local chandler, who in most cases will be pleased to help you out.

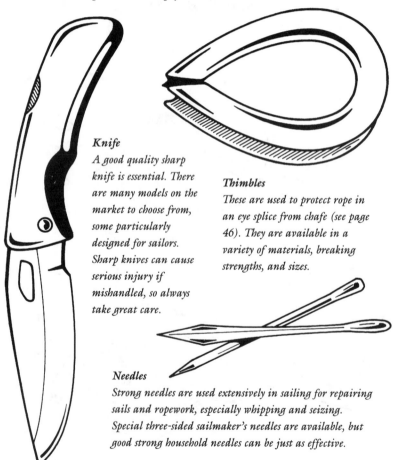

Knife
A good quality sharp knife is essential. There are many models on the market to choose from, some particularly designed for sailors. Sharp knives can cause serious injury if mishandled, so always take great care.

Thimbles
These are used to protect rope in an eye splice from chafe (see page 46). They are available in a variety of materials, breaking strengths, and sizes.

Needles
Strong needles are used extensively in sailing for repairing sails and ropework, especially whipping and seizing. Special three-sided sailmaker's needles are available, but good strong household needles can be just as effective.

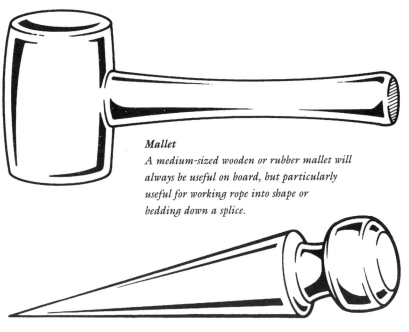

Mallet
A medium-sized wooden or rubber mallet will always be useful on board, but particularly useful for working rope into shape or bedding down a splice.

Fid
A fid is a sharp wooden spike used to splice or part twisted rope. It is made from hardwood and often has a decorative handle. Great care needs to be taken when using fids because, like knives, they can cause serious injury if mishandled.

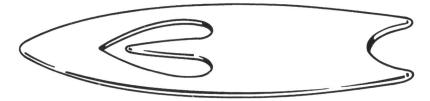

Net Needle
These are made from wood or more commonly these days, plastic. Netting twine is wound on to the center of the needle, which is then used to create a net (see page 516). It is possible to make nets by hand, but to construct a good quality large net a net needle is vital.

HOW TO USE THIS BOOK

The diagrams accompanying the descriptions of the knots are intended to be self-explanatory. Written instructions and special tying techniques and methods will accompany the more complex knots. There are arrows to show the directions in which you should push or pull the working ends of the rope or line. The dotted lines indicate intermediate positions of the rope. In many of the illustrations lines are shown faded out or cut short for clarity. When tying the knot you should always have a sufficient working end to complete the knot. The amount of working end required can often be calculated by looking at the illustration of the finished knot. Always follow the order shown of going over or under a length of line; reversing or changing this order could result in a completely different knot, which might well be unstable, unsafe, and insecure.

ROPE PARTS

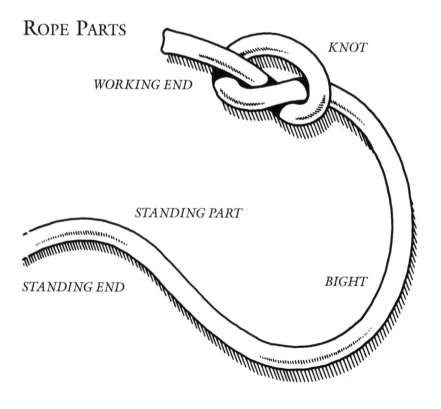

KNOT

WORKING END

STANDING PART

STANDING END

BIGHT

ROPE ENDS

A slowly unraveling rope with frayed ends is annoying, wasteful, and in some cases dangerous. But a rope with correctly sealed ends is safe, neat, and makes knots significantly easier to tie.

Artificial fiber ropes now are widely used in sailing and have many advantages, one of them being that the rope ends can be quickly and efficiently heat-sealed to prevent them from fraying. But natural fiber ropes are still used, and if left unseized, the ends will fray. A secure and easy way to prevent this is by whipping the ends. Use vegetable fiber twine or waxed polyester twine and always bind against the lay.

Common Whipping

This easily tied and practical whipping is, as its name suggests, one of the most widely used forms of whipping. But it should be remembered that if the rope end frequently becomes wet, most whipping twines will swell and stretch. This can lead to the whipping loosening and slipping off. So for rope ends that are subject to becoming wet, this should be seen as only a temporary whipping.

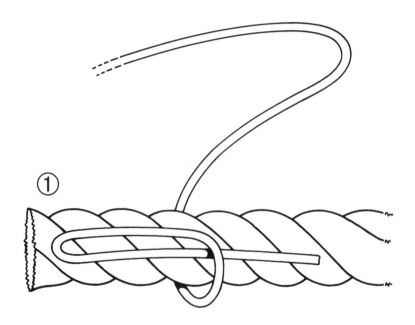

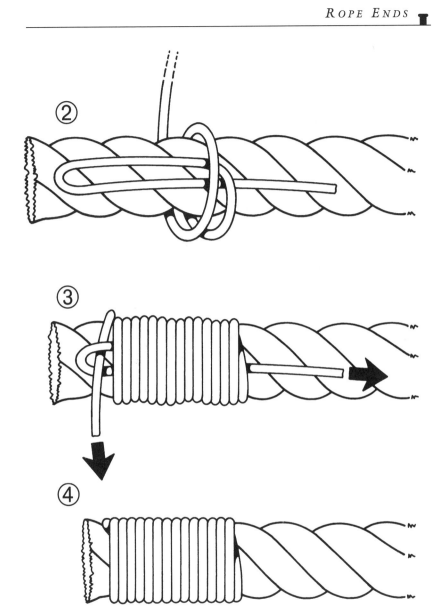

Trim the loose ends of the whipping twine and make neat the rope strand ends. With artificial ropes, the strand ends can be heat-sealed.

PALM-AND-NEEDLE WHIPPING

This durable and reliable whipping is especially suited to twisted natural fiber rope, but can also be tied on braided or artificial fiber ropes. It will stand up well to friction, so it can be employed for heavy usage. You will need a needle with an eye big enough to take whipping twine. Special sailmaker's needles are available for this purpose.

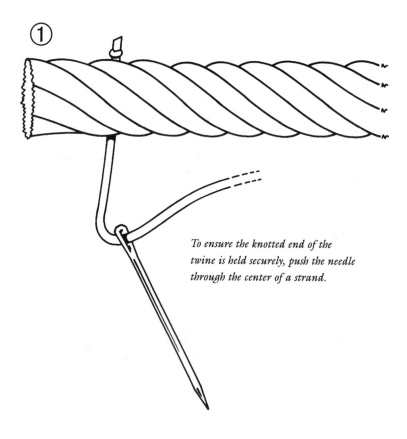

To ensure the knotted end of the twine is held securely, push the needle through the center of a strand.

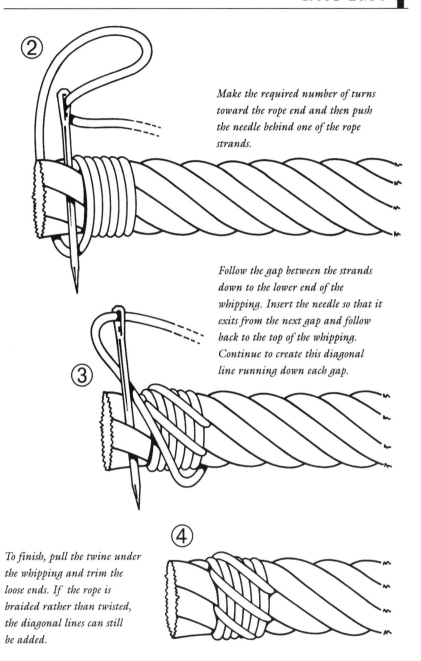

Make the required number of turns toward the rope end and then push the needle behind one of the rope strands.

Follow the gap between the strands down to the lower end of the whipping. Insert the needle so that it exits from the next gap and follow back to the top of the whipping. Continue to create this diagonal line running down each gap.

To finish, pull the twine under the whipping and trim the loose ends. If the rope is braided rather than twisted, the diagonal lines can still be added.

Snaked Whipping

This decorative and highly effective whipping is more suited to large-diameter ropes; it can prove difficult to tie on thinner ropes. It is important with all whipping, and especially snaked whipping, to make sure that each turn is pulled as tight as possible. Also, to make the snaking less likely to slip, as you pass the needle under the whipping, pick up a few fibers of the rope itself. The decorative appearance of this whipping makes it ideal for ropes that are left out on show or on board.

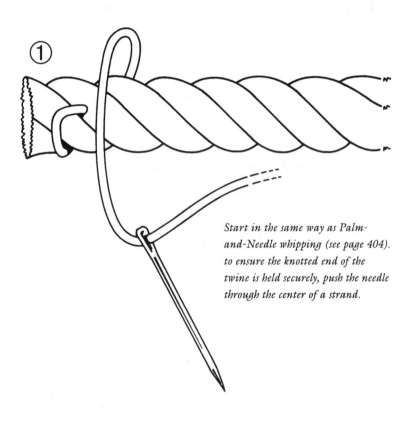

Start in the same way as Palm-and-Needle whipping (see page 404). to ensure the knotted end of the twine is held securely, push the needle through the center of a strand.

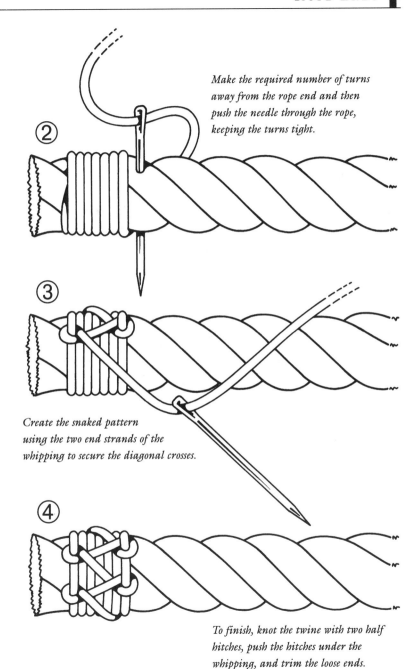

2 Make the required number of turns away from the rope end and then push the needle through the rope, keeping the turns tight.

3 Create the snaked pattern using the two end strands of the whipping to secure the diagonal crosses.

4 To finish, knot the twine with two half hitches, push the hitches under the whipping, and trim the loose ends.

Sealing Ends

Apart from whipping the ends of rope, there are three other options to consider to seal ends.

All synthetic rope ends can be sealed using heat. When you buy synthetic rope from a chandler they will cut it to the required length using an electrically heated knife, which gives a neat, sharp edge. When you cut synthetic rope yourself, use a sharp knife and then melt the end with a cigarette lighter or on an electric ring.

A quick and efficient method of creating a temporary seal is to use ordinary adhesive or electrical tape. And finally, on small stuff (any rope whose circumference is less than one inch), a simple stopper knot will provide an effective seal.

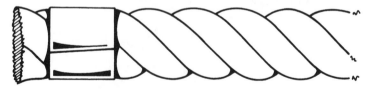

Heat-sealed synthetic rope

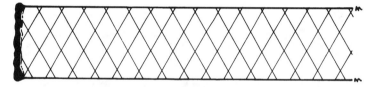

Rope sealed with adhesive or electrical tape

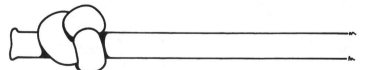

Rope sealed with a stopper knot

Seizings

A seizing is used to bind two ropes together. The same thickness and type of twine or small stuff used for whipping is generally applicable for seizing.

Seizing can be used to bind two separate parts of rope together, but it is most widely used to bind the same piece of rope together to form an eye.

FLAT SEIZING

This simple form of seizing is good for light loads and to temporarily bind two pieces of rope together. For this type of seizing, use twine or thin line that has been prepared with a small eye at one end.

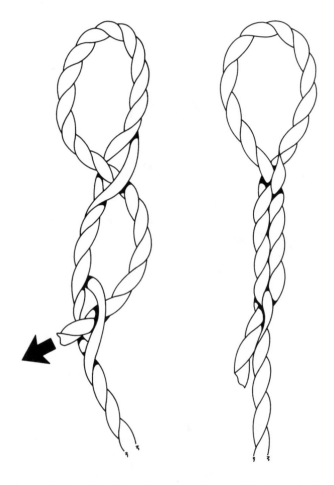

*Prepare the seizing twine by forming a small eye in one end.
This is done by opening up the strands and tucking the twine
end through a couple of times.*

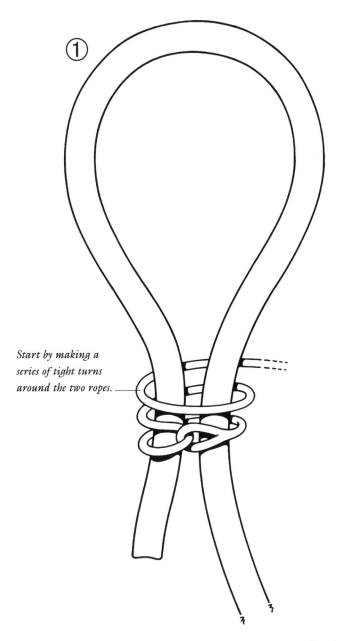

Start by making a
series of tight turns
around the two ropes.

continued on page 412

Flat seizing

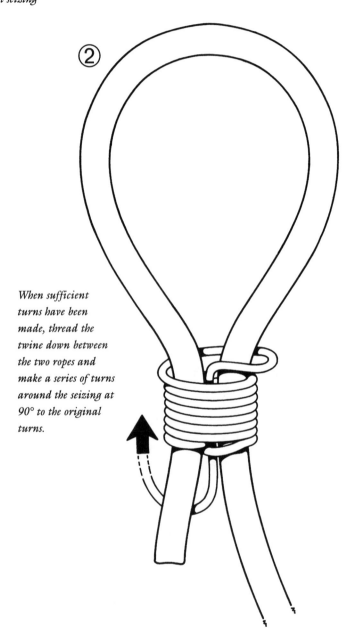

When sufficient
turns have been
made, thread the
twine down between
the two ropes and
make a series of turns
around the seizing at
90° to the original
turns.

③

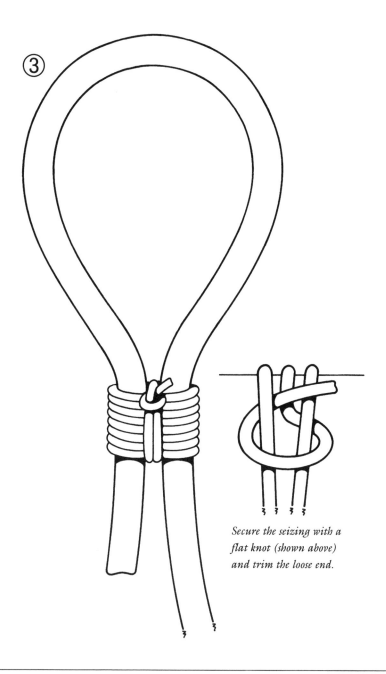

*Secure the seizing with a
flat knot (shown above)
and trim the loose end.*

PALM-AND-NEEDLE SEIZING

This method of seizing creates a strong grip on the rope, making it suitable for heavy loads. It is particularly useful for making eyes in the end of ropes. It is recommended that you use a sailmaker's needle to thread the twine through the rope.

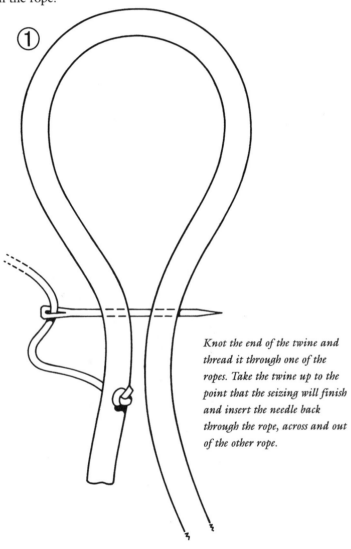

Knot the end of the twine and thread it through one of the ropes. Take the twine up to the point that the seizing will finish and insert the needle back through the rope, across and out of the other rope.

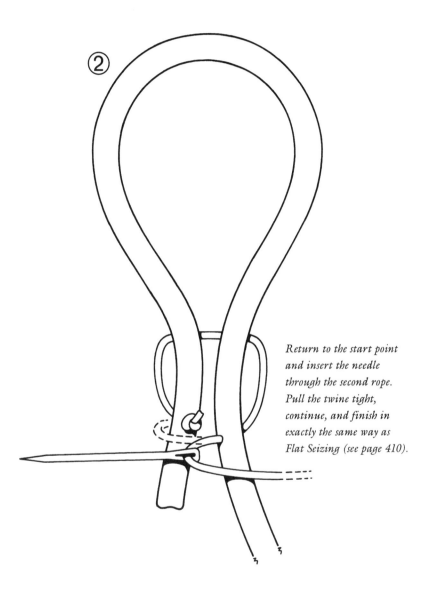

② Return to the start point
and insert the needle
through the second rope.
Pull the twine tight,
continue, and finish in
exactly the same way as
Flat Seizing (see page 410).

RACKING SEIZING

This form of seizing should be used if the seized rope parts are to be subject to excessive, uneven, or sideways loading. Instead of making complete turns, thread the twine over and under the ropes. This will substantially strengthen the seizing. Racking can be applied to Flat Seizing (see page 410) and Palm-and-Needle Seizing (see page 414).

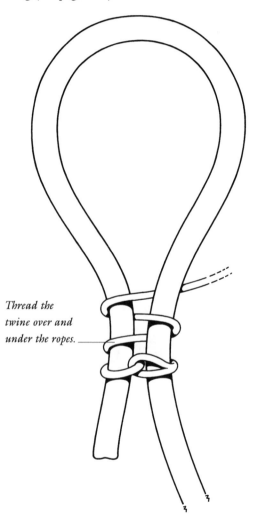

Thread the twine over and under the ropes.

SPLICINGS

Splicing is a method of joining rope to itself or to another rope by interweaving the separate strands. It is a very reliable method and one that every sailor should know.

If you encounter difficulty in separating rope strands, use a fid (see page 399). Most ropework, and especially splicing, benefits from being worked into shape and this can be done by being rolled underfoot or by using a wooden mallet or rubber-faced hammer. All the examples covered in this chapter are illustrated with the most commonly used three-stranded rope.

BACK SPLICE

This is one of the most widely used splices in the sailing world. It is also known as Spanish whipping. It creates a decorative and practical end to a rope and, unlike whipping, it becomes firmer and stronger with time.

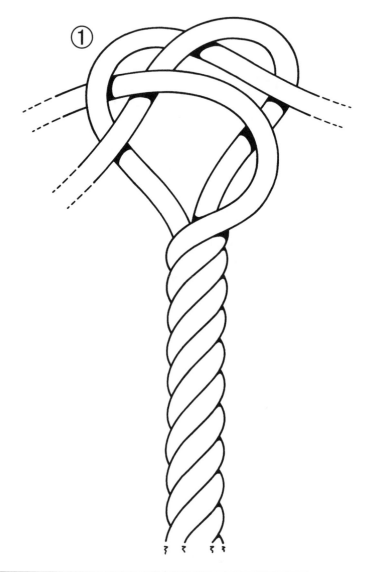

This splice starts with a crown knot, formed in step
1 and finished in step 2. Pull all the strands tight
to give the appearance of step 2 and then
the splicing can begin.

The crown knot.

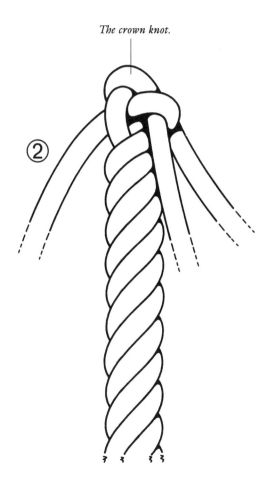

②

continued on page 420

Back splice

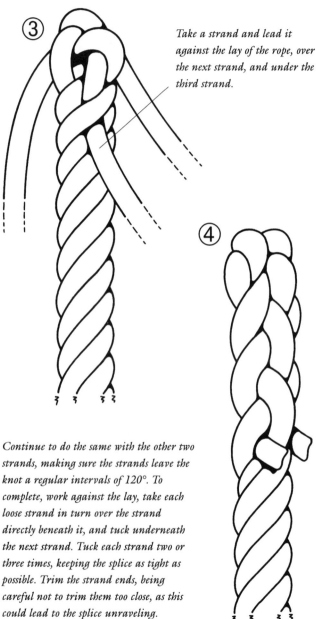

③ Take a strand and lead it against the lay of the rope, over the next strand, and under the third strand.

④

Continue to do the same with the other two strands, making sure the strands leave the knot a regular intervals of 120°. To complete, work against the lay, take each loose strand in turn over the strand directly beneath it, and tuck underneath the next strand. Tuck each strand two or three times, keeping the splice as tight as possible. Trim the strand ends, being careful not to trim them too close, as this could lead to the splice unraveling.

SHORT SPLICE

This splice provides the ideal solution for permanently joining the ends of two ropes with little loss of strength. It can also be successfully used to repair a break in a line.

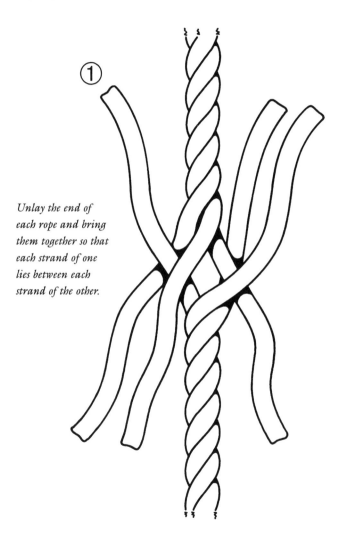

Unlay the end of each rope and bring them together so that each strand of one lies between each strand of the other.

continued on page 422

Short splice

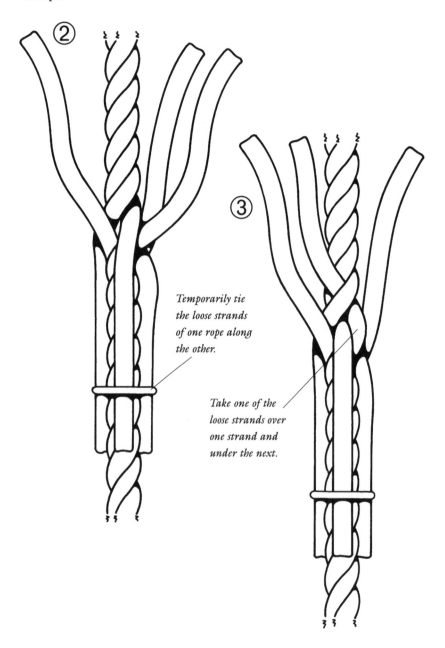

② Temporarily tie the loose strands of one rope along the other.

③ Take one of the loose strands over one strand and under the next.

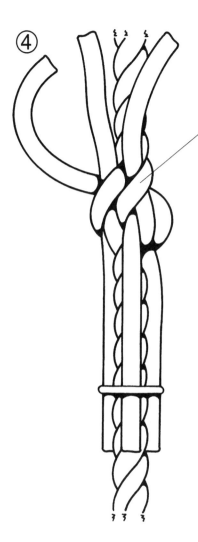

④

⑤

Repeat the over-one-under-one tuck with the second and third strand and then repeat the whole process, tucking each strand two or three times.

To complete, turn the assembly around, remove the temporary fixing, and tuck exactly the same as for the first half. Trim the loose ends, then place the splice on the floor and roll it under your shoe to make it uniformly round.

EYE SPLICE

This is one of the most important sailing knots and one that every sailor should learn. You will always need eyes in the end of your ropes and the eye splice is the most reliable way of achieving this.

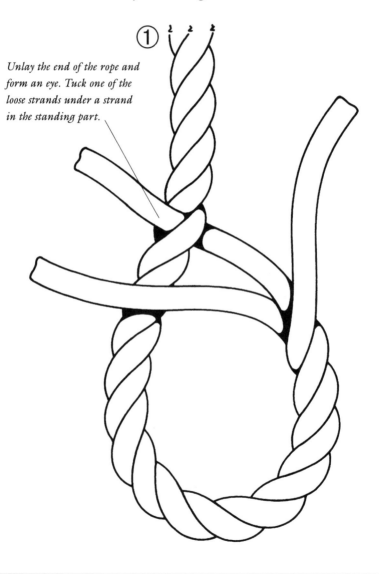

Unlay the end of the rope and form an eye. Tuck one of the loose strands under a strand in the standing part.

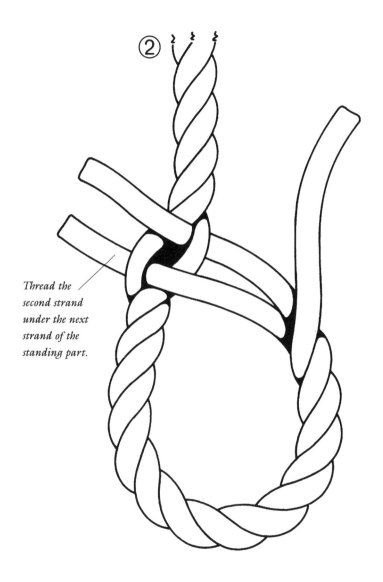

Thread the
second strand
under the next
strand of the
standing part.

continued on page 426

425

Eye splice

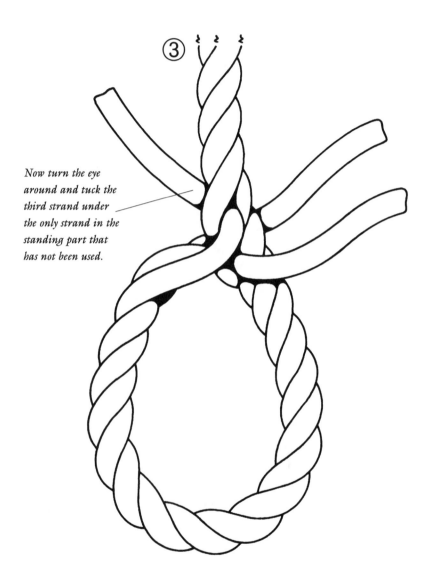

Now turn the eye
around and tuck the
third strand under
the only strand in the
standing part that
has not been used.

④

To complete, repeat the process, putting in two more tucks for each strand, making sure the splice is kept as tight as possible. Trim the loose ends and roll the splice between your hands to make it uniformly round.

EYE SPLICE WITH THIMBLE

If subject to heavy use and chafing, an eye splice can be reinforced and strengthened with a thimble. Thimbles are made from various metals or plastic and are available in a wide variety of sizes. The splice can be either tied around or stretched over a thimble.

Whipping that is kept well away from the working surface will secure a loose thimble.

Thimble _____

STOPPER KNOTS

Stopper knots, as their name suggests, are used to prevent the ends of a rope or line slipping through an eye, loop, or hole. They can be used to bind the end of a line so that it will not unravel and can also be used decoratively. At sea they are used to weight lines and at the ends of running rigging.

The most important knot of this type is the overhand. This is the simplest, and perhaps the oldest, knot known to man and is used as a basis for countless others.

Overhand Knot

Also known as the thumb knot, this knot forms the basis for many others. It is used in its own right as a stopper knot and is tied at regular intervals along lines to make them easy to grip. If a line develops an unwanted overhand knot, undo it immediately, as this knot is very difficult to untie, especially when wet.

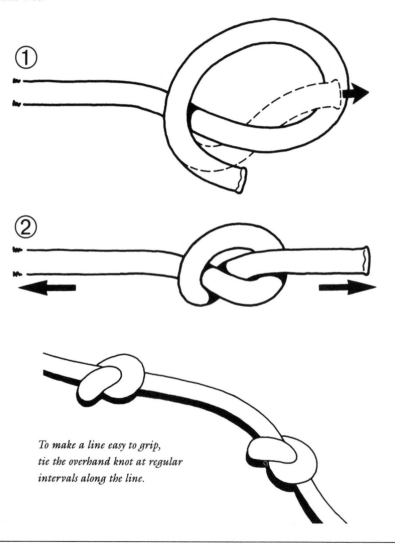

To make a line easy to grip, tie the overhand knot at regular intervals along the line.

FIGURE-EIGHT KNOT

The knot's name comes from its characteristic shape. It is the most important stopper knot for sailors, used on running rigging. (It is also known as the Flemish knot or Savoy knot).

The knot is made in the end of the line, with the upper loop around the standing part and the lower loop around the working end. When tying this knot you should leave a tail on the working end. This will enable you to grasp the knot should it become jammed.

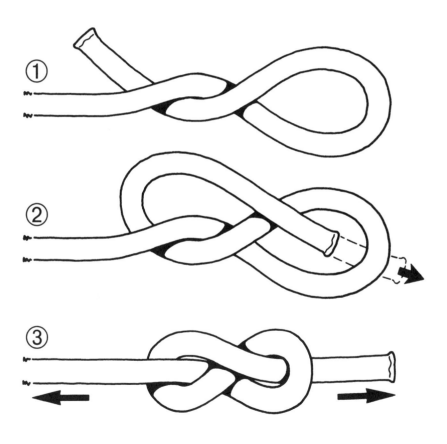

Multiple Overhand Knot

This knot, also known as the blood knot, earned its other name because it was the knot used to weight the ends of the lashes in the cat-o'-nine-tails, the whip used historically to flog soldiers, sailors, and criminals. Its main sailing uses are as a weighting or stopper knot made with small-diameter line.

When tying the knot, keep the loop open and slack as you make the turns and gently pull on both ends at the same time, twisting the two ends in opposite directions. Like many stopper knots, this knot is difficult to untie when the line is wet.

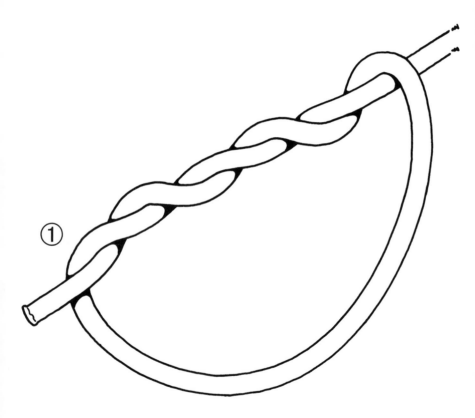

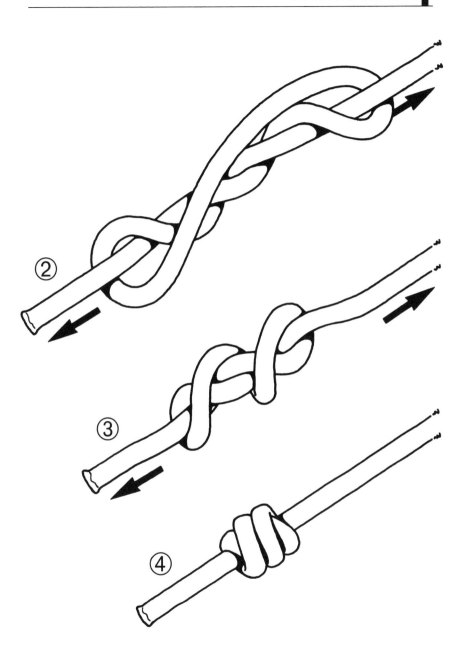

② ③ ④

HEAVING LINE KNOT

When a heavy line is thrown from boat to shore or to another vessel, a heaving line knot is used. The heavy line is attached to a *heaving* line, a lighter line that is thrown across the gap first so the heavier line can be drawn behind it. The heaving line knot is tied in the end of this lighter line to give it weight and aid in throwing. Heaving lines are usually one half to three quarters of an inch in diameter and may be up to eighty feet long. They should float, be flexible, and be strong enough to bear a man's weight.

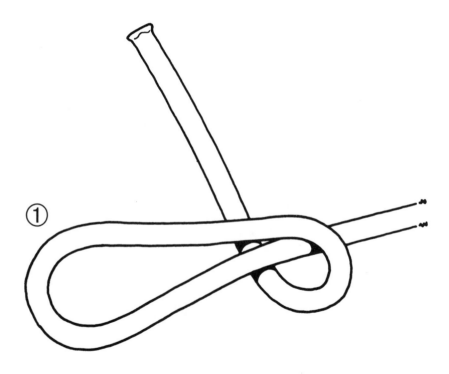

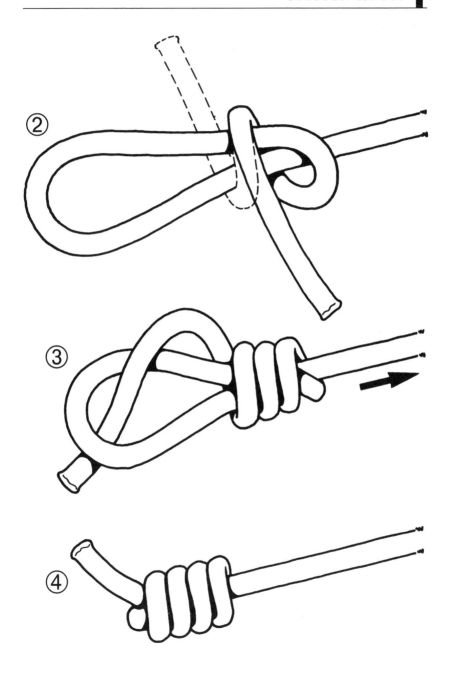

② ③ ④

Doughnut

This decorative heaving line knot has the obvious advantage that other lines can be easily tied to it or it can be hooked on or over objects. The weight of this knot can be increased by wrapping a narrow strip of sheet lead around the original three coils before making the final turns. The doughnut also has a very useful secondary use: When it is tied in small material without the sheet lead, it can be used at the end of any cord that you need to pull.

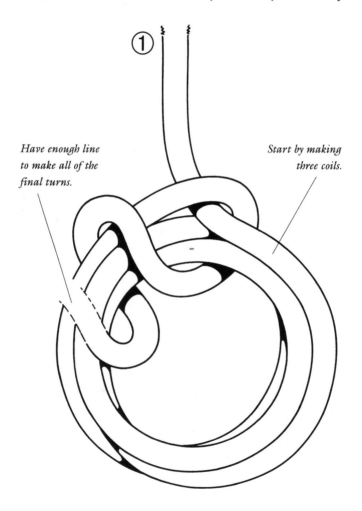

Have enough line to make all of the final turns.

Start by making three coils.

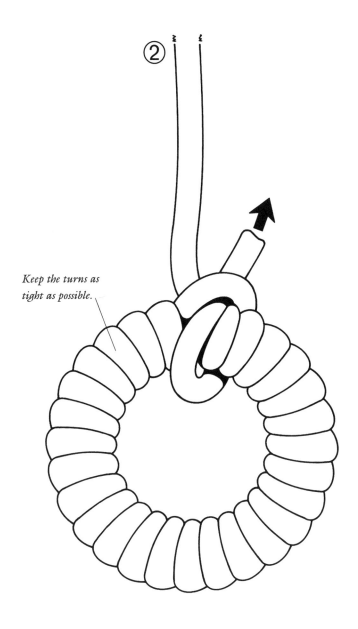

②

Keep the turns as
tight as possible.

continued on page 438

Doughnut

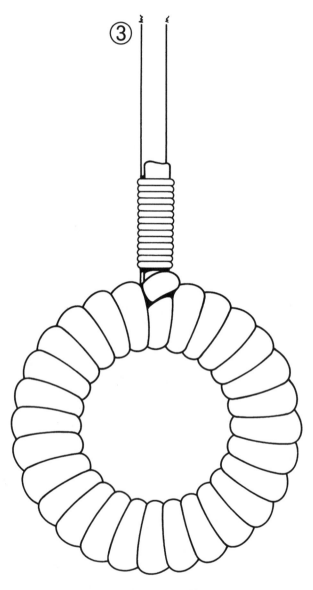

*Work the knot into its final circular shape and then trim
and seize the knot end to the standing part.*

BENDS

ends are used to join two lengths of rope at their ends to
form one longer piece. It is important, if bends are to be
secure, for the ropes joined in this way to be of the same kind
and the same diameter. The sheet bend (see page 442) is the
exception to this rule. It is secure, even when it is used to join
ropes of different diameters.

Bends used at sea can often be made totally secure and more
streamlined by seizing any loose ends.

REEF KNOT

The reef knot gets its name from its nautical use to tie two ends of a rope when reefing a sail. It is often the only knot many people know, apart from the granny knot.

The reef knot is not a secure bend and should not be used as one, certainly never with ropes of different diameter. Its true function is to join together the ends of the same rope or string. It should *only* be used to make a temporary join in lines of identical type, weight, and diameter where it will not be put under great strain. If the lines have to take strain, stopper knots should be tied in the short ends.

The knot is made up of two half knots. The first half knot starts left over right, the second is added right over left, and both short ends finish on the same side. A correctly tied reef knot is symmetrical. If the knot is raised and uneven, it is a granny knot, which is not secure and should be avoided.

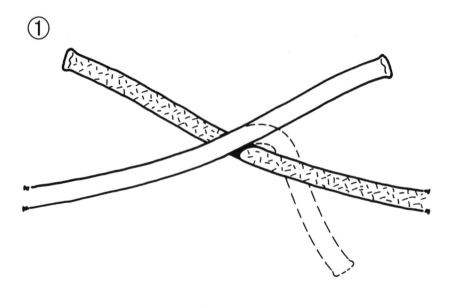

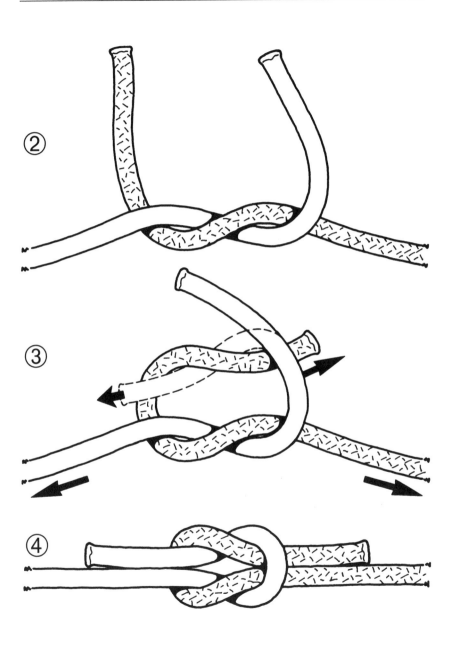

SHEET BEND

The sheet bend is probably the most commonly used of all bends and, unlike most other bends, it can safely join lines of different thickness. It is not, however, 100 percent secure, especially with synthetic rope, and should never be used in circumstances where it will be subjected to great strain. Its breaking strength also decreases in direct proportion to the difference of the lines joined.

The sheet bend derives its name from the way the knot was originally used on sailing ships to secure the ropes (known as sheets) to sails. When put to its other traditional use, as the knot used to join the corners of a flag to the rope when it is hoisted and lowered, it is known as the flag bend. It is quick to make and easy to untie, by rolling forward the bight encircling the single line, and is one of the basic knots that all sailors should know.

A slipped sheet bend is formed by placing a bight between the loop of the heavier rope and the standing part of the lighter one. The slipped knot is easiest to untie when the rope is under strain.

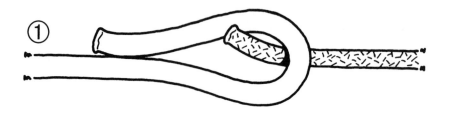

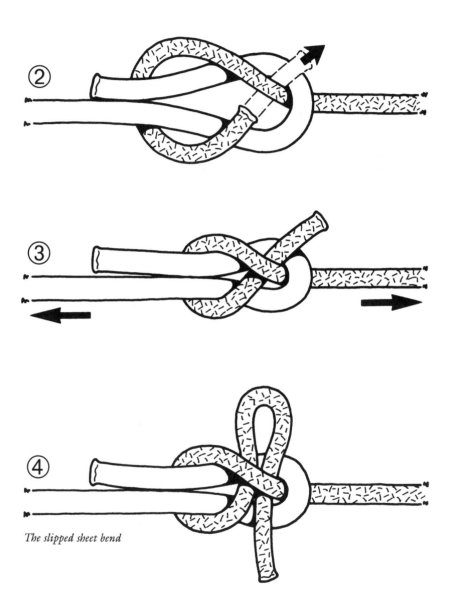

② ③ ④

The slipped sheet bend

CARRICK BEND

Its name probably derives from a medieval Western European ship, the carrack. The knot is formed from two overhand knots crossing each other. It is a very stable knot, does not slip, and is one of the most secure ways of joining two ropes of similar diameter but different type. It is rarely used as a temporary knot as it is very hard to undo when wet or if it has been subjected to very heavy strain. It can be used with larger-diameter ropes such as hawsers, tow lines, and warp ropes.

In its flat form it is valued for its distinctive symmetric appearance and has long been a favorite among artists and graphic designers. When it is drawn up it capsizes into an entirely different shape, but this has no detrimental effect on its strength or security.

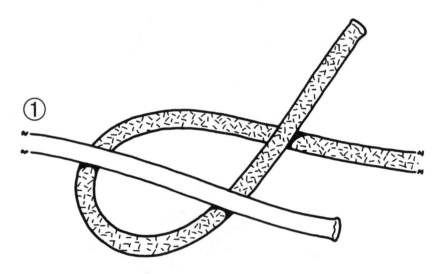

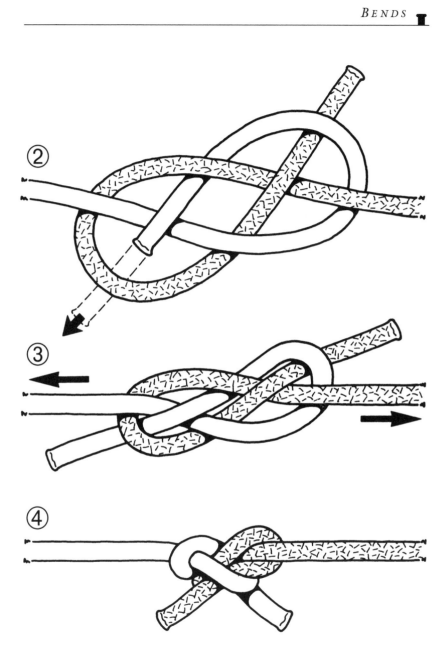

RIGGER'S BEND

The rigger's bend or Hunter's bend is based on two overhand knots. It is stable, has good grip, and is stronger than the sheet bend or the reef knot. It also has the advantage of being easy to untie.

The name Hunter's bend came from Dr. Edward Hunter, a retired physician, who was reported to have invented the knot in 1968. Subsequent research, however, revealed his knot to be the same as the rigger's bend described nearly twenty years earlier by Phil D. Smith in an American book called *Knots for Mountaineers*. He had devised the knot while working on the waterfront in San Francisco. Whoever first invented it, the rigger's bend or the Hunter's bend remains a good general-purpose sailing knot with many useful qualities.

①

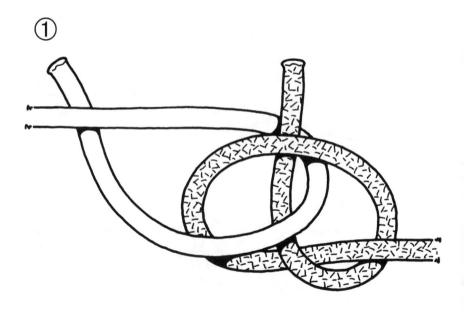

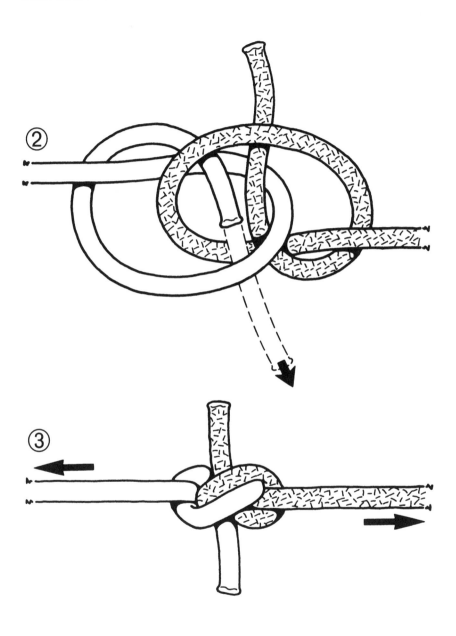

②

③

SURGEON'S KNOT

This knot, as the name suggests, is used by surgeons to suture wounds and tie off blood vessels. It is also an excellent sailing knot for joining two lengths of rope or line together. It is less bulky than other knots and has a good grip. It twists as it is drawn up tight and the diagonal is wrapped around it.

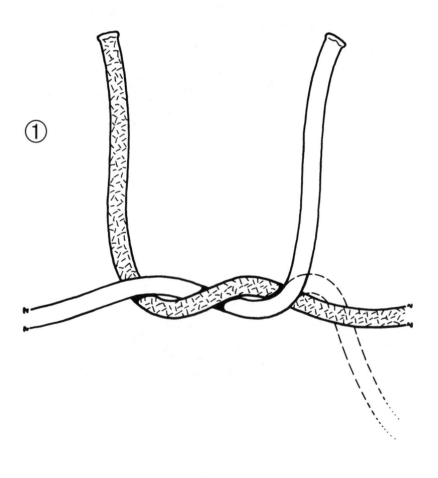

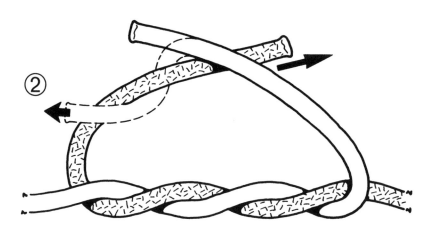

②

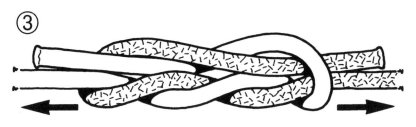

③

④

FISHERMAN'S KNOT

This knot is said to have been invented in the nineteenth century, but some authorities suggest it was known to the ancient Greeks. It is generally known as the fisherman's knot, but over the years it has picked up many different names (such as angler's knot, English knot, Englishman's bend, halibut knot, true lover's knot, and waterman's knot). It is formed from two overhand knots that jam against each other; the short ends are on opposite sides and lie almost parallel to their nearest standing part. After use, the two component knots are generally easily separated and undone.

The fisherman's knot is best suited to joining thin lines such as string, cord, twine, or small stuff, and as the name suggests, it is widely used by fishermen for joining the finest of fishing lines.

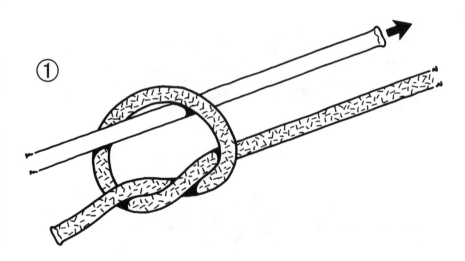

①

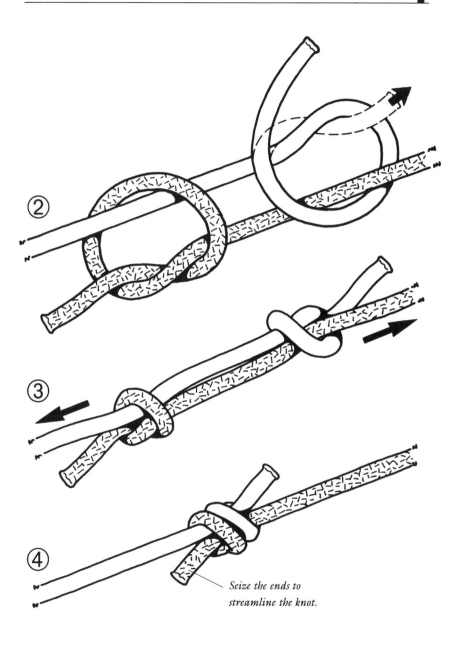

② ③ ④

Seize the ends to
streamline the knot.

DOUBLE FISHERMAN'S KNOT

This double version of the fisherman's knot is a very strong knot for joining
thin lines. It is also known as the grapevine knot. It is quite a bulky knot, so
often the ends are seized to streamline the knot and prevent it from catching.

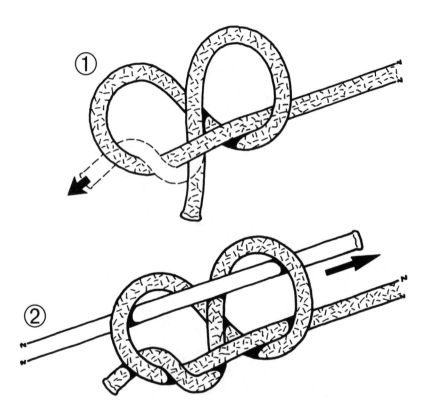

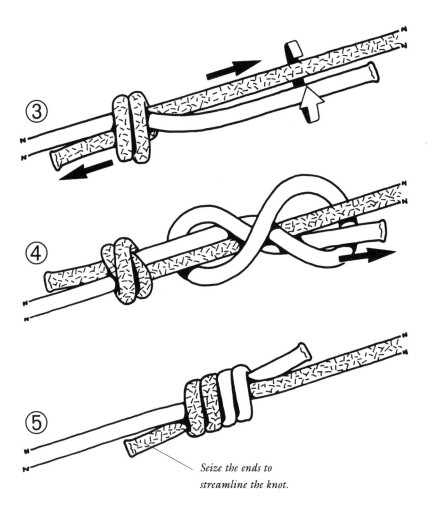

③

④

⑤

Seize the ends to
streamline the knot.

FIGURE-EIGHT BEND

This simple knot (also known as the Flemish bend or knot) is tied by making a figure-eight knot in one end of a line and then following it around with the other working end. It is, despite its simplicity, one of the strongest bends and holds equally well in string and rope.

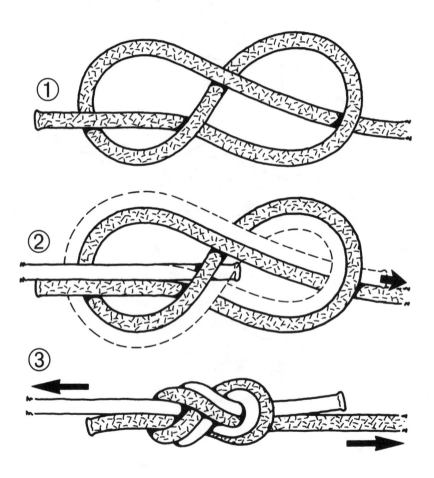

LOOPS

K nots made in the end of rope by folding it back into an eye or loop and then knotting it to its own standing part are called loops. Unlike hitches, which are formed around an object and follow its shape, loops are made in the hand, generally to drop over an object.

Loops are the most commonly used group of sailing knots, and are particularly important to sailors.

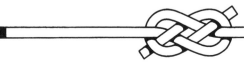

Figure-Eight Loop

This knot is relatively easy to tie and stays tied, even when stiff rope is used. It has many sailing applications, especially when a quick, but strong, eye or loop is required at the end of a rope. Its disadvantages—it is difficult to adjust and cannot easily be untied after loading—tend to be outweighed by its usefulness. It is also known as the figure-eight on the bight.

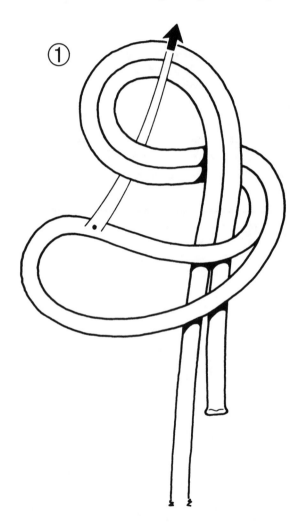

①

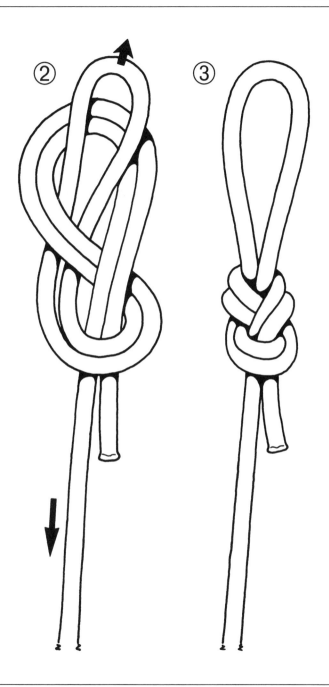

② ③

BOWLINE

The bowline is one of the best known and widely used knots and is particularly important to sailors. It is tied to form a fixed loop at the end of a line or to attach a rope to an object. It has many sailing applications, including use on running rigging and for hoisting, joining, and salvage work.

The bowline is simple to tie, strong, and stable. Its main advantages are that it does not slip or come loose, even in polypropylene ropes that allow other knots to slip. It is also quick and easy to untie, even when the line is under tension, by pushing forward the bight that encircles the standing part of the line.

For extra security, finish the bowline off with a stopper knot or an extra half hitch.

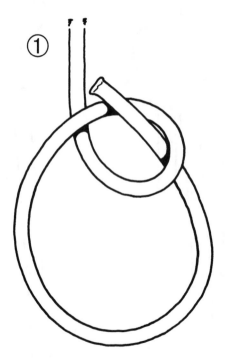

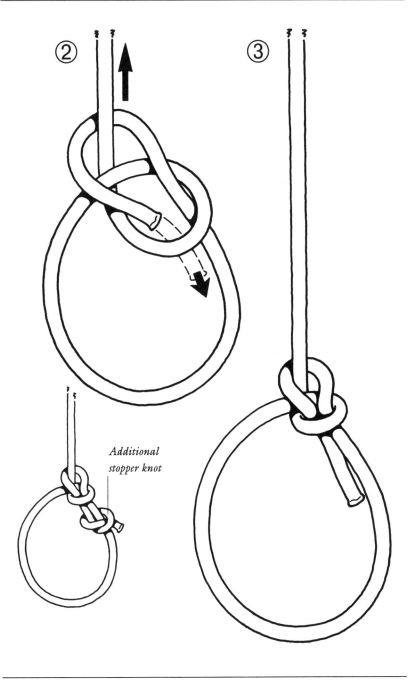

② ③

Additional stopper knot

Running Bowline

This is probably the only running knot used by sailors; it is used on running rigging and to retrieve floating objects that have fallen overboard. On the old sailing ships this knot was used in high winds to tighten the square sail to the yardarm.

The running bowline has many uses because it is strong and secure, does not weaken rope, is simple to untie, and slides easily. It is useful for hanging objects with ropes of unequal diameters—the weight of the object creates the tension that makes the knot grip.

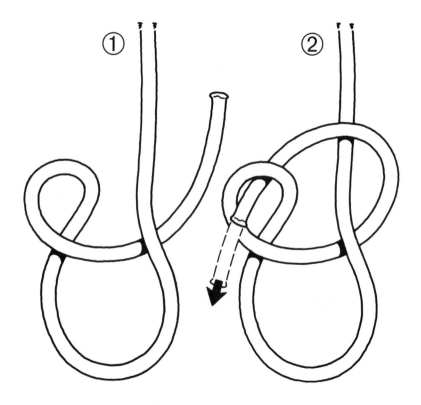

BOWLINE ON A BIGHT

The bowline on a bight forms two fixed loops that do not slide. They are of the same diameter and overlap each other but, when opened out, they can be used separately. Although an ancient knot, it is still used today—especially in sea rescues. If the person to be rescued is conscious, he or she puts a leg through each loop and holds on to the standing part. If the person is unconscious, both legs are put through one loop and the other loop goes under the armpits. This knot is equally effective in salvaging objects.

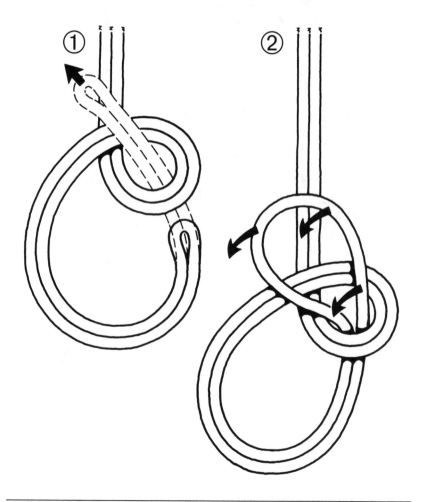

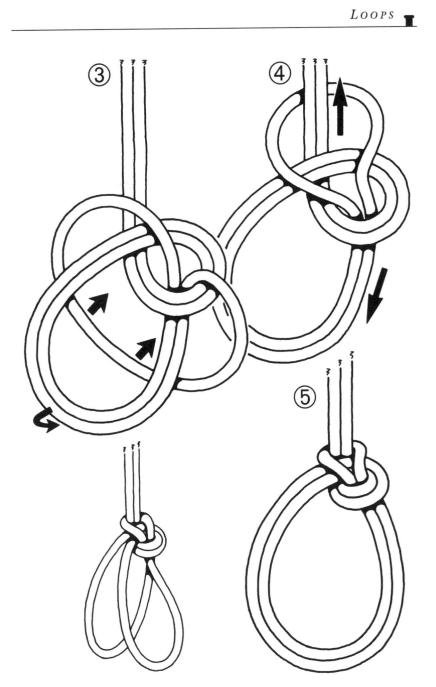

③

④

⑤

BOWLINE – ROPE UNDER TENSION

This variation for tying the bowline is particularly useful for attaching boats to rings. The standing part stays taut throughout while the working end is used to tie a secure fastening.

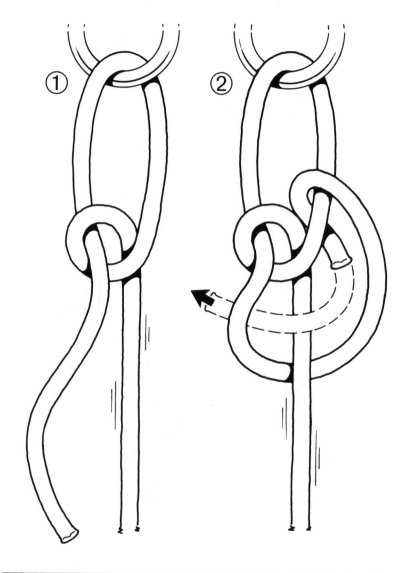

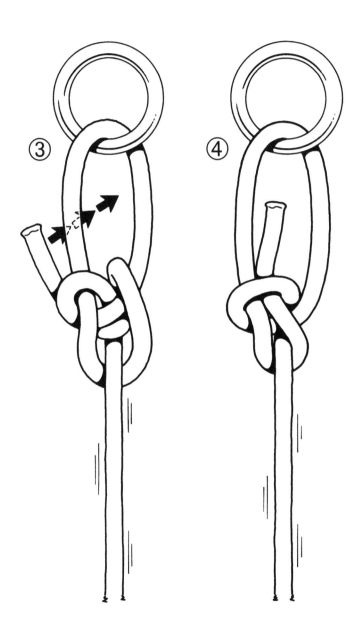

Three-Part Crown

This sturdy, secure, double loop knot can be used as a decorative knot from which to hang gear or equipment, aboard ship or on shore.

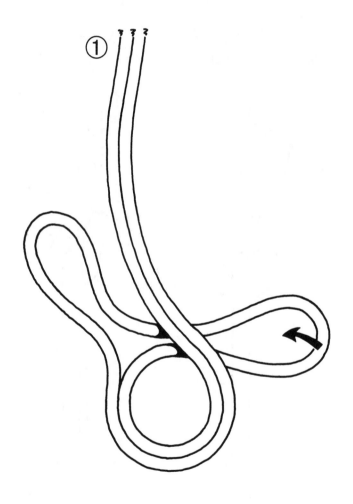

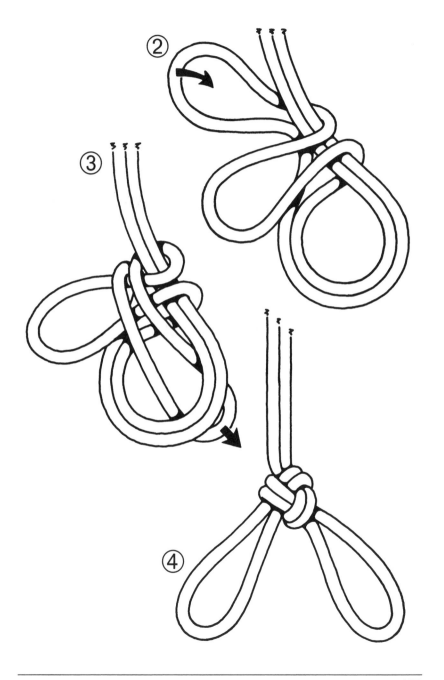

② ③ ④

SPANISH BOWLINE

This is a very strong knot that is widely used in rescue work at sea. The Spanish bowline can also be used to hoist large objects in a horizontal position.

Like the bowline on a bight (see page 462), it is a very old knot, formed of two separate and independent loops that will hold securely and are very safe, even under considerable strain. To effect a rescue, one loop is slipped over the casualty's head, around the back and under the armpits; the other loop goes around the legs behind the knees. It is vitally important that each loop is tightened to the individual's size and then locked into position. If this is not done properly, an unconscious casualty could easily fall through the loops.

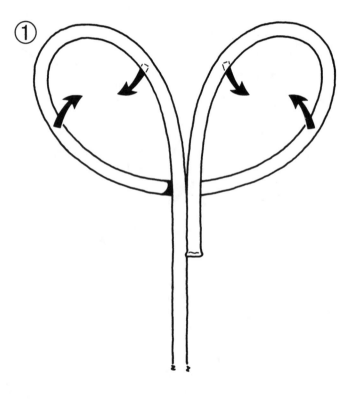

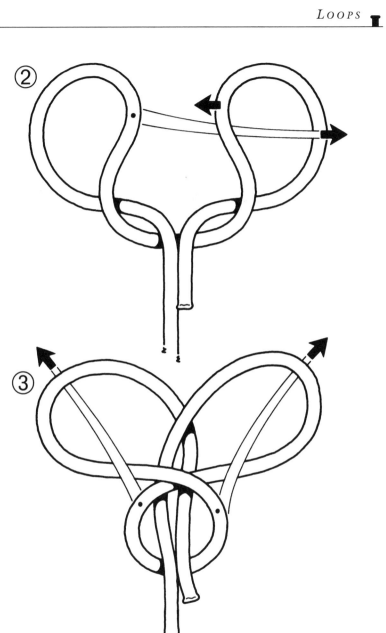

continued on page 470

Spanish bowline

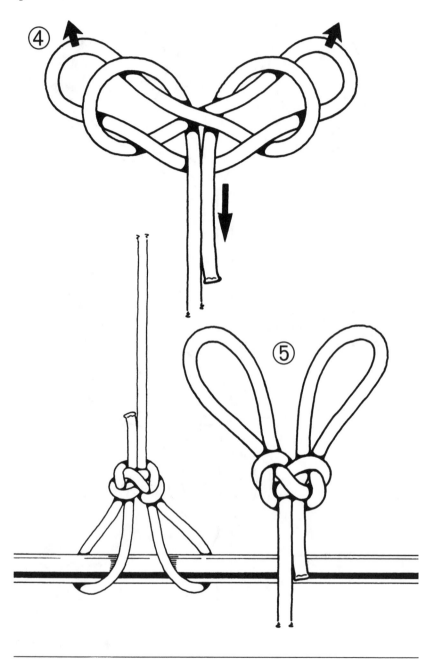

HITCHES

Hitches are knots used to secure a rope to another object (such as a post, hook, spar, rail), or another rope that does not play any part in the actual tying.

They are widely used in sailing for mooring boats, fastening lines, and lashing. They can stand parallel strain without slipping and have the advantage of once learned, being very quick to tie.

HALF HITCHES

The half hitch is a very widely used fastening. It is, in fact, a single hitch formed around the standing part of another hitch. It is used to complete and strengthen other knots—as in the round turn and two half hitches—which can then be used for tying, hanging, hooking objects, etc. The slipped half hitch is a useful variation of the simple half hitch; a sharp pull on the end releases the knot.

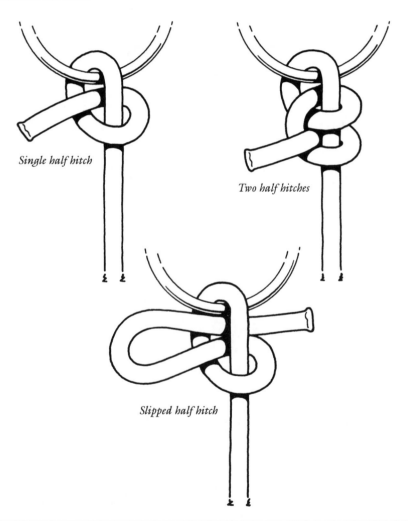

Single half hitch

Two half hitches

Slipped half hitch

CLOVE HITCH

The clove hitch is one of the best known and most valuable of hitches and is used extensively on most yachts. It can be used to fasten a line to a rail, post, or bollard, or on to another rope that is not part of the knot. It can, with practice, be tied with one hand. As one of its other names, the boatman's knot, suggests, it is particularly useful for sailors who may need to moor a dinghy to a dock with one hand while holding on to a rail with the other.

The clove hitch is not, however, a totally secure mooring knot, as it will work loose if the strain is intermittent and comes from different angles. It is best used as a temporary hold, and then replaced by a more stable knot. It can be made more secure by making one or two half hitches around the standing part of the rope, or by adding a stopper knot.

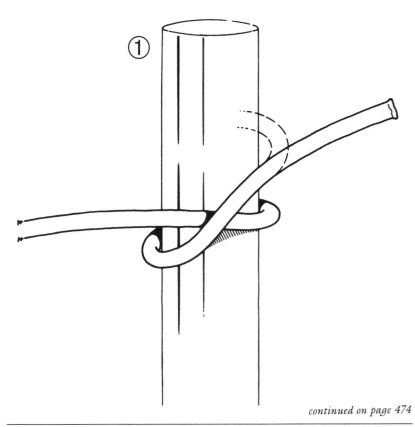

continued on page 474

Clove hitch

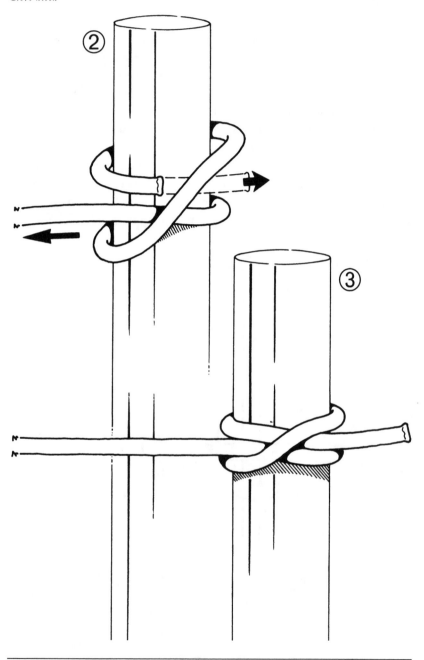

A useful alternative method of constructing a clove hitch is to form the knot before dropping it over a post or bollard.

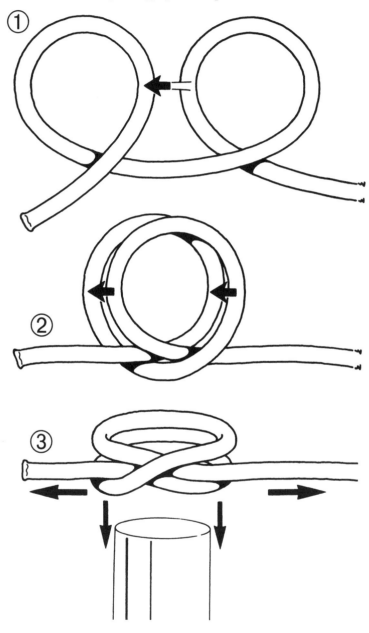

Constrictor Knot

This is a popular all-purpose knot because it is firm and does not slip. It is particularly useful for creating a quick temporary whipping on the ends of ropes.

The knot is made by taking two turns with the rope, forming an overhand knot in the second. The left end is then threaded under the first turn, trapping the overhand knot under a crosswise turn that holds it firmly in place. The constrictor knot grips firmly and stays tied. It may have to be cut free unless the last tuck is made with a bight to make a slip knot.

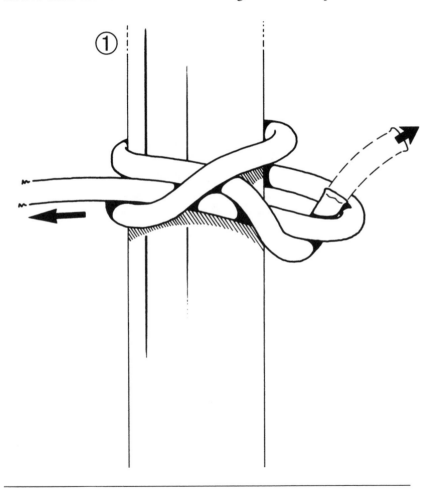

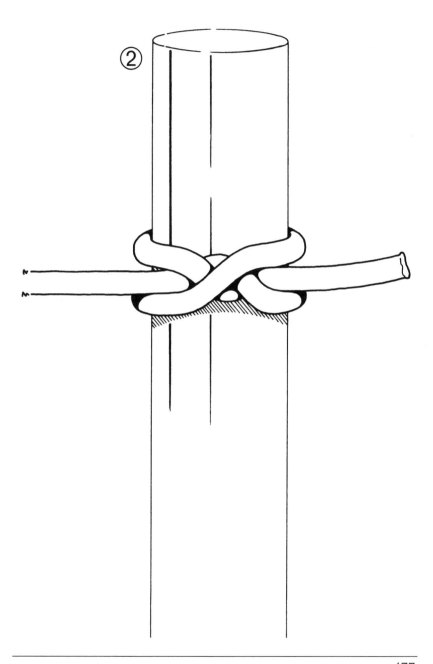

TRANSOM KNOT

This is similar to a constrictor knot (see page 476). It is used to fix together crossed pieces of rigid material and has a wide range of sailing uses; for example, to secure paddles to luggage racks. If used as a permanent knot, the ends may be trimmed off for neatness.

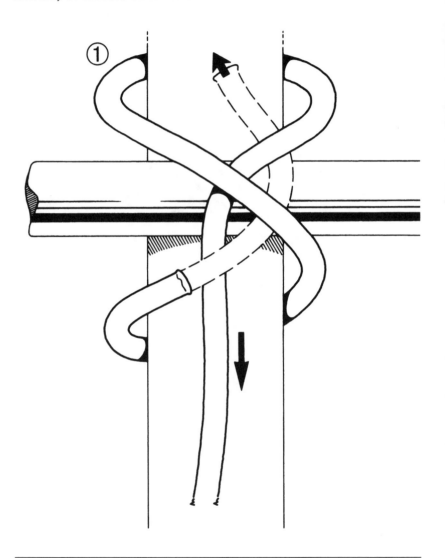

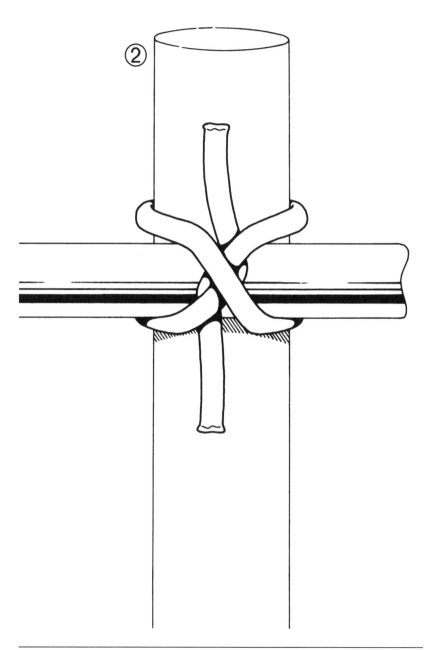

PILE HITCH

The pile hitch is a very neat and practical hitch for securing objects to a post. It is ideal for a temporary mooring of a boat. The big advantage of this hitch is that it is very easy to tie quickly.

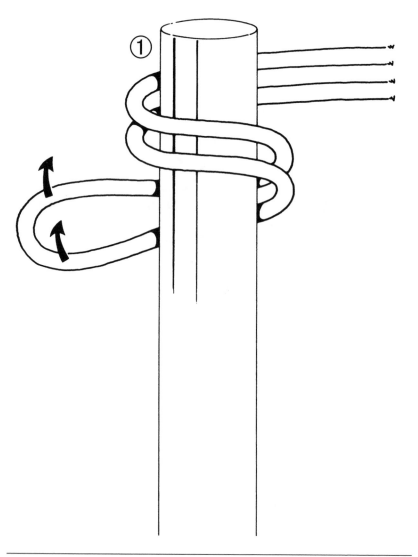

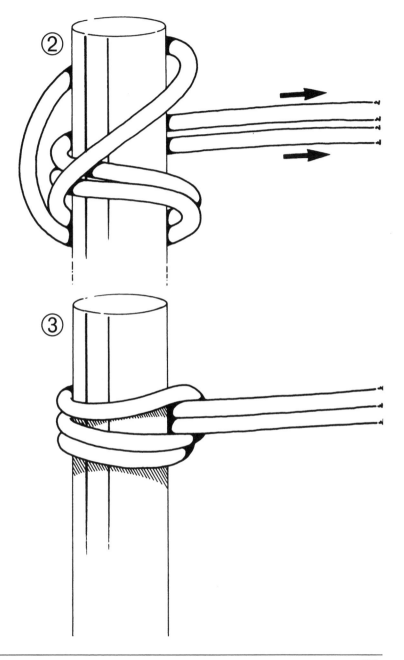

ROUND TURN AND TWO HALF HITCHES

This knot is strong, dependable, and never jams. This makes it a very versatile sailing knot; you can use it whenever you want to fasten a line to a ring, post, bollard, deck eye, rail, or beam. It moors boats safely and will support heavy loads. It has another advantage in that once one end has been secured with a round turn and two half hitches, the other end can be tied with a second knot. This is especially useful when fastening unwieldy, bulky objects.

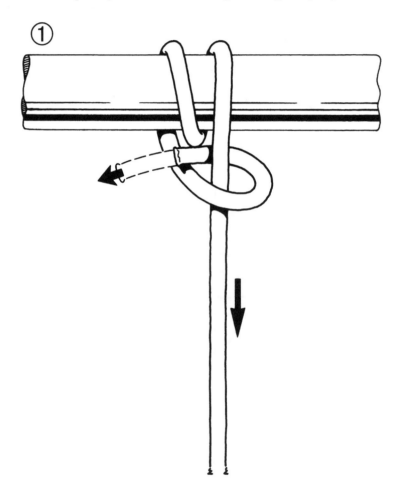

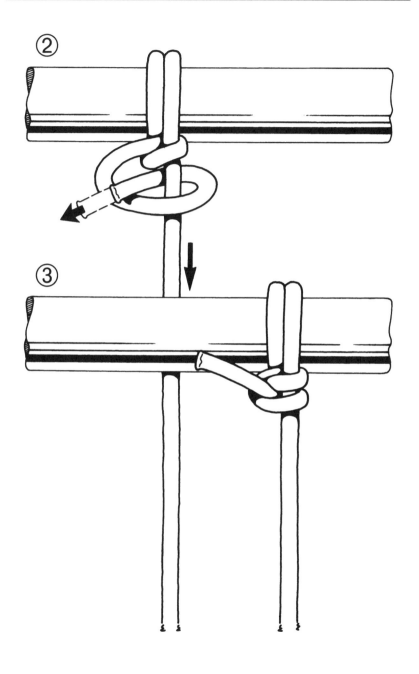

ANCHOR BEND

The anchor bend, also known a the fisherman's bend, is one of the most secure and widely used sailing hitches. It is formed by making two turns around a post or through a ring and then tucking the working end through both turns.

An additional stopper knot or half hitch can be used for added safety, but if the anchor bend is to be used as a long-term fixing (for example, to tie onto an anchor ring), the working end should be secured with a seizing for total security.

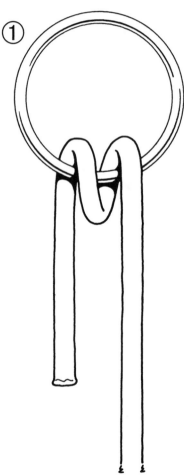

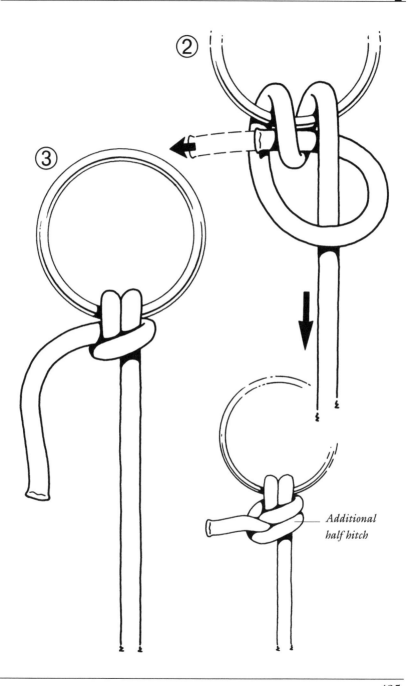

Additional
half hitch

BUNTLINE HITCH

This hitch is specifically used for attaching buntlines to to the eyes or eyelet holes on sails. The buntline hitch needs to be very secure so as to avoid loosening in strong winds that constantly buffet sails. Its strength comes from the short end being deliberately trapped inside the knot.

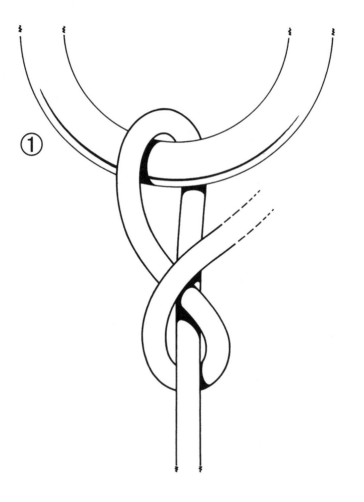

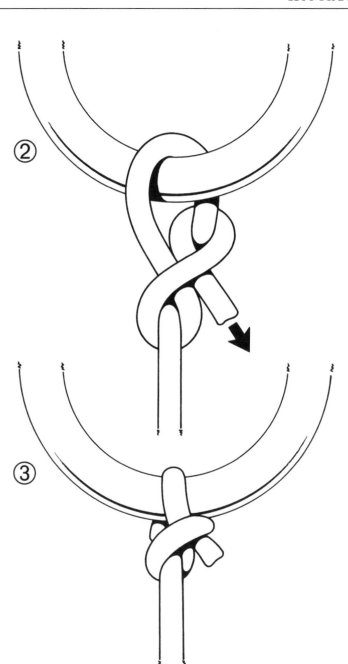

② ③

ROLLING HITCH

This is an essential knot for sailboarders. It is derived from the clove hitch but is significantly more secure. It is used on sailboards to secure the wishbone boom to the mast, but can equally well be used to make any line fast to other cylindrical objects. This very effective, reliable knot is easy to tie and it grips itself, but only in one direction.

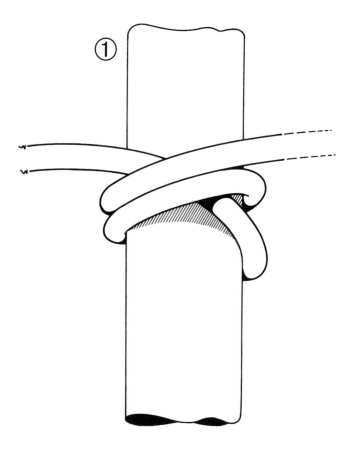

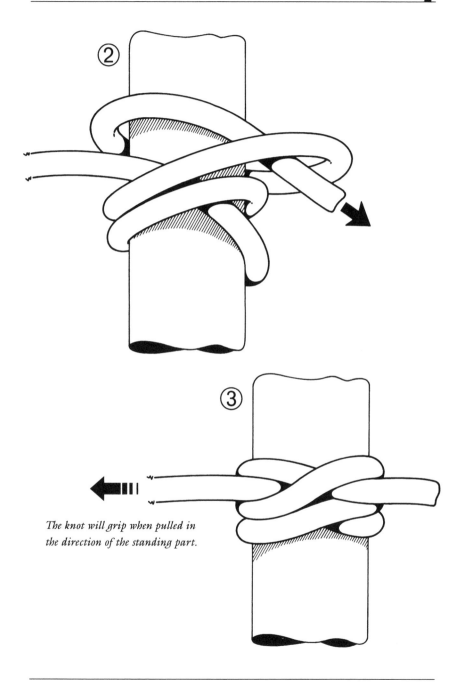

The knot will grip when pulled in the direction of the standing part.

WAGGONER'S HITCH

The waggoner's hitch is a very useful, practical knot that makes it possible to pull tight a line or rope yet leave it ready for immediate release. This makes it an ideal knot for securing loads or deck gear. Once the line has been heaved tight, it should be secured with at least two half hitches.

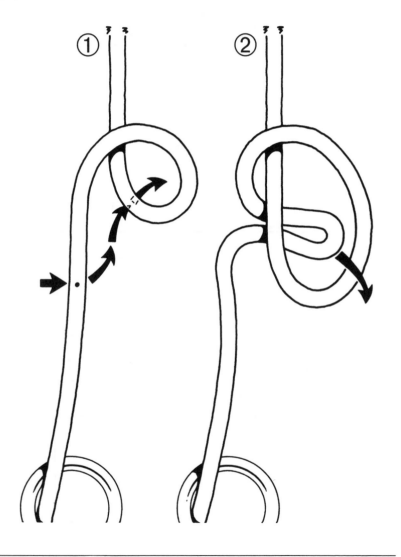

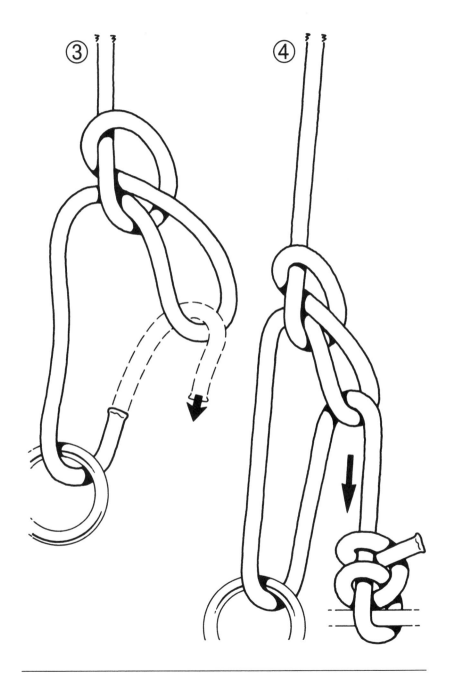

③

④

CAT'S PAW

This is the best hook knot for rope of medium diameter because the strain is equal on both sides. It has a long history of use on the docks and at sea for lifting and slinging heavy loads. This very secure knot can be used, for example, on the hook of a crane in the marina.

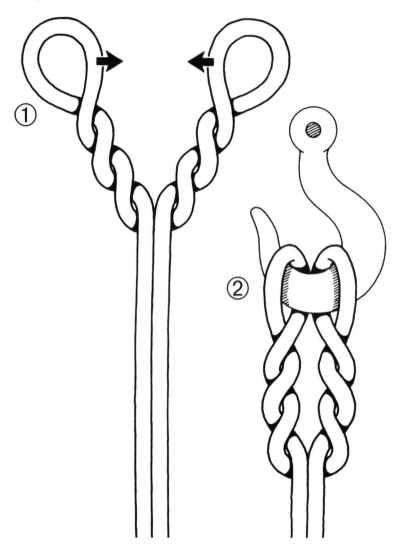

DECORATIVE KNOTS

D ecorative knots can be used individually or in elaborate combinations; they can be used for pure decoration or in the case of sailing for some very practical purposes.

Many decorative knots have long nautical traditions, and seamen and sailors, particularly those who served aboard the great sailing vessels of the eighteenth and nineteen centuries, made decorative knot tying into a branch of folk art.

KNIFE LANYARD KNOT

A lanyard is usually worn around the the neck or attached to a belt for the purpose of holding a wide variety of objects—from knives and whistles to watches and binoculars. Lanyards have a long nautical tradition and because the cord is left in view, sailors often decorated them with a range of elaborate knots. The knife lanyard knot is one of the most attractive and subsequently one of the most widely used. At first sight it may appear difficult to tie, but be patient, follow the step-by-step instructions, "work" the knot into its final form, and you will be rewarded with a beautiful and functional decorative knot.

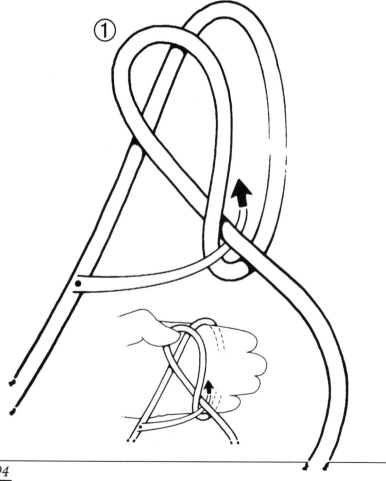

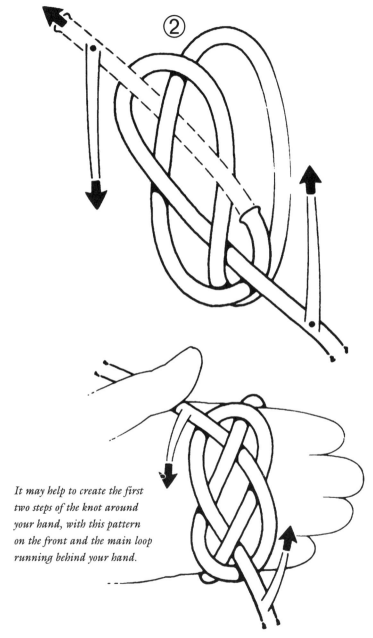

②

It may help to create the first
two steps of the knot around
your hand, with this pattern
on the front and the main loop
running behind your hand.

continued on page 496

Knife lanyard knot

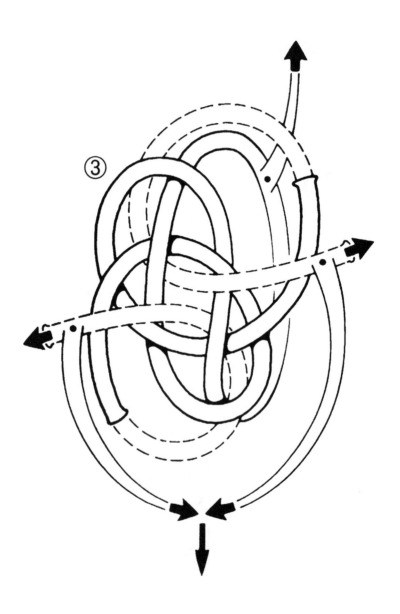

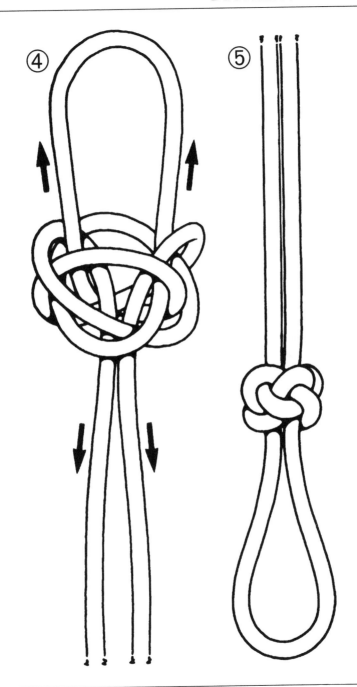

④

⑤

FLAT SINNET

Sinnets are one or more intertwined strands that can be tied from a wide variety of materials. They have a vast range of decorative applications, but also have many practical advantages. In the past sailors exploited the excellent "cling" and surface wear qualities of "sinnet lines."

This simple, three-strand, plait or braid sinnet is also know as the English or common sinnet. Arrange the three strands as in step 1 and if necessary secure them in a straight line with a clip or clamp. To achieve a neat, compact sinnet as in step 6, tighten and arrange the plait at each step of the tying. Sinnets can be finished off in a variety of ways, depending on their final use. The simplest method is by clamping or seizing with thin string and then trimming off the excess.

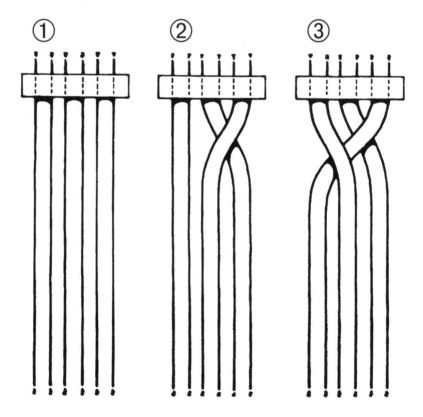

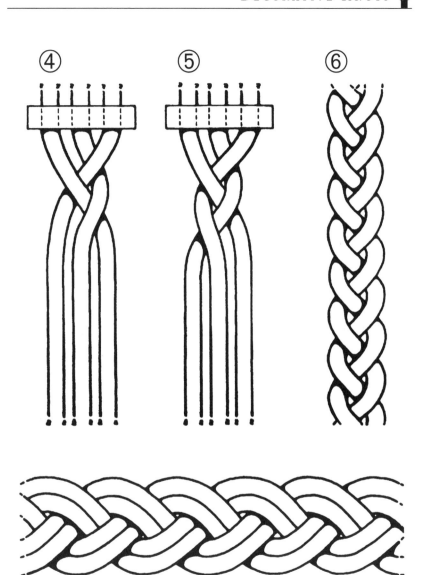

This attractive variation of the flat sinnet is created by doubling the strands. Use six strands, arranged in three pairs, and follow exactly the same tying procedure.

Monkey's Fist

The monkey's fist is a decorative knot that also has many practical uses, the most common being the knot at the end of a heaving line. To give the monkey's fist more weight, it is often tied over a spherical object such as a heavy ball or stone. Smaller knots can be tied over golf balls and if the line is required to float, use a rubber ball. Decoratively, it makes an attractive end to any cord, and is regularly used at the end of pull cords.

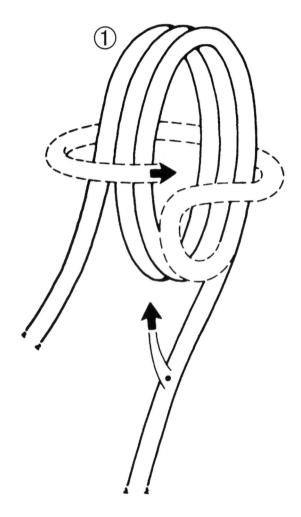

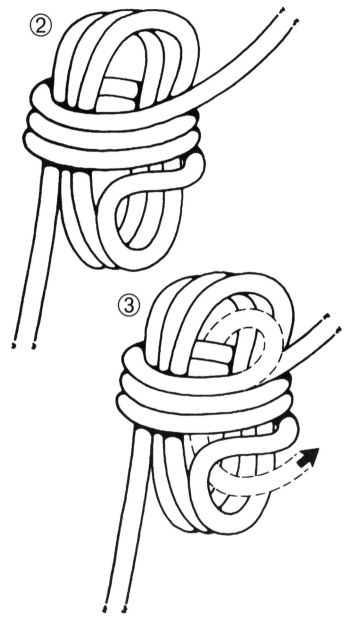

continued on page 502

Monkey's fist

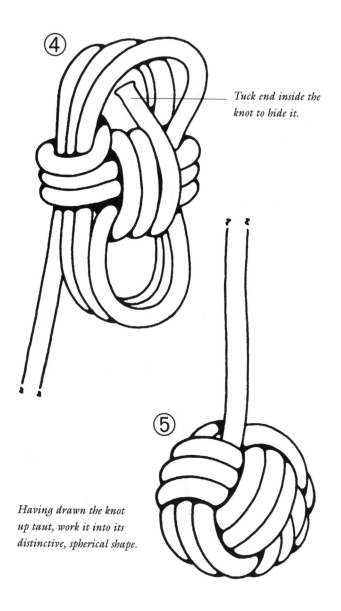

④

Tuck end inside the
knot to hide it.

⑤

*Having drawn the knot
up taut, work it into its
distinctive, spherical shape.*

This alternative way of tying a monkey's fist
brings both ends out of the knot.

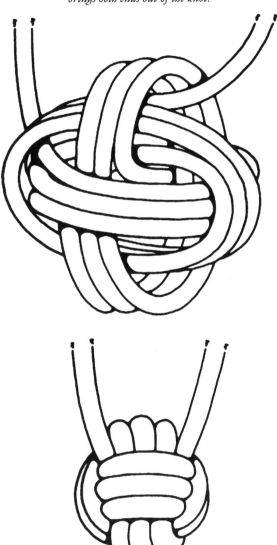

Turk's Head

Turk's head knots have long been recognized for their highly decorative attributes. Leonardo da Vinci drew them in the fifteenth century and they are still widely used today. They are usually tied around cylindrical objects—in most cases as pure decoration (for example, to decorate a tiller). But they can also serve many practical sailing purposes, and are often used to mark the position of center rudder on the ship's wheel.

There are many recorded variations of these knots. The Turk's head shown here, a single-strand, four-lead, three-bight version, is one of the most popular. To create the finished compact knot as in step 6, the slack will need to be worked out. This is done gradually, by starting at one end of the cord and progressing right through the knot to the other end. It may also help to use a pair of thin-nosed pliers.

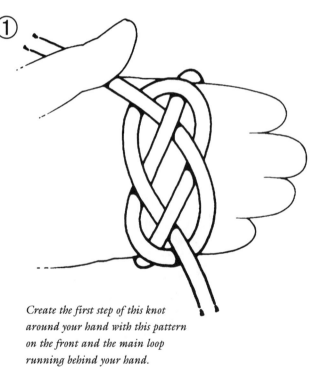

Create the first step of this knot around your hand with this pattern on the front and the main loop running behind your hand.

②

Remove the knot from your hand and
place the thumb and forefinger though
the spaces indicated by the black dots
(see step 3, page 124).

continued on page 506

Turk's head

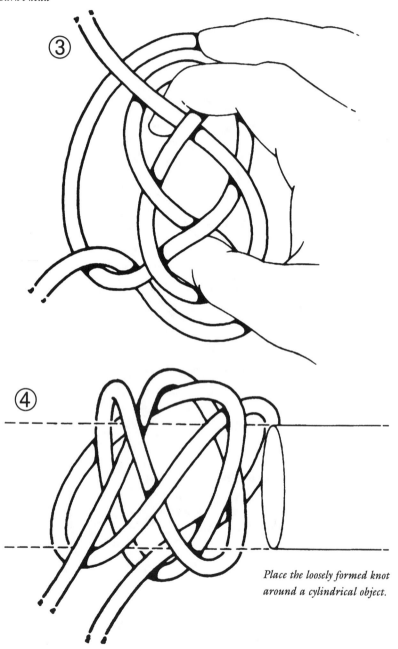

③

④

Place the loosely formed knot
around a cylindrical object.

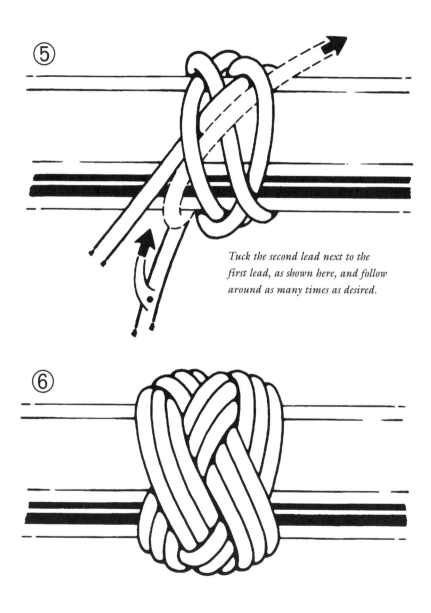

⑤

Tuck the second lead next to the first lead, as shown here, and follow around as many times as desired.

⑥

TURK'S HEAD – FLAT FORM

This method shows how to tie a Turk's head in a flat form. The knot can be left in this form to create, for example, a mat or decorative fender. Alternatively, it can be turned down and worked over a cylindrical object to form a decorative covering.

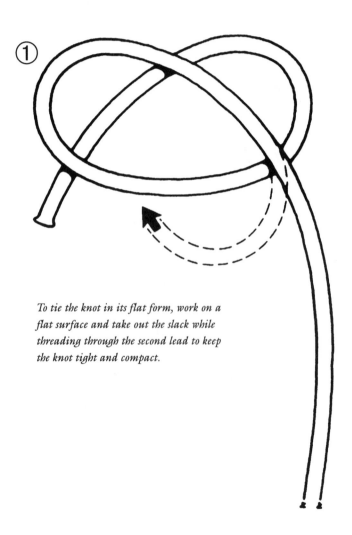

To tie the knot in its flat form, work on a flat surface and take out the slack while threading through the second lead to keep the knot tight and compact.

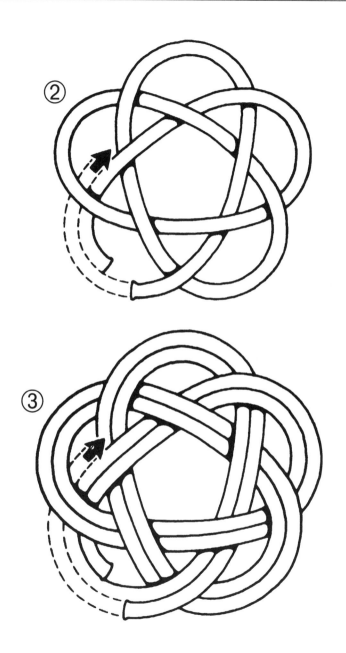

continued on page 510

Turk's head – flat form

The first lead can be followed around by the second lead
as many times as required to create the finished knot.
Always keep the second lead on the same side as the first
lead (the lead that created the pattern) and tuck
the ends in neatly to hide them.

OCEAN PLAT

This classic flat knot is found all over the world in a surprising number of situations but its use as a mat or tread aboard ship or boat is one of the common and practical uses.

The size of the example shown here, which is one of the most widely used, is based on three side bights. The pattern can be made more solid by increasing the number of times the lead is followed around, but the actual size of the knot cannot be increased. To increase the size of the knot, the number of bights has to be increased. For example, increase to six or nine bights to create a long, narrow ocean plat for a companionway aboard ship or boat.

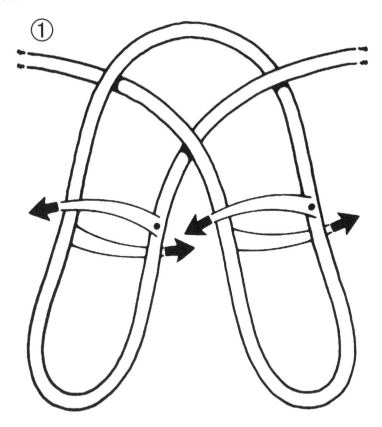

continued on page 512

Ocean plat

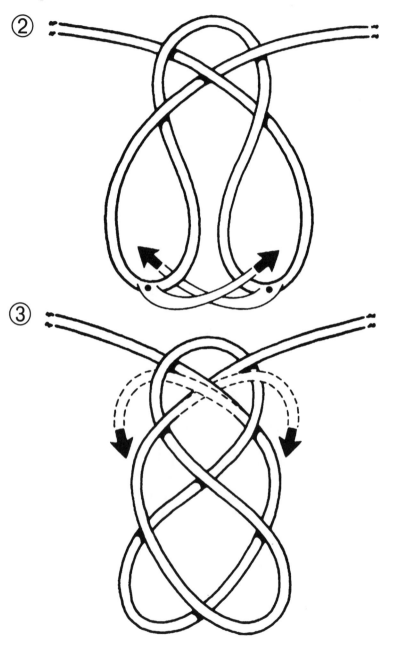

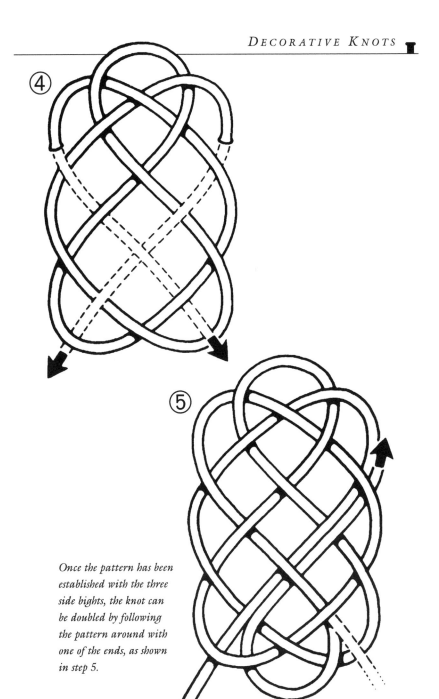

④

⑤

*Once the pattern has been
established with the three
side bights, the knot can
be doubled by following
the pattern around with
one of the ends, as shown
in step 5.*

continued on page 514

Ocean plat

The knot can be doubled or followed around as
many times as desired. It can also be left loosely
formed as shown above, or it can be tightened
and made solid, as in step 7.

⑦

To finish, hide the ends by tucking them into the weave on the
underside of the knot. If the knot is to be used as a mat, the
whole structure can be greatly stengthened by sewing together
all of the intersecting points with strong thread.

NET MAKING

Nets can be tied in a variety of sizes for many different uses, from fishing to storage, and it is always useful to be able to construct your own custom-sized net. One of the most popular, and important, sailing uses is safety netting between guardrails and deck. This does not only prevent people, especially small children, from falling overboard, but it also prevents the loss of important equipment that can often prove impossible to recover.

To construct a net you will require a reel of good netting twine, a net needle, and a piece of wood with straight edges.

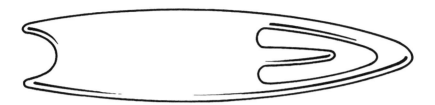

*A net needle will make it easy to thread the twine
and save you from having to pull the whole line
through at each turn.*

*A wooden straightedge will enable you to
hold and check the mesh to give a
uniform pattern.*

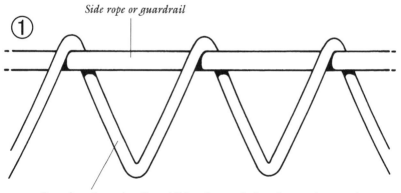

Side rope or guardrail

①

*Looped netting twine. For additional strength the twine can be secured
to the side rope or guardrail by using a clove hitch at each apex.*

continued on page 518

Net making

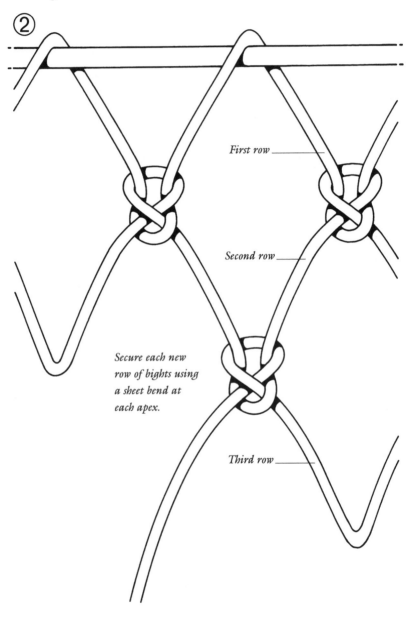

First row

Second row

Secure each new
row of bights using
a sheet bend at
each apex.

Third row

③

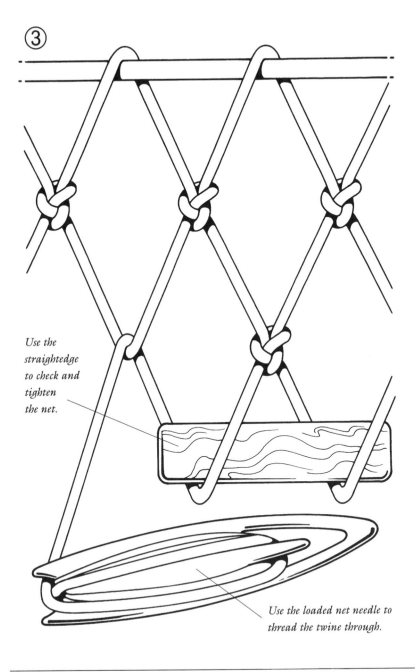

Use the straightedge to check and tighten the net.

Use the loaded net needle to thread the twine through.

DECORATIVE KNOTS

CONTENTS

INTRODUCTION

· ·

Decorative or "Fancy" knots and knot work have held in the past, as they do today, a particular fascination in the way they combine what is useful with the aesthetically pleasing. Few knots included in this category are purely decorative. Most have practical applications and are derived from or based on well known standard knots, but they all allow for individual creativity through personal ingenuity and inventiveness and, in the complexity and precision of their formation, can be as absorbing and satisfying as any puzzle.

Decorative knotting has a long and distinguished history and is one of the oldest and most widely distributed of the folk arts. It is still widely practised. Over the years, it has retained wide popular appeal and fascination, and now has the status of a recognized art form.

In the past, the intricacies of knot formation could take a long time to acquire; the knowledge being passed on from one individual to another, often under pledge of secrecy. *The Book of Decorative Knots* gives you the opportunity, through clear instructions and easy to follow step-by-step illustrations, to master 50 classic decorative knots within a few hours. The knots, meticulously explained and described, are not just decorative and attractive in their own right, but have a multitude of modern applications in all walks of life as well – from sailing, fishing, hunting and outdoorsmanship, to the worlds of fashion and interior design.

· ·

HISTORY

The art of knotting is as ancient as humankind. Stone Age peoples used knots to secure and fasten their traps, clothing and housing; coiled and braided rope was found in the tomb of Tutankhamun; the Inca people of Peru used knotted string instead of written figures and the Greeks, Romans, and other ancient civilizations probably knew as much about knots as we do today.

Throughout this long history, the decorative potential of the knot has been almost as important as its practical function. This aspect of knot making can be found in many places and many ages, from the elaborate patterning on Celtic artifacts to the fringe on the gown of Leonardo da Vinci's Mona Lisa. It was, however, seamen and sailors, particularly those who served aboard the great sailing vessels of the eighteenth and nineteenth centuries, who made decorative knot tying a branch of folk art peculiarly their own.

The length of the voyages undertaken by sailing ships left sailors with little to do for much of the time; this was particularly true on whalers which were at sea longer than other ships and were heavily overmanned. Isolated on board, unable for the most part to read and write, sailors had to find some way to fill their idle hours and knotting was an ideal way of passing the time.

There was no shortage of raw materials. Sailing ships carried miles of rigging, and there was always a plentiful supply of spoiled rope (known as "junk") available for knotting and thin string or twine for finer work. Sailors used their leisure hours to develop ways of tying knots that were both decorative and highly functional.

Lanyards (see pg. 537), for example, were used to secure anything movable that had to be carried aloft and could be made fast round the neck, shoulder, wrist or attached to a belt, allowing the sailor to work with both hands and minimizing the danger of losing irreplaceable articles overboard. Lanyards could be knotted in many different ways, allowing the individual sailor to mark any personal articles as his own.

The inventiveness and creativity can also be seen in the way sailors combined different knots to make netting for fishing nets and hammocks, or to form something as complex as a ladder (see pg. 648) from a single piece of rope.

Flat knots (see pg. 633) were used to make matting, which was found everywhere on board – to prevent chafing and slipping, nailed to the deck at gangways and companionways, to the sides of smaller boats to act as buffers, and rails and spars. Vitally necessary and absolutely functional, mats were often as elegant in their patterns and formation as works of art.

Knotting on board ship was often very competitive and the secrets and intricacies of particular knots jealously guarded. Sailors were also responsible for the colourful descriptive names still given to particular knots, the Turk's Head (see pg. 607) and Monkey's Fist (see pg. 597), for example.

The Turk's Head, a tubular binding knot, combines a highly decorative appearance with a great diversity of practical uses. It is formed around a cylindrical object and was used as a foot hold on ladders, as a hand hold on life lines and guard rails, a hand grip on oars and fishing rods, a hand guard, drip guard and handle. The knot is so decorative, however, it was also commonly used, as it is today, in making bracelets, anklets, rings and napkin holders.

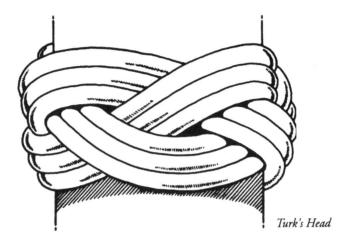

Turk's Head

The Monkey's Fist, the highly descriptive name refers to its shape, superficially resembles the Turk's Head but is formed around a small heavy ball and was used to carry the weight of a heaving line. It can be used to cover any small round objects, from paperweights to cane heads and door handles.

Sailors also spent their time in the plaiting or braiding of rope, which is termed Sinnet (see pg. 617). On board ship sinnet served many purposes; as lashing, as belting and to prevent chafing. It has excellent "cling" qualities and is resistant to surface wear. The intricacy that can be introduced into the plaiting or braiding process meant that sinnet work was often highly decorative.

By the middle of the nineteenth century, the great days of sail were coming to an end. Fast clipper ships and then the advent of steam meant sailors no longer had the time or the raw materials available for knot making. These changes did not mark the death of the craft, however, for sailors were not the only people interested in, or open to the functional and decorative possibilities of fancy knot work.

Their inland counterparts, working canals and rivers, made similar knots, adapted to their own style and purpose, as did other groups of workers with rope and time on their hands, from riggers to cow hands.

Decorative and fancy knotting had always been a part of the domestic arts and handicrafts. Knots were commonly used in dress making and the design of accessories, belts, bags, etc, even jewelry. The knots were not there just to decorate and enhance but to hold and fasten. The classic knot of this type was the Chinese Button Knot (see pg. 589). Worn throughout China, particularly on underwear and nightclothes, the Chinese Button Knot could be used as a fastening, replacing buttons of wood or bone. It was often matched with frogging – a variant of flat knotting – to provide decorative and unusual fastenings on coats.

Another knot frequently used in dress and jewelry design was the Bowknot (see pg. 570). Bowknots were often formed of ribbon and the material, together with the loops and loose ends characteristic of this kind of knot, made them highly attractive.

Sinnets, flat matting and all kinds of fancy knotting were freely used to decorate and embellish in all areas of fashion, from clothes to hair design.

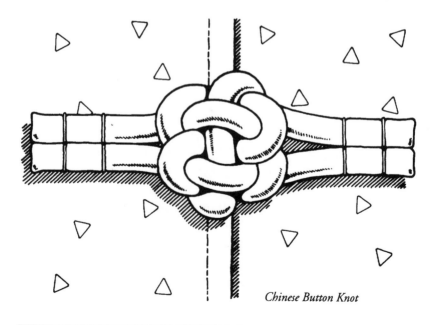

Chinese Button Knot

THE PRESENT DAY

D ecorative knots are as popular now as they were in the past. Modern sailors and boat owners rarely go to sea in fully rigged tall ships but they use the same knots as were used in the days when all craft were under sail. This is not just because of the proven reliability of knots developed in those times, but also because they recognise the knots' decorative potential. A knotted boat fender, for example, might do the same job but it looks significantly more attractive than an old tire. The Turk's Head, sinnets and lanyard knots all have their place on modern boats. Hammocks and rope ladders are just as important on board today as they were in the days of sail. Decorative knots are not only serviceable and functional but also enhance the ship-shape appearance of any vessel.

Knife Lanyard Knot

Outdoorsmen also find many uses for decorative knots. Lanyards are as useful halfway up a mountain as they are in the rigging of a ship, allowing free use of the hands while keeping vital belongings or equipment safe and secure. Knots, such as the Turk's Head again, or the Monkey's Fist, provide useful coverings and bindings, and sinnets and lanyard knots can be used to make belts and strong, attractive handles and strapping for gear.

Decorative knotting is not just found outdoors. It has become well established in arts and crafts generally and has a particularly strong place in interior design. Plant holders, curtain cords and tiebacks, cord pulls, light pulls, tassels and fringing, place mats on tables, even door mats and flooring are just some of the modern applications described in *The Book of Decorative Knots*. Many of the knots to be found in the book can be a help around the house generally, from wrapping gifts and parcels more attractively to getting the tail of a kite to fly right.

Similarly, decorative knots are still widely used in dress making, tailoring and the manufacture of personal accessories from belts and key fobs to hair ornaments. Knowing how to tie them, and when and where to apply them, allows the individual scope for ingenuity and creativity in making gifts and personal items and can, in fact, become a whole hobby area in its own right.

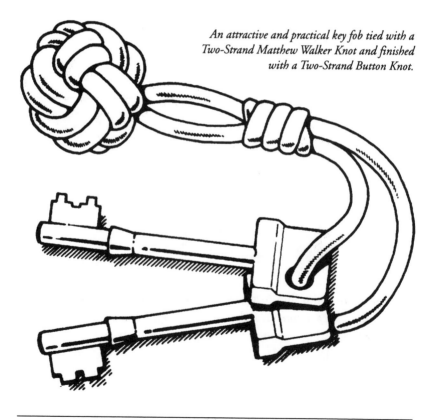

An attractive and practical key fob tied with a Two-Strand Matthew Walker Knot and finished with a Two-Strand Button Knot.

MATERIALS

It is possible to make decorative knots out of almost anything from rope and leather to human hair, but the most common materials are rope of different thicknesses, along with yarn, braid, string, cord, thread and twine (known as small stuff). Decorative knotting also utilizes materials not generally associated with ordinary knot formation, such as flat tape and ribbon.

NATURAL FIBER ROPES

Traditionally, rope was made from vegetable fibers and on the old sailing ships this was what would be used for decorative knotting. Sailors would use whatever material was at hand, the most commonly available being manila, sisal, coir and hemp. Flax and cotton were highly prized for their fine quality and manageability, but they were expensive and more likely to be used to rig a rich man's yacht than on an ordinary sailing vessel.

Three-strand natural fiber rope.

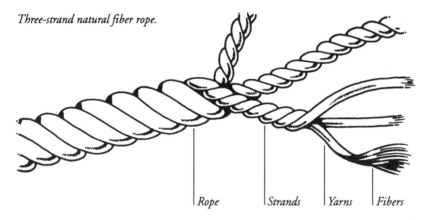

| Rope | Strands | Yarns | Fibers |

Natural fiber rope is normally three-strand and right laid and is made by twisting fibers of natural materials together. The fibers were twisted first into yarn, then into strands, and finally into rope, in a process called laying up. Sailors often had to use spoiled or junk rope which could be any size for their own knot tying and would carefully unravel the laid up rope and then work it up themselves into the size they required.

Nowadays, natural rope is little used for conventional knots, but for decorative purposes many still prefer vegetable fibers for their traditional appearance and beauty of their natural colors and textures. The finest natural fibers are cotton, linen and silk.

SYNTHETIC ROPES

Synthetic materials have widely replaced natural fibers in the manufacture of rope. Man-made filaments can be spun to run the whole length of a line, do not vary in thickness, and do not have to be twisted together to make them cohere. This gives them superior strength.

Nylon, developed toward the end of the Second World War, was the first man-made material to be used in this way. Since then a range of synthetic ropes have been developed to meet different purposes, but they all share certain characteristics. Size for size they are lighter, stronger and cheaper than their natural counterparts. They can also be made in a range of colors, and this makes them particularly attractive for the tying of decorative knots.

Nylon (Polyamide) fibers make ropes that are both strong and elastic. They are also used in fishing line, and are tough, flexible, easily knotted and hold knots well.

Polyester ropes are nearly as strong as nylon and give very little stretch. They are widely used in sailing for sheets and halyards. Polyester is also used in small stuff for whipping twine.

Polypropylene is not as strong as nylon or polyester but it makes a good, inexpensive, all-purpose rope.

The other types of synthetic rope are plaited or braided. Plaited describes four- or eight-stranded solid plaits. Braided rope has an outer sheath of sixteen or more strands round an inner core that is either braided and hollow or made up of solid parallel, or slightly twisted, filaments. Braided rope is the softer and more flexible of the two types of rope.

Both natural fiber and synthetic ropes are suited to and used for different types of decorative knotting. Natural fiber ropes are usually only available from ship and boat chandlers or specialist rope suppliers. Synthetic ropes are more widely available, from camping and climbing shops to D.I.Y stores.

SMALL STUFF

Small stuff, the name given to any rope under an inch (25mm) in circumference, is used for fine work. It includes cord, string, thread, twine and yarn. Again it can be either man-made or natural fiber and is available from craft shops, camping shops, hardware stores, fishing tackle shops. Thread and yarn can also be bought in haberdashers, knitting and dressmaking shops.

RIBBON AND TAPE

Ribbon and different widths of tape are also used in decorative and fancy knot work and are available in a wide variety of colors. They would normally be bought in dressmaking, knitting and craft shops.

CHOOSING MATERIALS

The choice of materials very much depends on the type of knot you want to tie, what it will be used for, and the effect you wish to create. The same knot can look startlingly different, depending on the material used. Ribbon, for example, works up very differently from rope.

A Bowknot tied with ribbon.

A Bowknot tied with cord.

SEALING ENDS

Sealing the ends, if necessary, of your tying material makes knots significantly easier to tie as well as giving a neater appearance. When you buy synthetic rope from a chandlers, they will cut it to the length you require with an electrically heated knife. This seals the ends and gives a sharp edge. When you cut synthetic rope yourself, use a sharp knife and then melt the end with a cigarette lighter or on an electric ring.

Natural fiber rope will fray if left unseized. A neat, secure and easy way to prevent this is by whipping the ends. Use vegetable fiber twine and always bind against the lay of the rope. In general whipping needs to be as long as the width of the rope.

Two other quick and efficient methods of sealing ends is to use ordinary adhesive tape or on small stuff, a simple stopper knot.

Whipping the end of a rope.

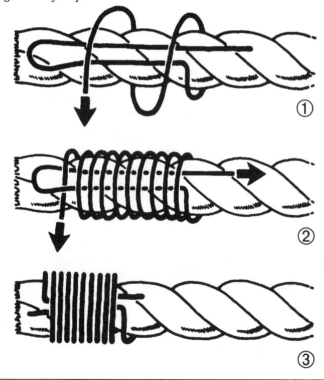

SELECTING KNOTS

Knots are selected according to function, purpose and decorative effect. *The Book of Decorative Knots* illustrates 50 of the best known and commonly tied knots, clearly explains how to tie them and describes their uses, functions and applications. No amount of theoretical knowledge, however, can compensate for practical experience. Mastering anything takes practice and tying knots is no exception. A beginner should not be discouraged if he or she is not immediately successful with a complicated knot, but it does make sense to master the simpler versions of each knot first.

A loosely tied Chinese Button Knot (left) *and the final 'worked' version* (right).

Finally, never try to complete an elaborate knot in one operation or draw it up in one movement. A knot should be loosely tied or projected and then "worked", molded carefully to keep its shape as it is gradually drawn up to final tightness. Slack should be worked out evenly and gradually. In decorative knotting this is as important as correct tying and requires both patience and practice.

HOW TO USE THIS BOOK

The diagrams accompanying the descriptions of the knots are intended to be self-explanatory. Written instructions, special tying techniques and methods will accompany the more complex knots. There are arrows to show the directions in which you should push or pull the working ends of the rope or line. The dotted lines indicate intermediate positions of the rope. Always follow the order shown of going over or under a length of line; reversing or changing this order could result in a completely different knot.

ROPE PARTS

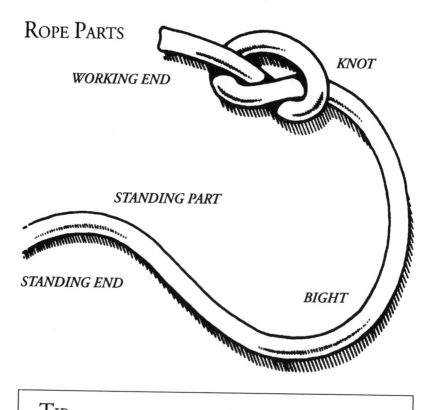

KNOT

WORKING END

STANDING PART

STANDING END

BIGHT

TIP . . . .

Metal or plastic tipped round shoelaces are excellent for knot practice. They are obtainable in a range of colors and different lengths.

1

LANYARD KNOTS

· ·

A lanyard is usually worn around the neck or attached to a belt for the purpose of holding a wide variety of objects – from knives and whistles to watches and binoculars. Because the cord is left in view it is often decorated with a range of elaborate lanyard knots and sinnets (see pg. 617).

The lanyard knots illustrated in this chapter divide into two groups, single-strand and two-strand.

Double Knife Lanyard Knot

MULTIPLE OVERHAND KNOT

This knot, also known as the blood knot, can be tied with any number of turns. A small knot, as shown here with four turns, can be gently drawn together by keeping the knot open and loose and pulling on both ends at the same time – it also helps to form the knot by twisting the two ends in opposite directions as you pull. Larger knots with more turns must be slowly "worked" together in order for the knot to settle into its final form.

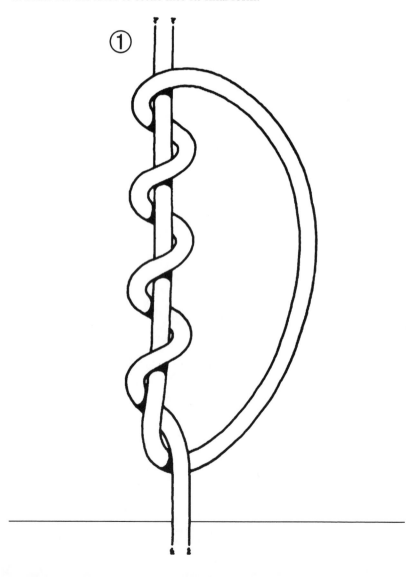

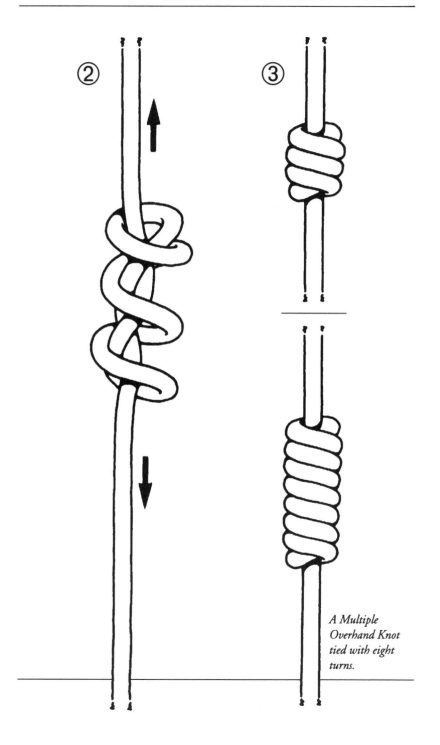

② ③

A Multiple Overhand Knot tied with eight turns.

LANYARD KNOT

This is a simple and effective single-strand knot based on a Figure-Eight Knot. It is particularly useful for decorating small stuff and is often tied in a series of knots, providing a decorative appearance and serving the useful purpose of preventing a cord or lanyard from slipping through the fingers.

If the knot is tightened at this stage it would form a Figure-Eight Knot, which is a commonly used stopper knot.

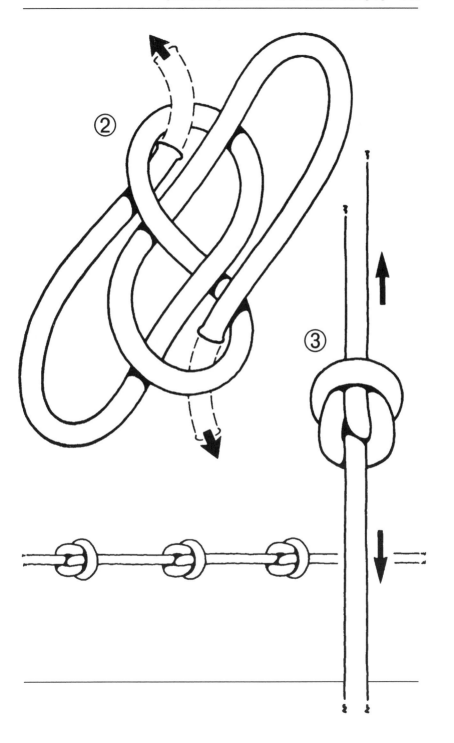

FOUR-PLY KNOT

This simple knot can be deceptively difficult to tie if the step-by-step instructions are not followed exactly. After creating the series of small turns in step 1, and forming step 2 as shown, it is important to methodically work out the surplus material before attempting to tighten the knot.

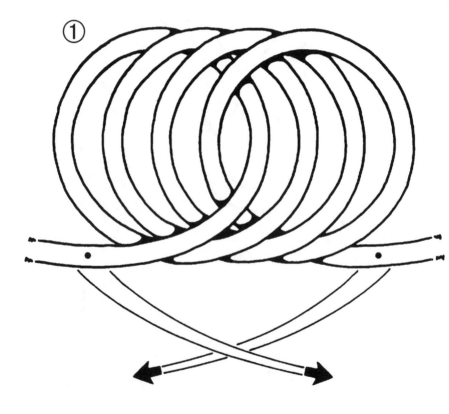

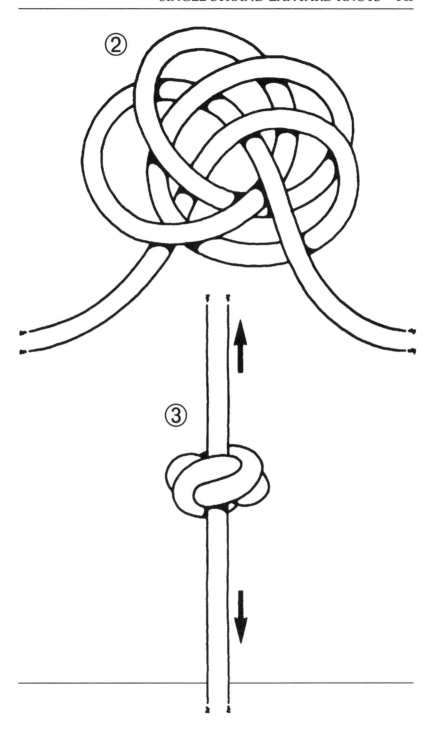

FIVE-LEAD FLAT-SINNET

Arrange the cord as in step 1, then proceed to plait by twisting the outside left strand over into the center. Then twist the new outside left strand over to form step 2. To finish the knot, tuck the outside right strand down through the center, gradually work out the surplus material and tighten.

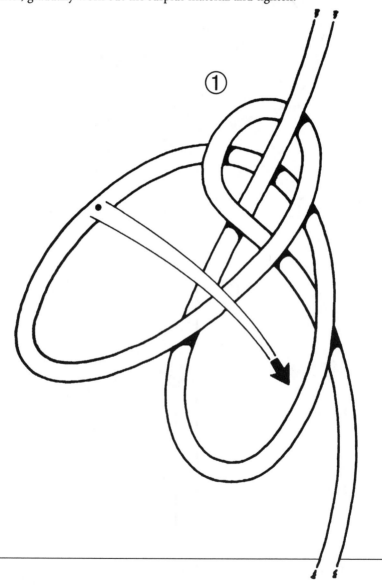

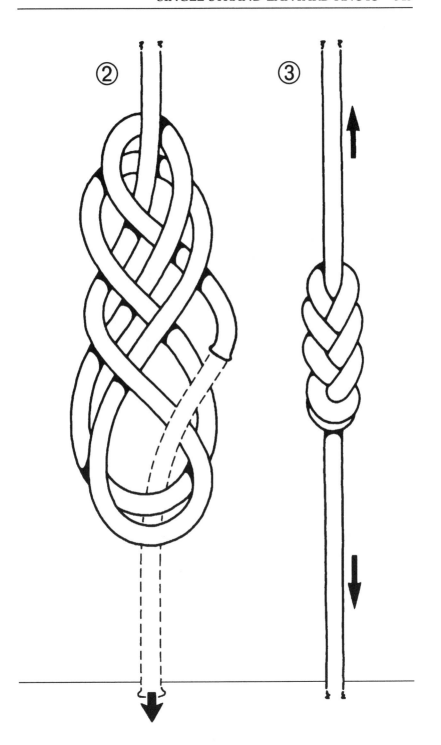

DOUBLE-TWIST BRAID KNOT

This knot, based on an Overhand Knot (step 1), is tied by twisting the outside left strand over and tucking the right-hand strand down through the center as in step 2. Then continue to plait alternately over and under as in step 3. To finish the knot, gradually work out the surplus and tighten.

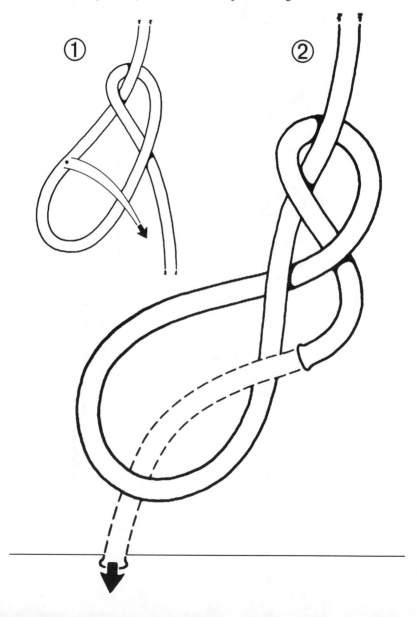

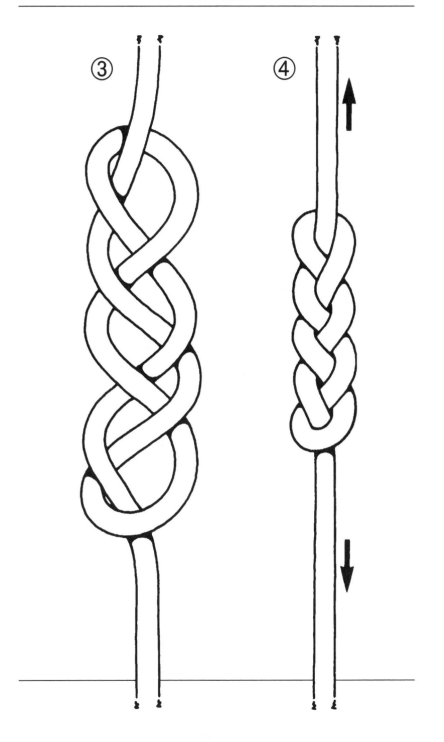

CROWN WITH SINGLE LOOPS

When this knot is firmly drawn up, the two single loops lie at right angles to the cord, making it an attractive single-strand knot. Simple crown knots can be difficult to keep together, but if care is taken at step 2, to methodically draw up this knot while forming the crown and loops, it will prove to be a firm knot.

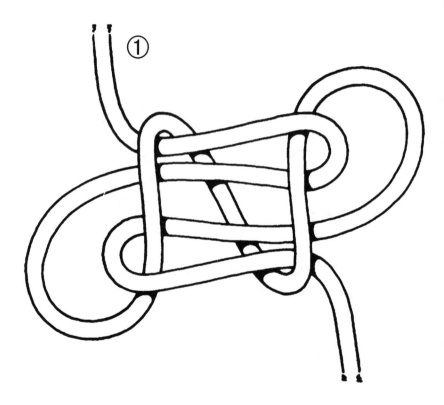

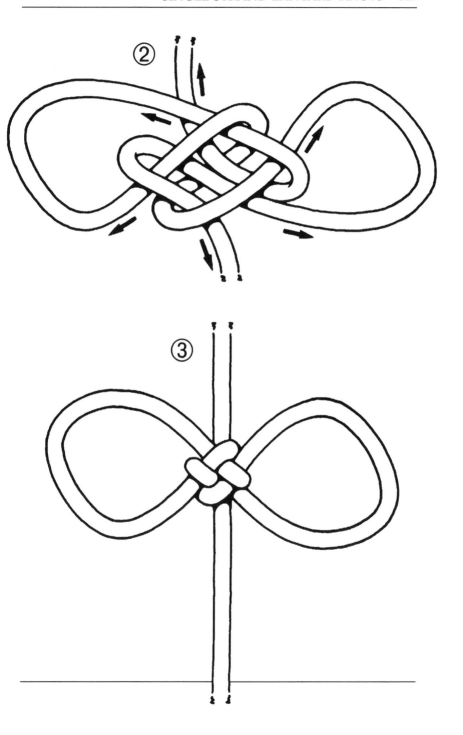

ONE-CORD LANYARD KNOT

Similar in many ways to a Crown with Single Loops (see pg. 548) this knot has the advantage of displaying a crown at both the front and back of the knot. For maximum effect, care should be taken when drawing up the knot to ensure that both loops are equal and both crowns balanced.

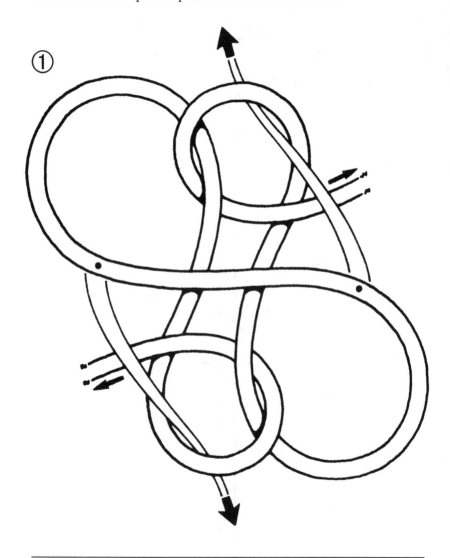

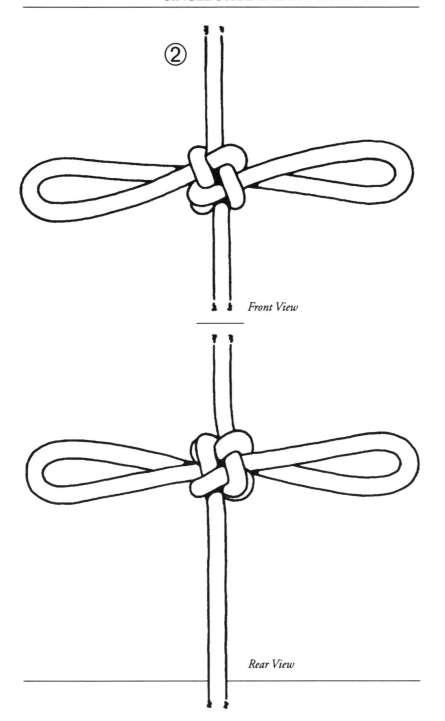

②

Front View

Rear View

TWO-STRAND MATTHEW WALKER KNOT

The precise history of Matthew Walker is not known, though he is thought to have been a master rigger in the British naval dockyards around the turn of the eighteenth century. One certainty about him, is that he is one of the few individuals who still retains credit for his knot tying. There are many variations of "Matthew Walker" knots; the one illustrated here is a simple but effective lanyard knot that can be easily extended by increasing the number of turns.

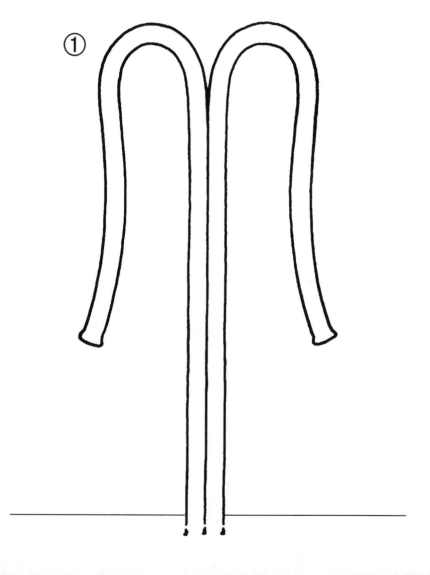

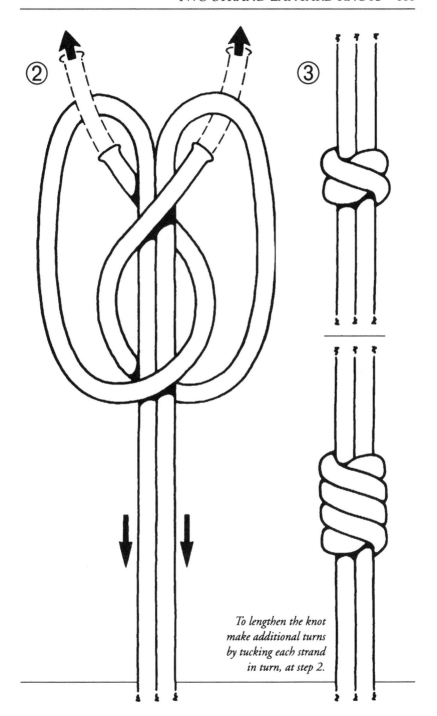

② ③

*To lengthen the knot
make additional turns
by tucking each strand
in turn, at step 2.*

DOUBLE WALL KNOT

The very neat appearance of this knot, combined with its simplicity, make it a very popular lanyard knot. It also has the added attraction of displaying an identical form when viewed from either side of the knot.

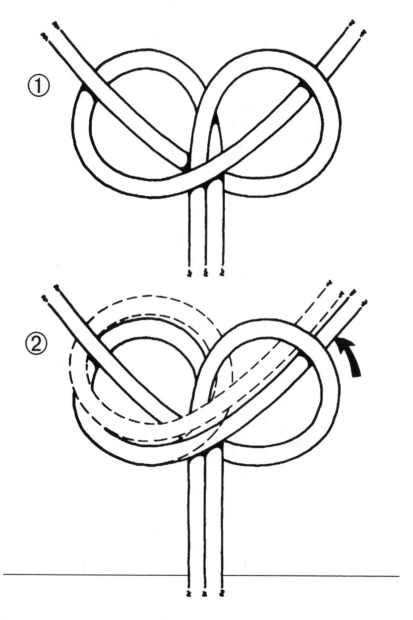

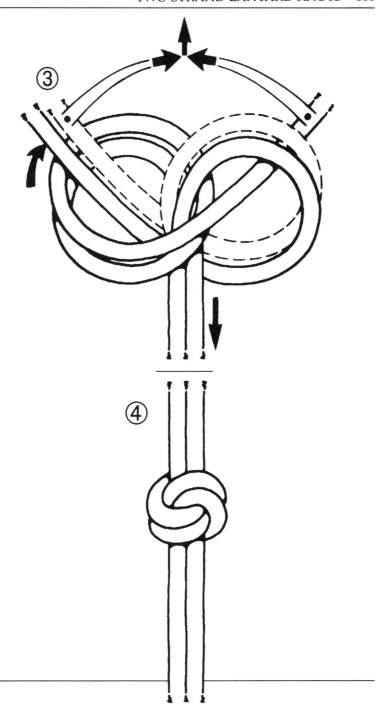

TWO-STRAND STOPPER KNOT

As its name suggests, this flat, wide, decorative lanyard knot can also act as a stopper knot. Stopper knots are useful if an object needs to slide along a certain length of a lanyard.

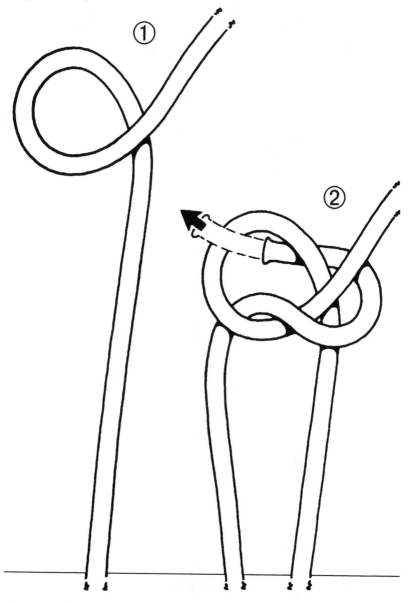

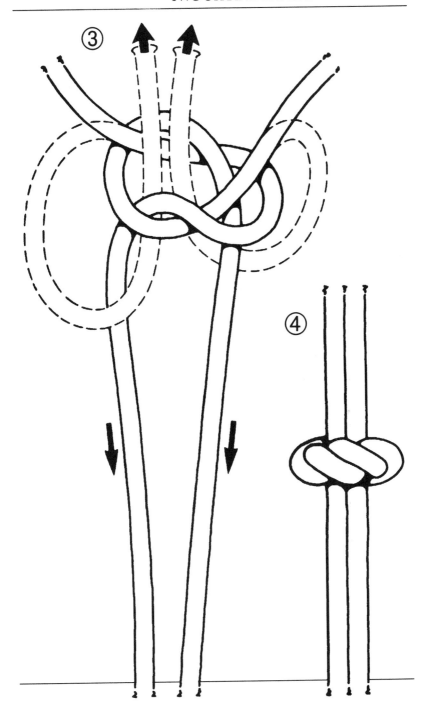

FLAT LANYARD KNOT

This attractive knot, which is based on two Overhand Knots, enables the two lanyard cords to be parted. In order to achieve the distinctive symmetrical form, the knot must be methodically "worked" together, after step 2 has been completed.

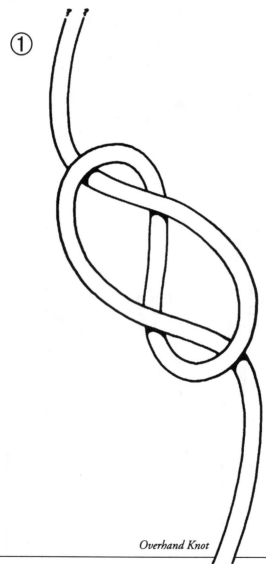

Overhand Knot

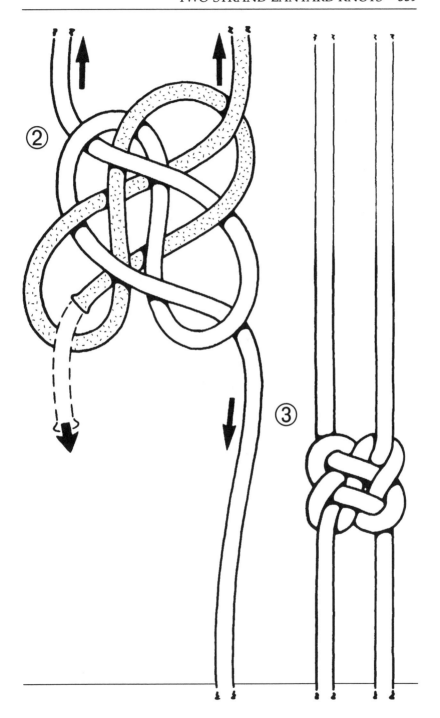

CHINESE BUTTERFLY KNOT

This knot can be tied and arranged in many different sizes and forms. The knot illustrated here is one of the smaller versions and is tied in lanyard form to achieve a bight, or curve, at each of the four corners. To successfully tie this type of knot, lay the cords on a flat surface and arrange as in steps 1 and 2. After step 2 has been completed, "work" the knot into its final form.

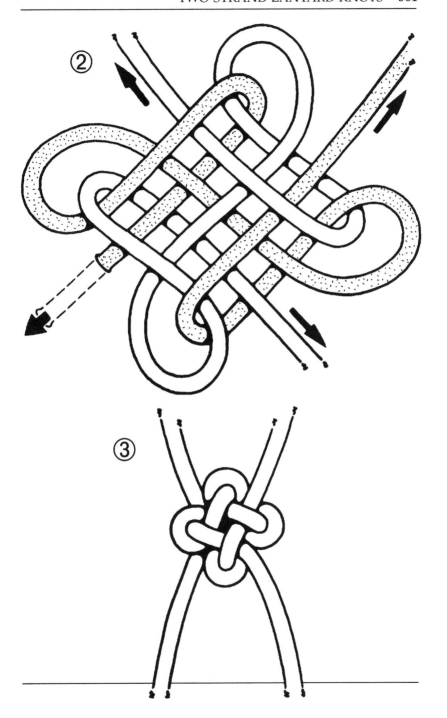

KNIFE LANYARD KNOT

This is one of the most attractive lanyard knots and subsequently one of the most widely used. Also known as the Two-Strand Diamond Knot and the Bosun's Whistle Knot, it is excellent for forming the loop at the end of a lanyard. At first sight it may appear difficult to tie and, as with many of the more complicated knots, the first attempt will probably result in failure. But be patient, follow the step-by-step instructions, "work" the knot into its final form and you will be rewarded with a beautiful and functional decorative knot.

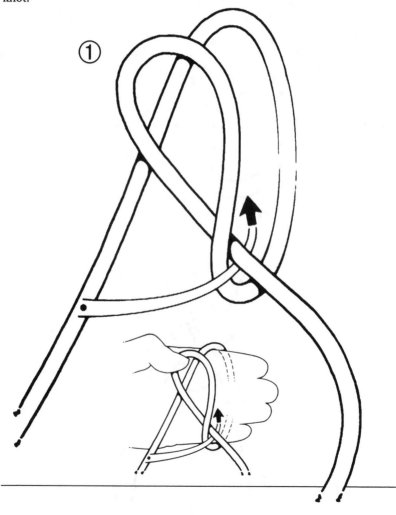

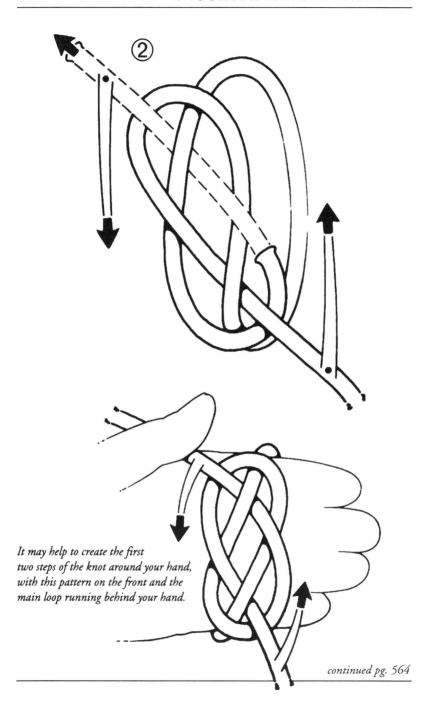

②

It may help to create the first
two steps of the knot around your hand,
with this pattern on the front and the
main loop running behind your hand.

continued pg. 564

Knife Lanyard Knot

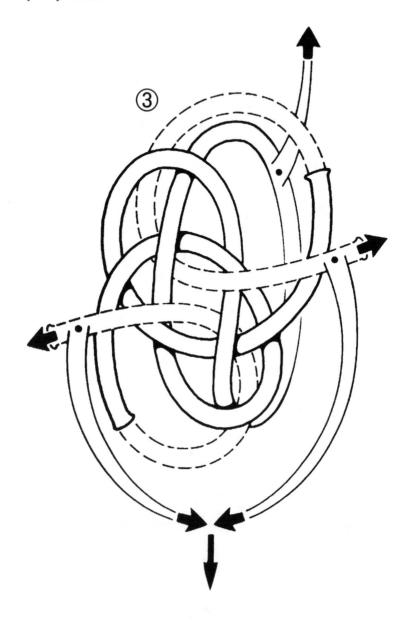

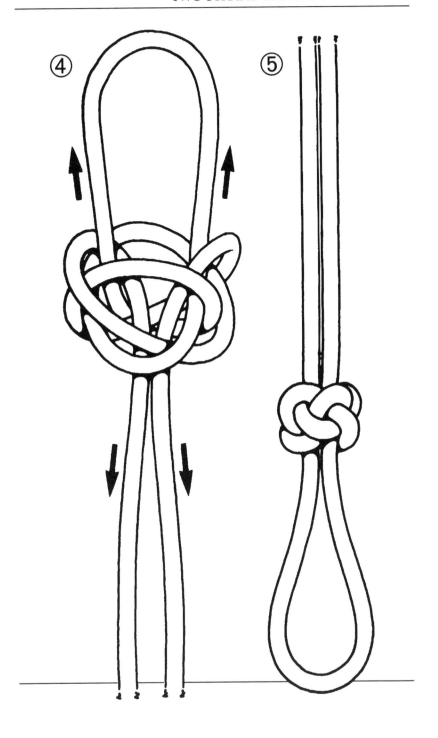

DOUBLE KNIFE LANYARD KNOT

The appearance of many decorative knots can be enhanced by "doubling" — literally following the initial lead of a strand around for a second time. The example illustrated here is a "double" version of the Knife Lanyard Knot. Follow steps 1, 2 & 3 of the Knife Lanyard Knot (see pgs. 562, 563 & 564) but instead of bringing the ends out of the knot as in step 3 (see pg. 564) double both ends by leading them along the inner side of the initial lead, as in step 1, below. Create step 2 and bring the ends out as shown, draw up the knot and "work" it into its final form, step 3, taking care to keep the doubled strands neatly together.

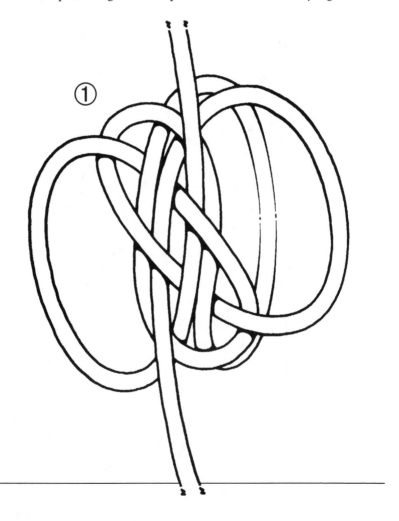

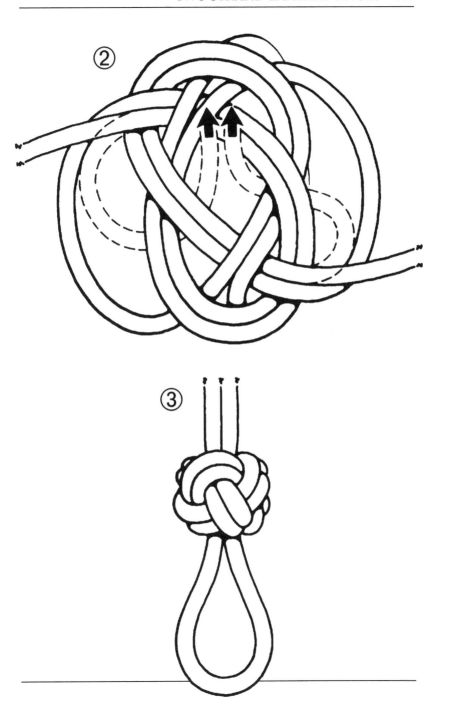

MULTIPLE OVERHAND SLIDING KNOT

Occasionally a sliding loop can be a useful addition to a lanyard. A simple and effective way of achieving this is to use a Multiple Overhand Knot (see pg. 538) but before tightening, slide a second strand through the knot as in step 1. The loop can then be altered to the required size.

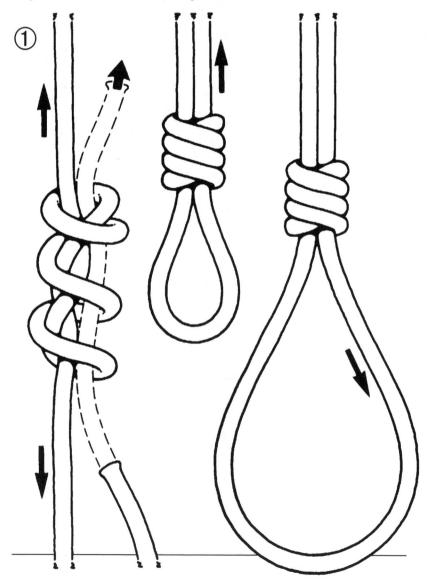

2
BOWKNOTS
· · · · · · · · · · · · · · · · · · ·

The common characteristics of Bowknots, often called "Fancy" knots, are the harmonious and symmetrical forms that are created from bows, loops and crowns. They are regularly used to give that "final touch" when wrapping gifts or parcels. The following examples can be tied in a wide variety of materials, keeping in mind that if ribbon or a patterned material having one definite right side is used, it will be necessary to twist the material and arrange the knot to keep that side uppermost.

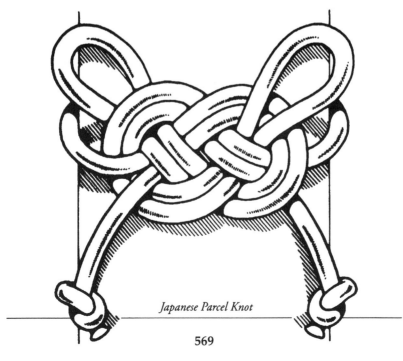

Japanese Parcel Knot

BOWKNOT

The common or ordinary bowknot is one of the most widely used of all knots. It can be used in any situation that requires two working ends to be quickly and easily tied together, plus it has the added advantage of being equally as easy to untie, by simply pulling on one of the working ends.

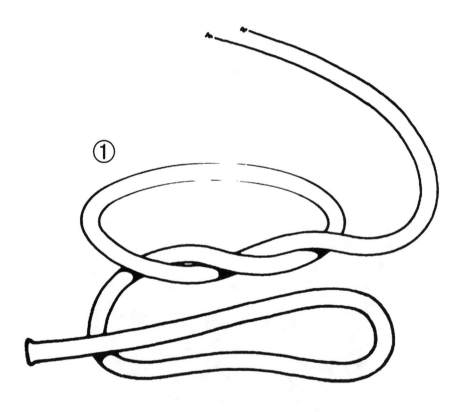

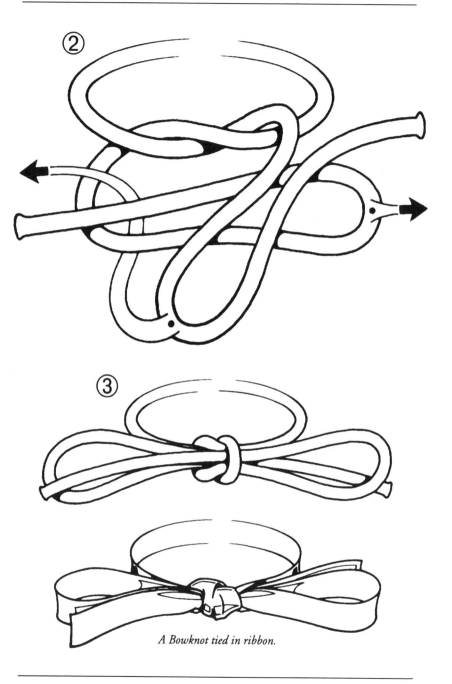

A Bowknot tied in ribbon.

SHEEPSHANK KNOT

The sheepshank knot is primarily used as a method of shortening a piece of rope or cord without cutting it, as shown in step 2, however when the two parts of the knot are pulled together it forms a simple but effective bowknot.

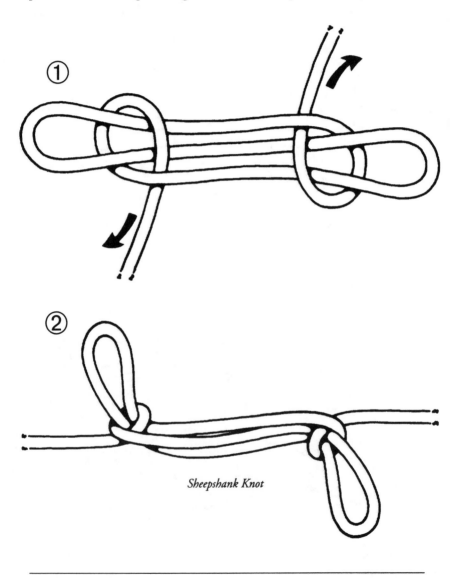

Sheepshank Knot

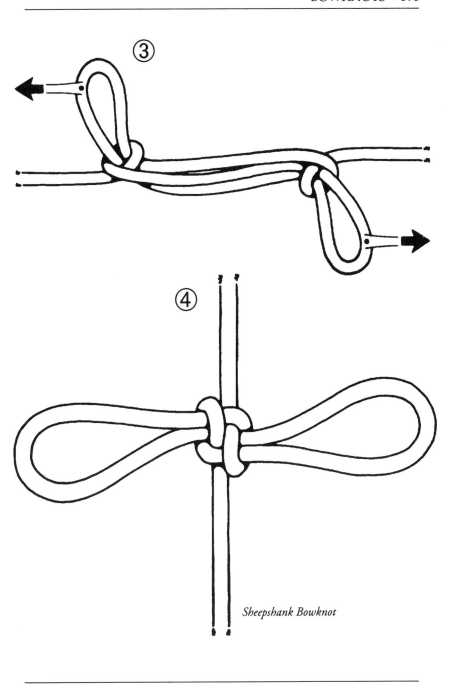

Sheepshank Bowknot

JAPANESE KNOT

This knot is used to decorate the end of a cord, often making a very effective and practical end to a window shade pull or light pull. The knot has a four-part crown in the center and two loops which can be adjusted to the required size while "working" the knot together during step 2.

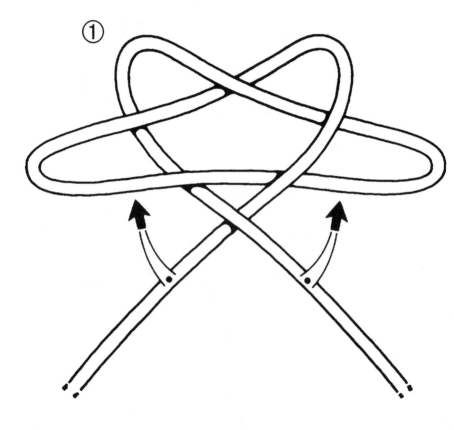

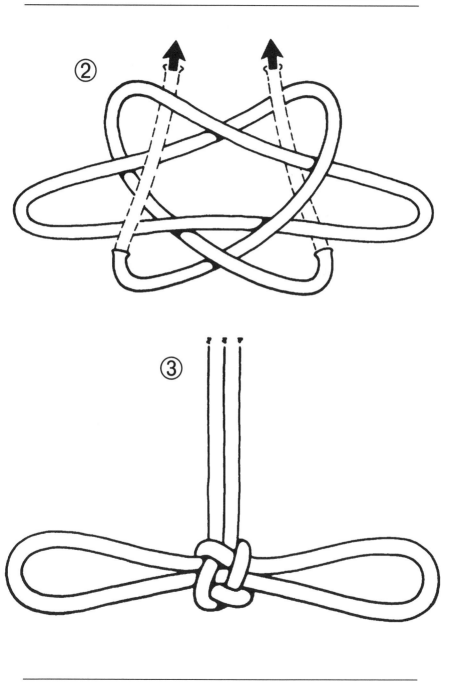

TRUE-LOVER'S KNOT

The name "True-Lover's Knot" has proved to be very popular over the years and can be traced back as far as 1664. Since then many knots have carried the name and it is generally agreed that one point is common to all of these knots – that two Overhand Knots are intertwined together to form one symmetrical knot, hence the name "True-Lover's Knot." In the example illustrated here the basic knot is shown in step 1 and then in a more decorative bow form – with two bights pulled through in steps 2 and 3.

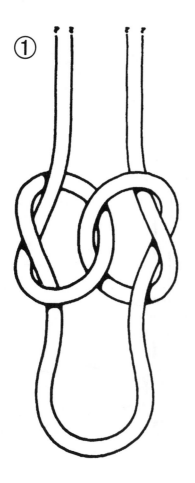

The True-Lover's Knot can be drawn up tight to create an attractive Two-Strand Lanyard Knot.

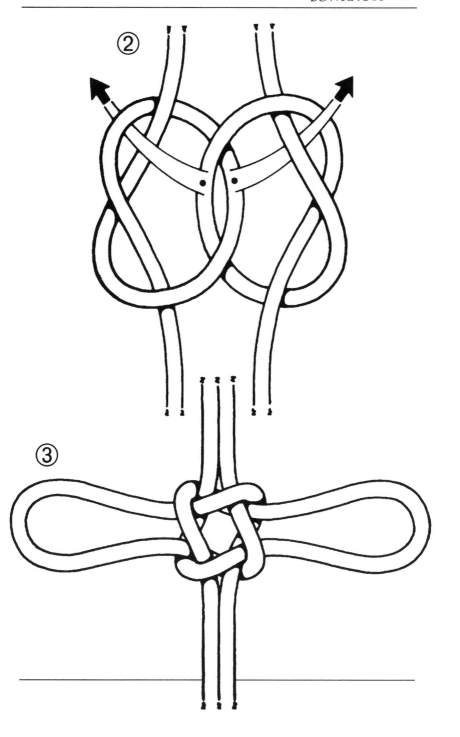

JAPANESE PARCEL KNOT

This attractive knot, tied in double ends, is based on the distinctively symmetrical Carrick Bend Knot. It is an ideal knot for gift tying and is often referred to as the "Gift Knot." If tied in ribbon the two ends can be cut or trimmed into a diagonal or swallowtail shape, and if tied in cord the ends can be finished off with a simple overhand knot.

Uncut ribbon *Diagonal cut* *Swallowtail cut*

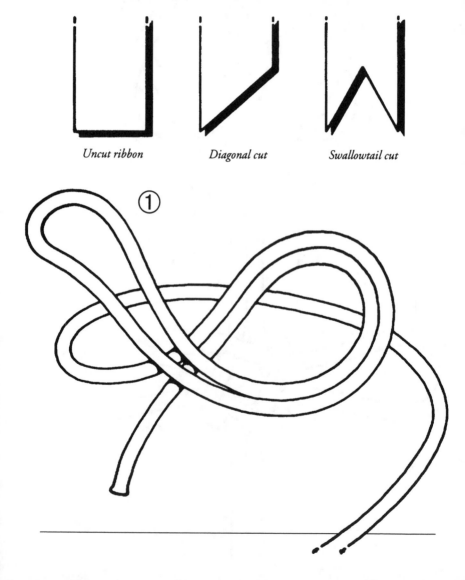

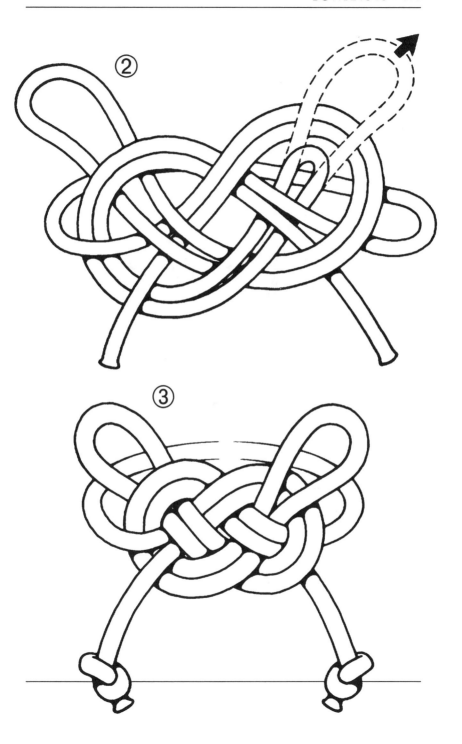

FOUR-LOOP CROWN

This very decorative parcel or gift knot is created by "crowning" four loops. Start by arranging the tying material as in step 1, then crown loop one by bringing it down to the right of loop two, cross loop two to the right and crown it with loop three as in step 2. Finally crown loop three with loop four and tuck under, as in step 2, the double bight created by loop one. Arrange all parts of the knot to give an equal and pleasing appearance, and draw up tight.

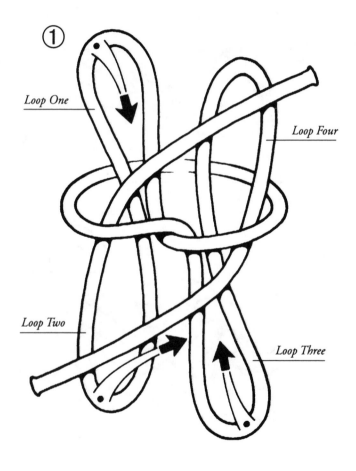

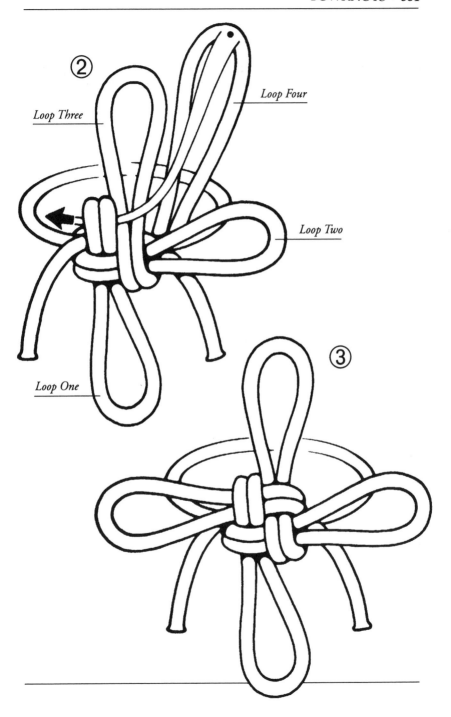

②

Loop Three

Loop Four

Loop Two

Loop One

③

SHAMROCK KNOT

This distinctive knot is constructed by "crowning" (see pg. 580). Begin by arranging the tying material into four loops as in step 1 – the two working ends being treated as one of the loops. Crown the loops, in order, in an anti-clockwise direction to create step 2. Then, without moving this structure, crown the loops again but this time in a clockwise direction, starting with loop three, followed by two, one and four. Work the knot into its final structure, see step 3.

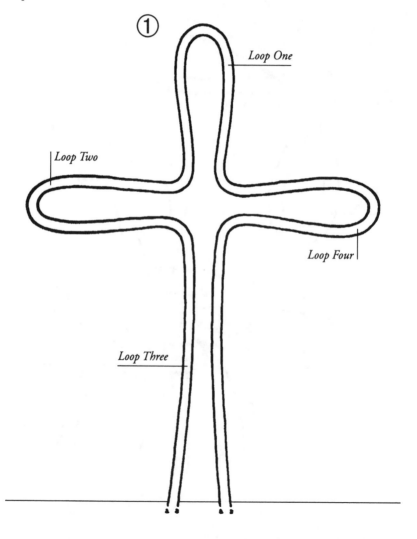

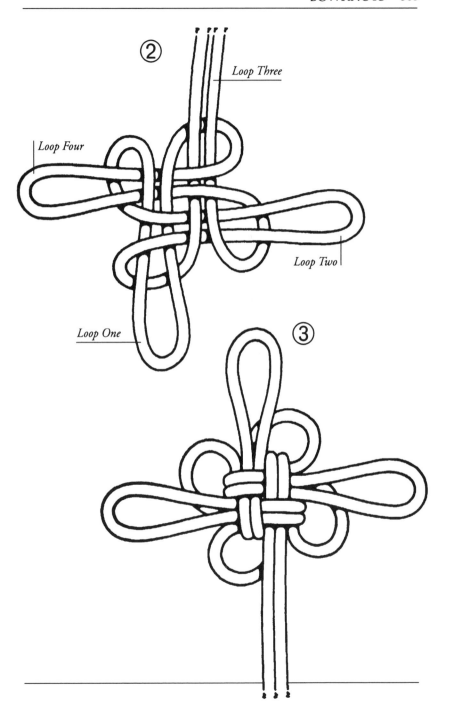

② Loop Three

Loop Four

Loop Two

Loop One

③

BUTTERFLY KNOT

This knot has a three-part crown center and, in its simplest form, two loops which make a bowknot with the appearance of a butterfly, as shown in step 3. A third loop can be created by tucking the working end through, as in step 4, to create a three looped terminal knot, as in step 5.

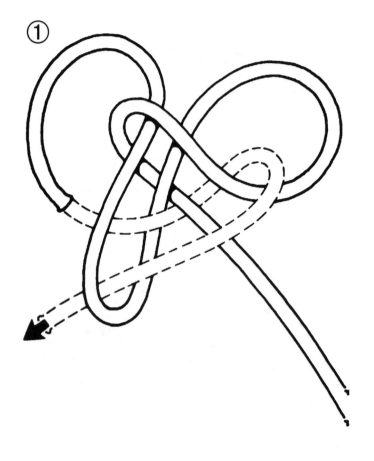

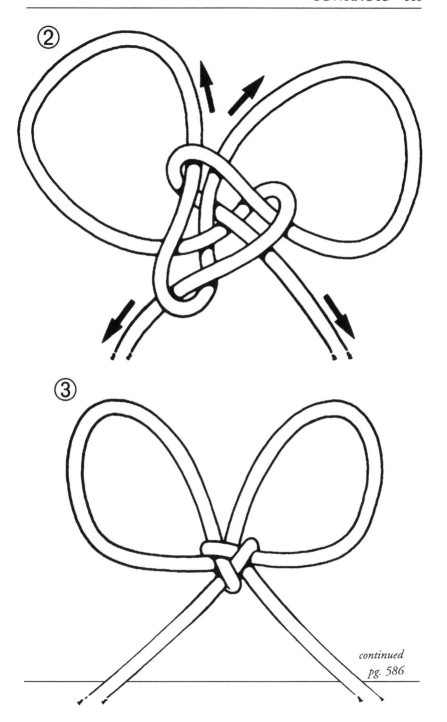

② ③

continued
pg. 586

Butterfly Knot

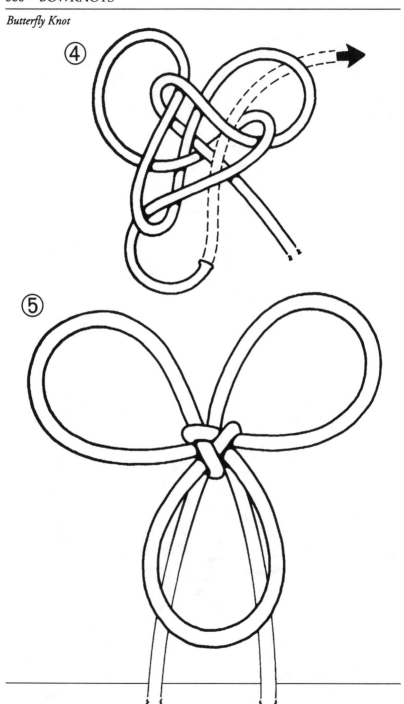

3

BUTTON KNOTS

· ·

B utton knots, or Pajama knots, are exactly as their name suggests – round, symmetrical knots used to form buttons to hold or fasten garments together, in particular, underwear and night clothes. Buttons of this type are still worn throughout China and are often seen as fashionable accessories elsewhere in the world. As well as being highly decorative, these buttons are softer and more comfortable to wear than bone or plastic buttons and have the advantage of being virtually unbreakable.

Chinese Button Knot

587

CHINESE BUTTON KNOT

Tying the traditional Chinese Button Knot as shown here may require a few attempts before the necessary technique is achieved. Start by creating step 1 on a flat surface. Then let the two ends drop down to form a stem as in step 2. Slowly work out the surplus material, at first keeping the knot flat, then as the knot draws up, allow it to form a mushroom shape as in step 3. The mushroom shape is formed by the rim of the knot closing down and the center of the knot rising up. Work the knot into its final form, step 4, by drawing the knot up tightly. This is best achieved by using a pair of thin nosed pliers or, if the tying material is small and delicate, a pair of fine tweezers.

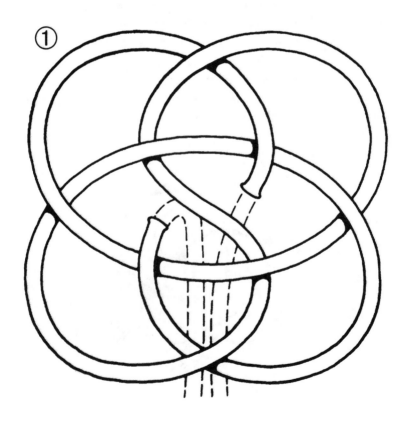

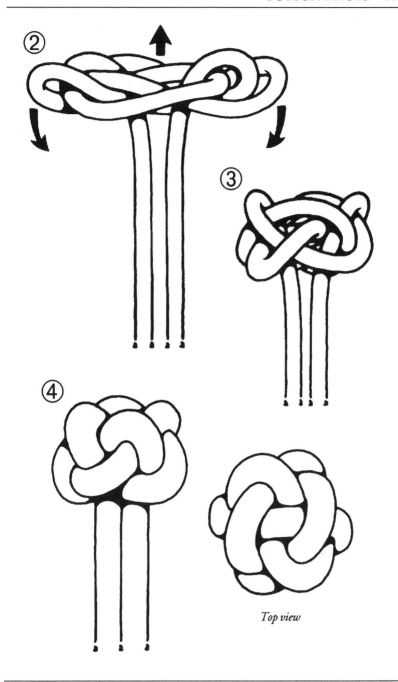

Top view

DOUBLE CHINESE BUTTON KNOT

Often tied with silk cord, this is one of the most commonly used and most decorative button knots. Follow the basic tying instructions for the Chinese Button Knot (see pg. 588) but continue to lead the cord around for a second time as indicated in steps 1 and 2 to create a two strand or "doubled" knot. When working the knot into its final form, care should be taken to keep the doubled strands together.

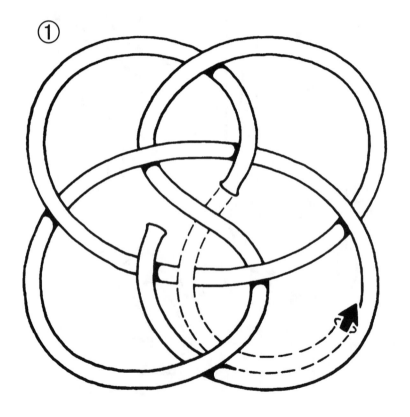

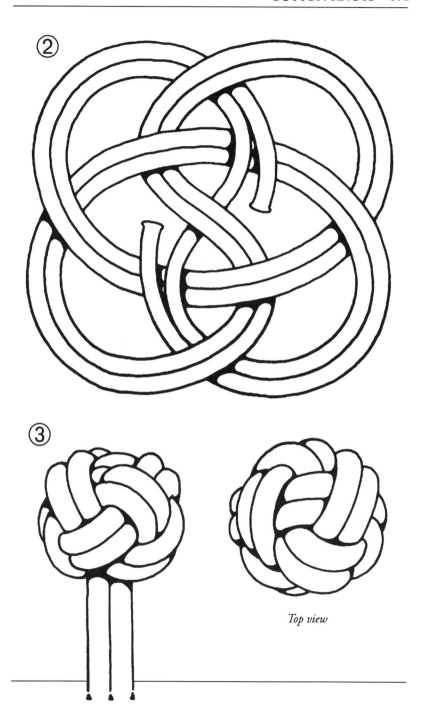

Top view

EIGHT-PART BUTTON KNOT

This knot is an interesting variation of the Chinese Button Knot and is created by changing the final tuck of the ends in step 1 – the rest of the tying instructions are as shown on page 588. The traditional Chinese Button Knot has nine surface parts, this knot has eight, altering the appearance enough to make it an alternative worth considering. Like the traditional knot, this one can also be "doubled."

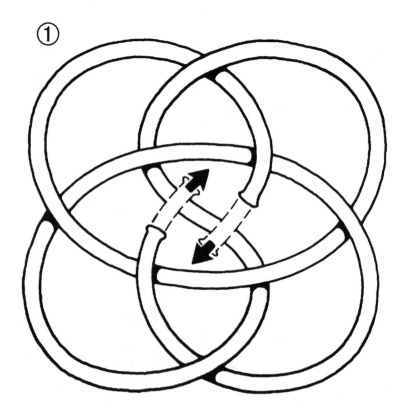

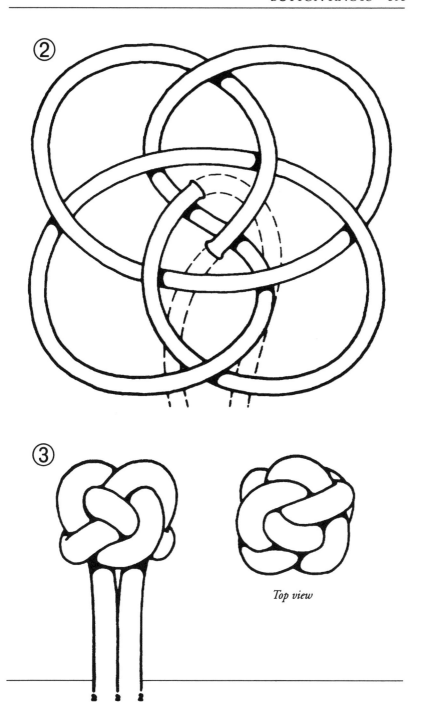

Top view

CHINESE BUTTON - KNIFE LANYARD METHOD

This is exactly the same as the Chinese Button Knot shown on page 588, but tied by a method that some might find quicker and easier, especially when tying a quantity of buttons. The method is based on tying a Knife Lanyard Knot (see pg. 562) around the hand.

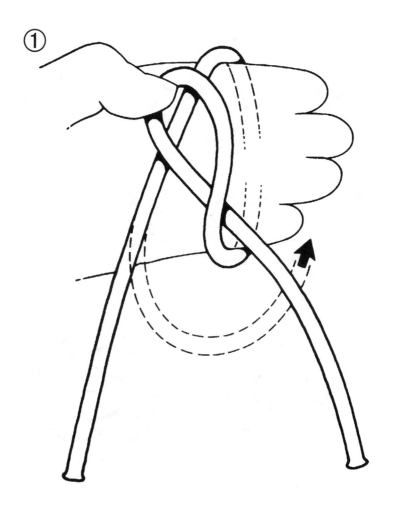

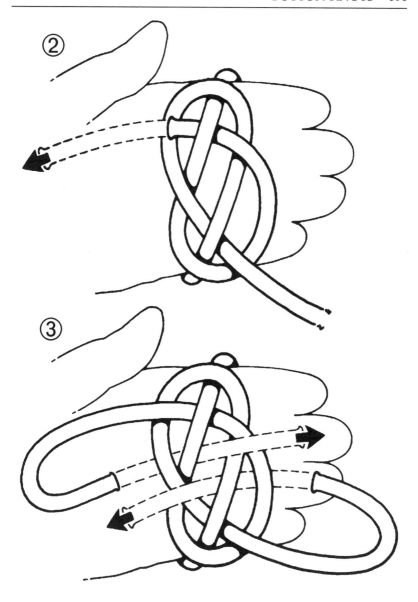

*When the two ends have been pushed through, remove
the knot from the hand, turn it completely over, and place
the two ends between the two middle fingers as shown in step 4.*

continued pg. 596

Chinese Button - Knife Lanyard Method

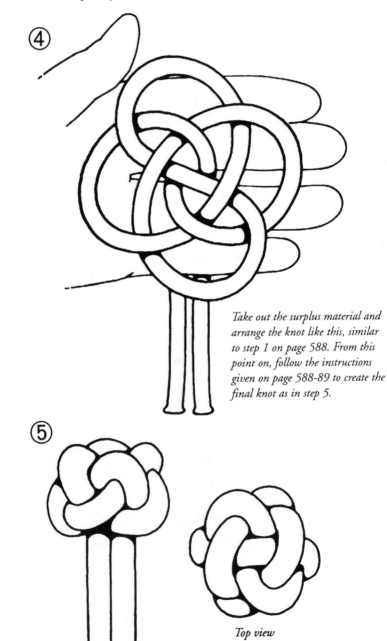

④

Take out the surplus material and arrange the knot like this, similar to step 1 on page 588. From this point on, follow the instructions given on page 588-89 to create the final knot as in step 5.

⑤

Top view

4

MONKEY'S FIST KNOTS

. . . .

The Monkey's Fist is a decorative knot that also has many practical uses, the most common being as the knot used at the end of a "heaving line," the line that is thrown from boat to shore or to another vessel. The purpose of the heaving line is to draw behind it a heavier line or rope to use for tying up. To give the Monkey's Fist more weight it is often tied over a spherical object such as a heavy ball or a stone, smaller knots can be tied over golf balls or marbles. Decoratively, it makes an attractive end to any cord, and is regularly used at the end of pull cords.

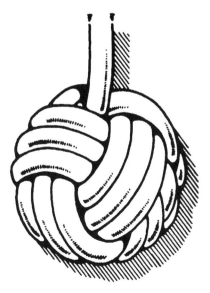

Monkey's Fist

MONKEY'S FIST - METHOD ONE

When using the traditional method of tying the Monkey's Fist, the knot is tied in two or three-ply. The illustrations here show a two-ply knot, but the tying instructions for three-ply are exactly the same. If required, a weight or core can be inserted at step 3. The knot needs to be carefully and methodically worked into its final symmetrical form, and if only one strand is required from the knot, the other strand can be worked around and tucked inside the knot to hide it.

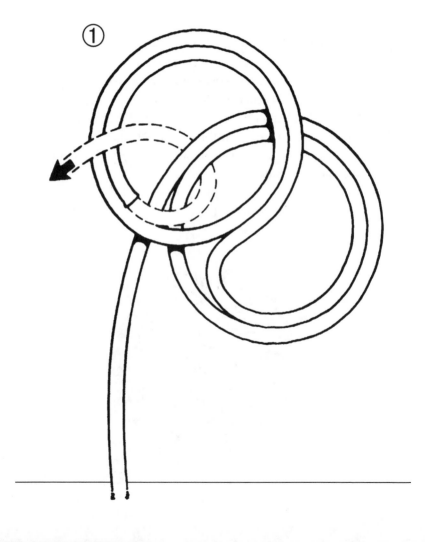

②

continued pg. 600

Monkey's Fist - Method One

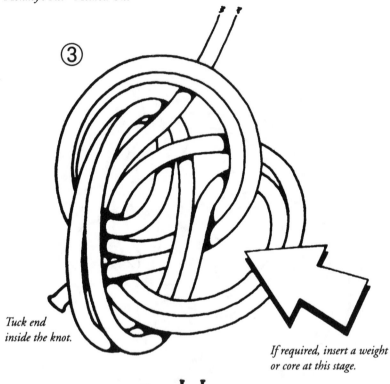

③

Tuck end
inside the knot.

If required, insert a weight
or core at this stage.

④

MONKEY'S FIST - METHOD TWO

This alternate way of tying a Monkey's Fist is shown in three-ply and with both ends being brought out of the knot. As with the first method, this knot can be tied around a weight or core object.

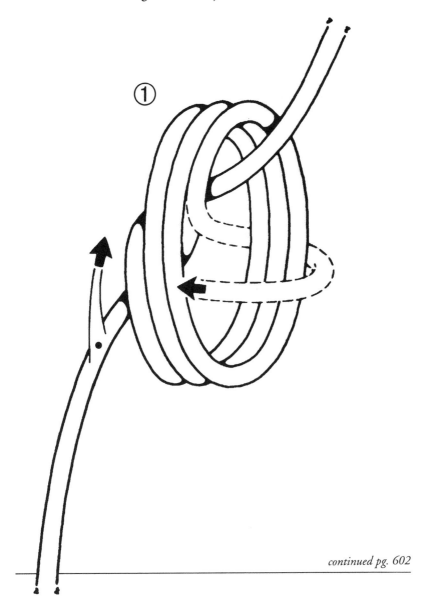

continued pg. 602

Monkey's Fist - Method Two

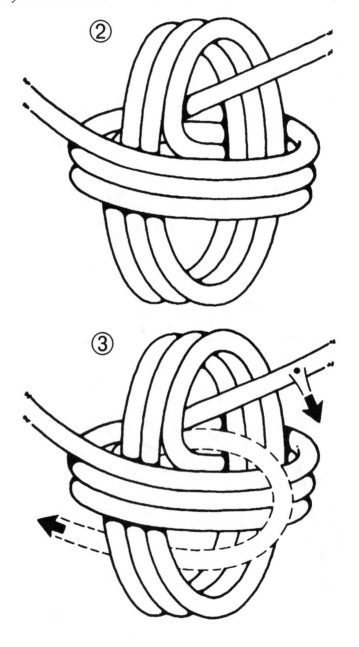

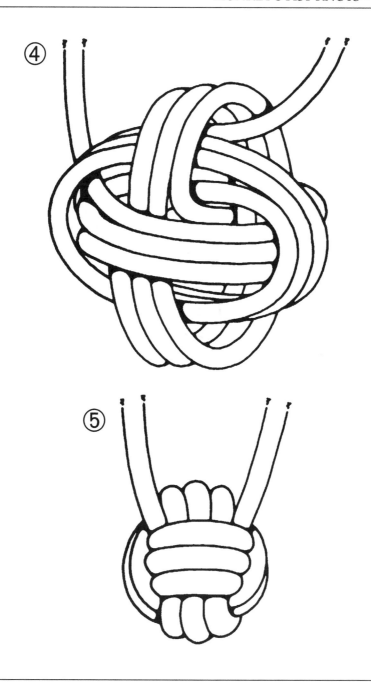

MONKEY'S FIST - SAILOR'S METHOD

This third alternative for tying a Monkey's Fist has long been the preferred method of sailors. The knot is tied, three-ply, around the fingers. If a weight or core is required, the knot can be tied around a spherical object – usually a rubber ball to help the line float in water.

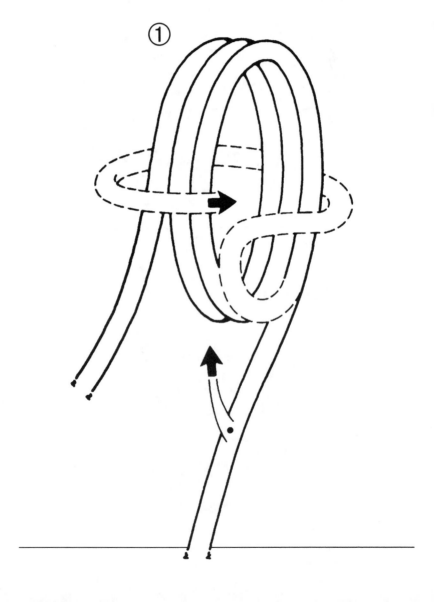

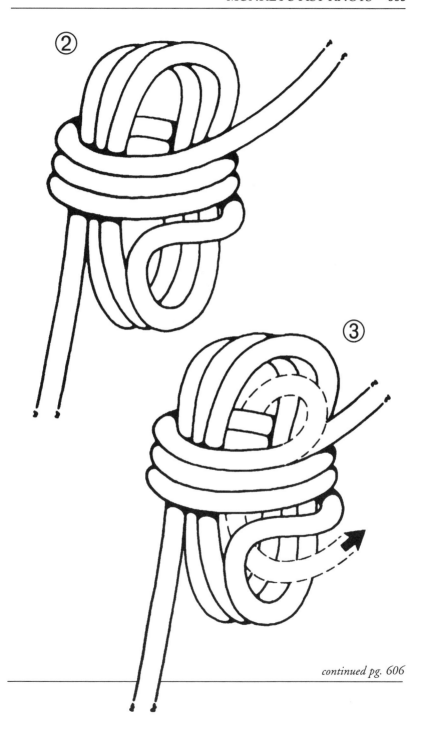

continued pg. 606

Monkey's Fist - Sailor's Method

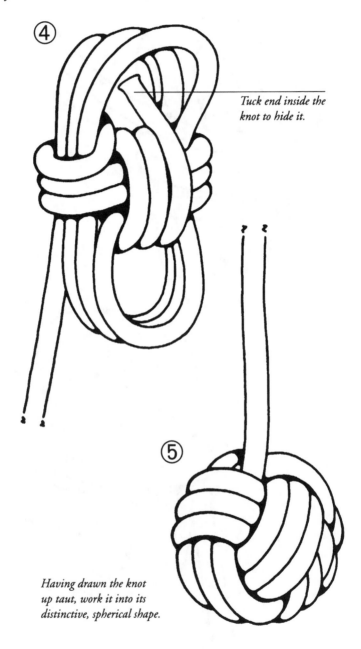

Tuck end inside the
knot to hide it.

Having drawn the knot
up taut, work it into its
distinctive, spherical shape.

5

TURK'S HEAD KNOTS

· ·

Turk's Head knots have long been recognized for their highly decorative attributes. Leonardo da Vinci drew them in the fifteenth century and they are still widely used today. They are usually tied around cylindrical objects – in most cases as pure decoration but also to serve many practical purposes from handgrips to napkin rings. There are many recorded variations of these knots, however the examples shown in this chapter are the most common variations whereby the first stages of the knot are constructed around the fingers or in the hand with a single strand of cord or rope, and then placed around a cylindrical object to be completed.

Four Lead, Three Bight Turk's Head

TURK'S HEAD - THREE LEAD, FOUR BIGHT

Single-strand Turk's Head knots are tied by many different methods, producing a wide variety of sizes. The size of this particular knot is "three lead, four bight." The term "lead" refers to a single circuit of the cord around the cylinder or object, and the term "bight" refers to the number of "scallop" shapes formed. The knot is initially formed around the hand as in step 1, then removed to form steps 2, 3 & 4. At this point it is placed around the chosen object to be completed. To create the finished compact knot as in step 6, the slack will need to be worked out. This is done gradually, by starting at one end of the cord and progressing right through the knot to the other end. It may also help to use a pair of thin-nosed pliers.

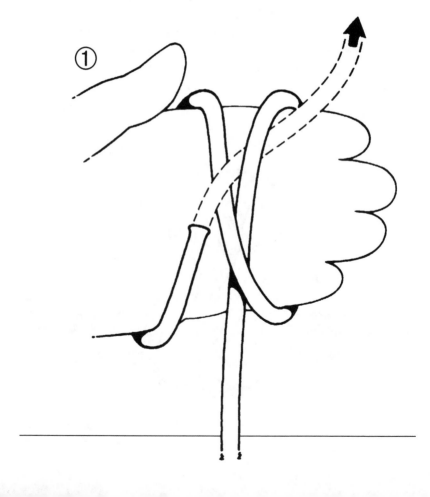

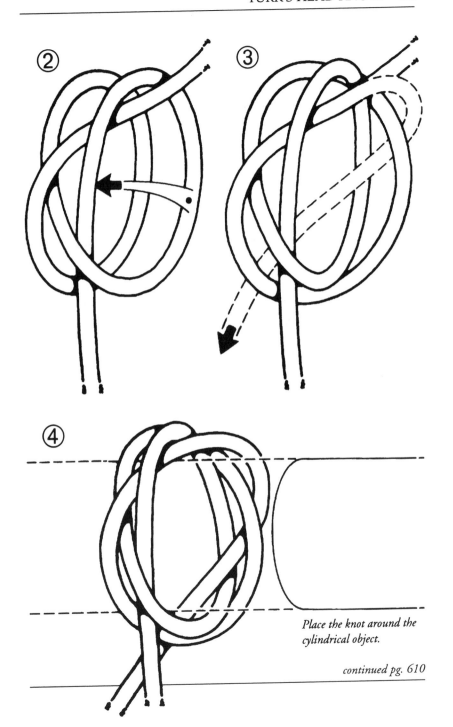

Place the knot around the
cylindrical object.

continued pg. 610

Turk's Head - Three Lead, Four Bight

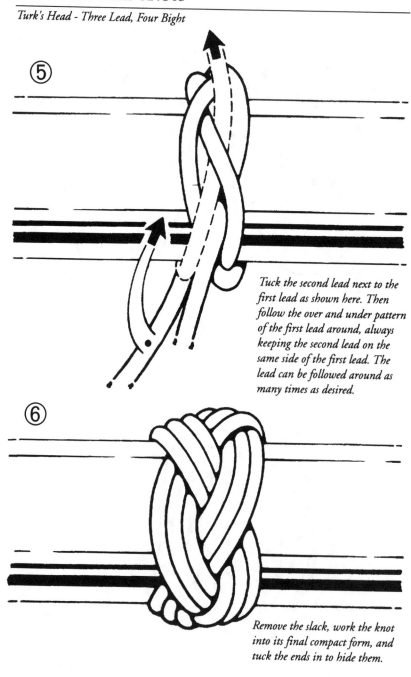

⑤

Tuck the second lead next to the
first lead as shown here. Then
follow the over and under pattern
of the first lead around, always
keeping the second lead on the
same side of the first lead. The
lead can be followed around as
many times as desired.

⑥

Remove the slack, work the knot
into its final compact form, and
tuck the ends in to hide them.

TURK'S HEAD - THREE LEAD, FIVE BIGHT

This method shows how to tie a "three lead, five bight" Turk's Head in a flat form. The knot can be left in this form to create, for example, a mat or drink coaster, or turned down and worked over a cylindrical object to form a decorative covering.

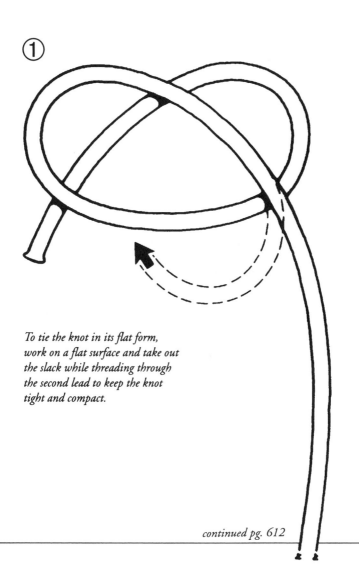

To tie the knot in its flat form, work on a flat surface and take out the slack while threading through the second lead to keep the knot tight and compact.

continued pg. 612

Turk's Head - Three Lead, Five Bight

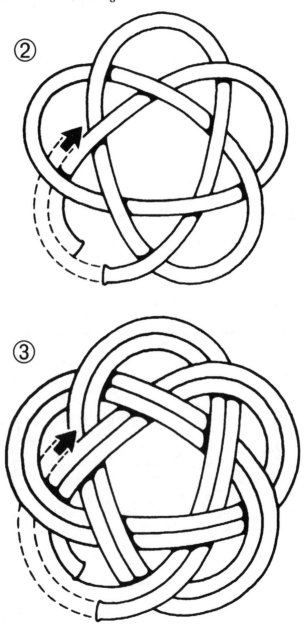

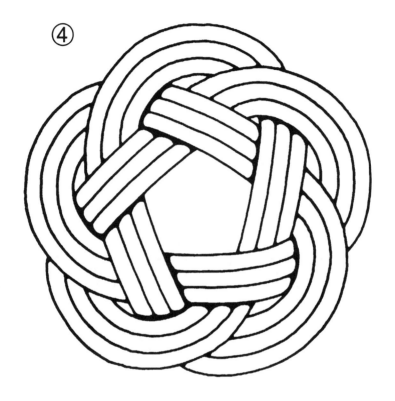

④

*The first lead can be followed around by
the second lead as many times as required to
create the finished knot. Always keep the second
lead on the same side of the first lead (the lead
that created the pattern) and tuck the ends
in neatly to hide them.*

TURK'S HEAD - FOUR LEAD, THREE BIGHT

To create step 1 of this "four lead, three bight" version, start as if you are tying a Knife Lanyard Knot (see pg. 562) around the hand. Use the forefinger and thumb as shown in step 2 to create the loose form of the knot before placing it on the chosen object as in step 3. To complete the knot follow the instructions given for the Turk's Head - Three Lead, Four bight (see pg. 610).

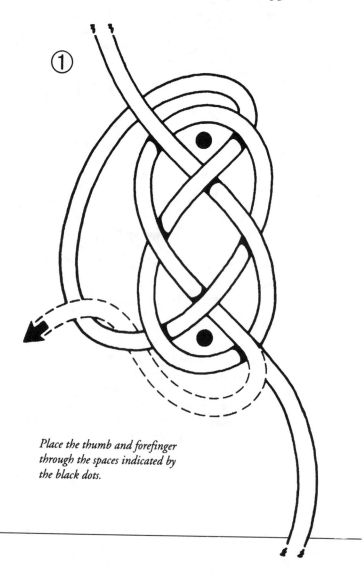

①

Place the thumb and forefinger through the spaces indicated by the black dots.

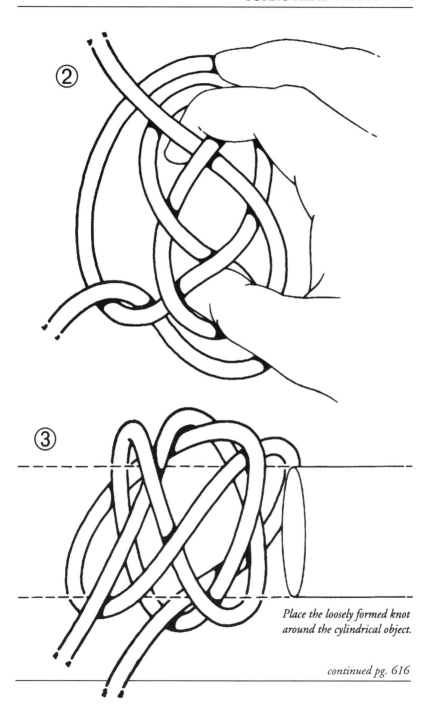

② ③

Place the loosely formed knot around the cylindrical object.

continued pg. 616

Turk's Head - Four Lead, Three Bight

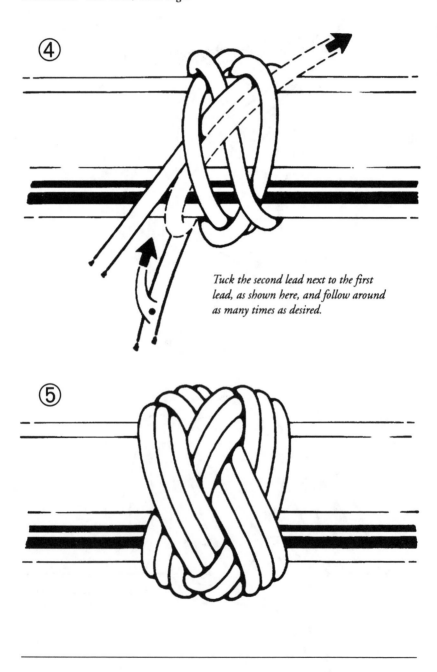

④

Tuck the second lead next to the first
lead, as shown here, and follow around
as many times as desired.

⑤

6

SINNETS

· · · · · · · · · · · · ·

S innets are one or more intertwined strands that can be tied from a wide variety of materials. They have a vast range of decorative applications – from belts and bracelets to schoolgirls' pigtails. There are three main types of sinnets: plait or braid sinnets, chain sinnets, and crown sinnets. Within these groups are many variations; this chapter shows some of the most decorative and commonly used examples.

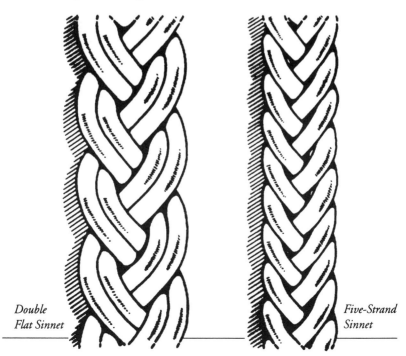

Double Flat Sinnet

Five-Strand Sinnet

FLAT SINNET

This simple, three-strand, plait or braid sinnet is also known as the English or Common Sinnet. It has a vast range of decorative applications, but undoubtedly the most popular is to plait schoolgirls' pigtails. Arrange the three strands as in step 1, (if necessary secure them in a straight line with a clip or simple clamp). The method of tying is to alternately cross the outside strands over the center strand; start with right-hand strand as in step 2, next the left-hand strand as in step 3. Now keep repeating this process as in steps 4 & 5, until you reach the desired length of sinnet. To achieve a neat, compact sinnet as in step 6, tighten and arrange the plait at each step of the tying. Sinnets can be finished off in a variety of ways depending on their final use. The simplest method is by clamping with a thin string, cord, or an elastic band and then trimming off the excess if necessary.

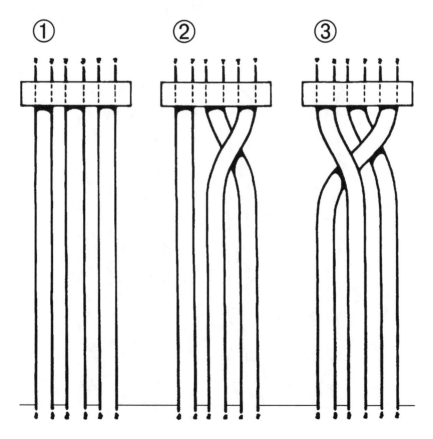

④ ⑤ ⑥

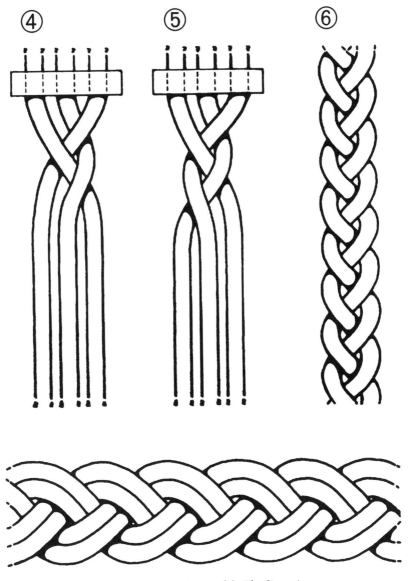

*This attractive variation of the Flat Sinnet is
created by doubling the strands – use
six strands, arranged in three pairs, and follow
exactly the same tying procedure.*

FOUR-STRAND SINNET

This very attractive, four-strand, plait or braid sinnet is created by always weaving the strand on the right-hand side as shown in step 1. Continue to weave only the right-hand strand, as shown in steps 2 & 3, until the desired length of sinnet has been created. To achieve the final result as in step 4, the sinnet must be tightened and arranged at each step of the tying procedure.

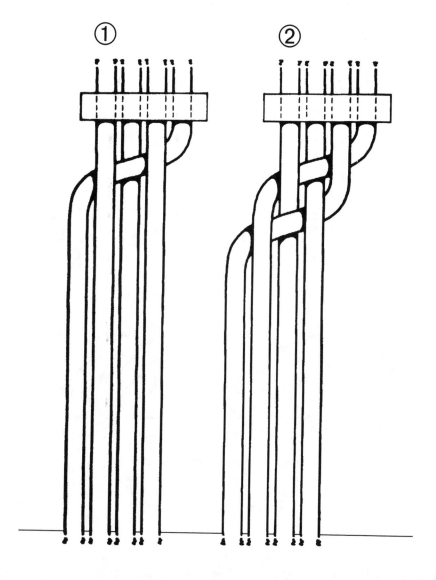

③

④

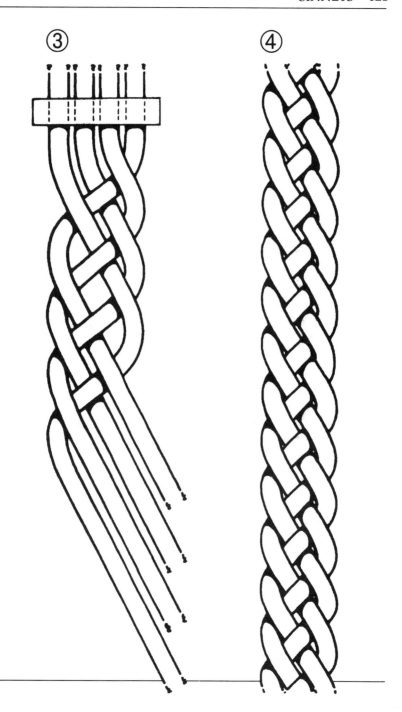

FOUR-STRAND WOVEN SINNET

This four-strand, plait or braid sinnet is an excellent example of the variations that can be achieved. This very ornamental sinnet is created by weaving just one strand through the other three. Arrange the four strands with the right-hand strand woven through as in step 1. Now continue to weave that strand as shown in steps 2 & 3. To create the final result as in step 4, tighten and arrange the sinnet at each step of the tying process.

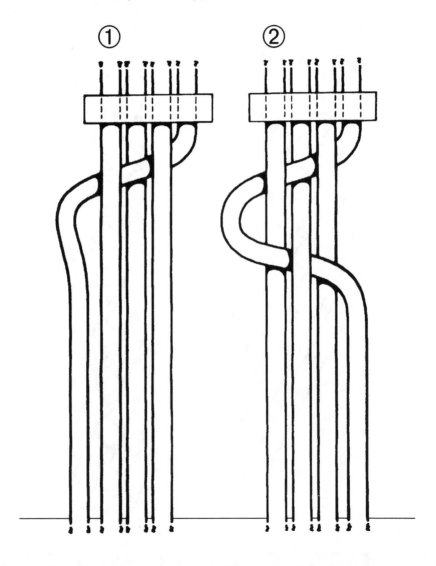

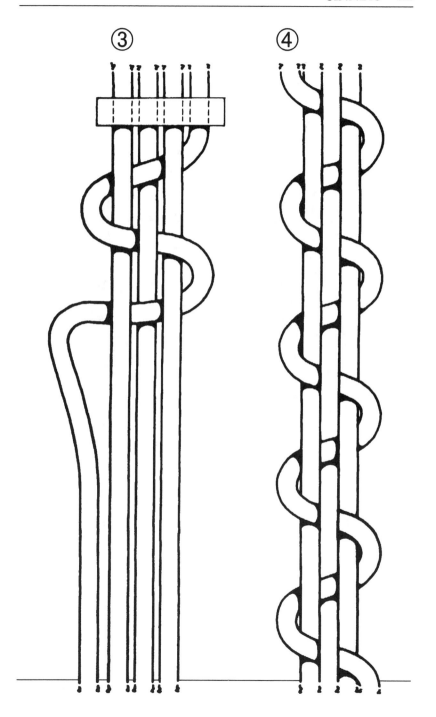

FIVE-STRAND SINNET

The method for tying this five-strand sinnet is exactly the same as that for the Flat Sinnet (see pg. 618) with one exception – alternately cross the outside strands over two strands instead of one. For the best appearance, keep this sinnet tight and compact at each step of the tying procedure.

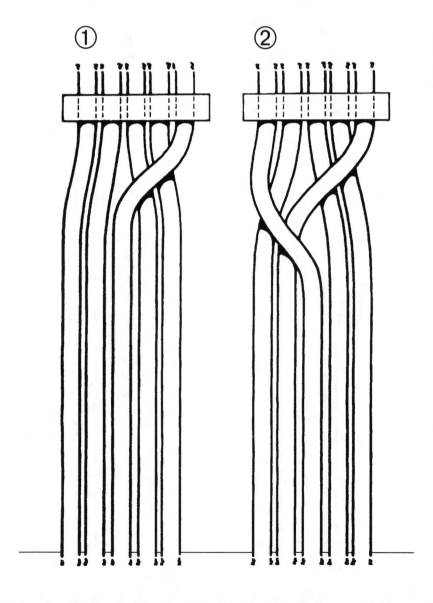

CHAIN SINNET

Chain sinnets are made of one or more strands that are formed into successive loops which are tucked through each other. The single-strand example shown here is the most commonly used and is also known as the Monkey Chain or Trumpet Cord. It is often seen tied in gold braid on dress uniforms and is an excellent way to decoratively shorten a rope or cord. This particular sinnet has one other interesting attribute – if a length of rope or cord is tied into a chain sinnet it acquires an elastic quality.

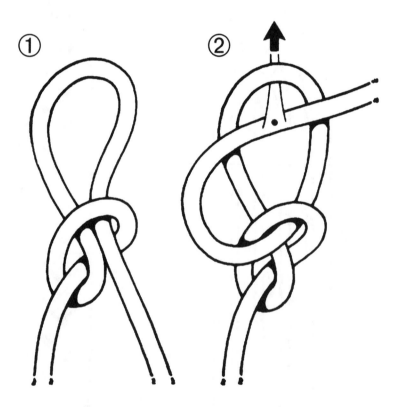

Arrange the cord as in step 1 and then
tuck the first loop as in step 2.

Continue to create the loops until the
desired length of sinnet has been achieved.
For the best results, tighten and arrange at
each step of the tying procedure. To finish
the sinnet, thread the working end through
the last loop and tighten as shown in step 4.

CROWN SINNET

Crown sinnets, as their name suggests, are built up by "crowning" (see pg. 580). Each strand in regular turn passes over an adjacent strand and under the bight of another. A variable number of strands can be used; the example shown here uses three but the tying method is exactly the same for sinnets with more strands. They can be used as cords or decorative coverings for cylindrical objects. A successful crown sinnet is dependent on methodical tying and drawing up the crowns – tight and even.

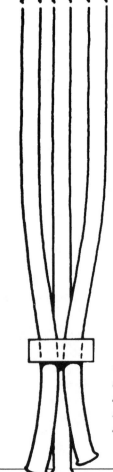

①

Clamp or tie three strands together with thin cord or an elastic band, or tie all three strands together with a simple overhand knot.

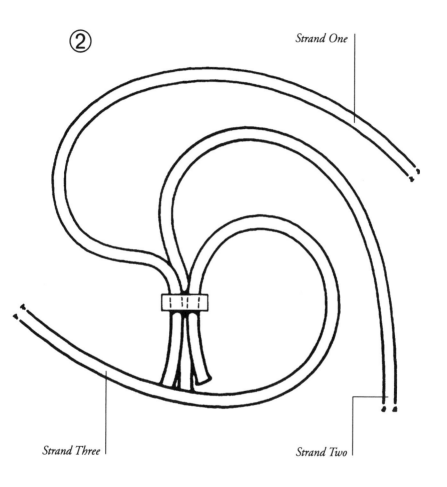

②

Strand One

Strand Three

Strand Two

*Arrange the three strands like this,
in preparation for crowning to begin.*

continued pg. 630

Crown Sinnet

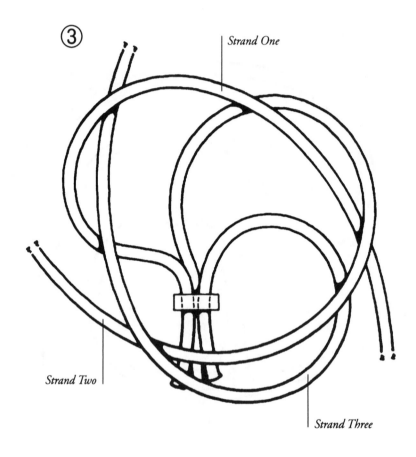

③ Strand One

Strand Two

Strand Three

As shown in this illustration, create the first crown by placing strand one over strand two, strand two over strand three, and strand three over and then under strand one. Draw the strands tight and the first crown is formed.

④

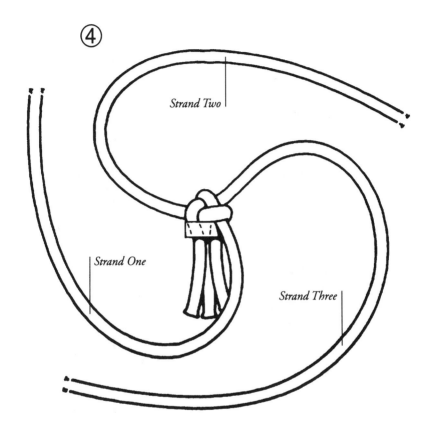

Strand Two

Strand One

Strand Three

*Now continue to build the sinnet with
successive crowns. To create this particular Crown
Sinnet the crowns must always be worked
in the same direction, in this case, clockwise.*

continued pg. 632

Crown Sinnet

⑤

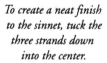

To create a neat finish to the sinnet, tuck the three strands down into the center.

This interesting variation of the Crown Sinnet is created by alternating clockwise and anti-clockwise crowns to form a triangular-shaped sinnet.

7

FLAT KNOTS

· · · · · · · · · · · · · · · · · · · ·

The highly decorative appearance of flat or two-dimensional knots may look complex, but if the tying instructions are followed correctly they should present no great difficulties. The most common use for this type of knot is as household or marine mats, but they also have a very practical use in protecting objects from wear by rubbing or chafing – as boat fenders for example. To create round matting or drink coasters, use the Turk's Head - Three Lead, Five Bight (see pg. 611) in its flat form.

Ocean Plat

OCEAN PLAT

This classic flat knot is found all over the world in a surprising number of situations – the most common being as a door mat or matting found aboard a ship or boat. The size of the example shown here, which is the one most widely used, is based on three side bights. This pattern can be made more solid by increasing the number of times the lead is followed around, but the actual size of the knot can not be increased. To increase the size of the knot, the number of side bights has to be increased. For example, increase to six or nine bights to create a long, narrow mat or tread for a companionway aboard a ship or boat.

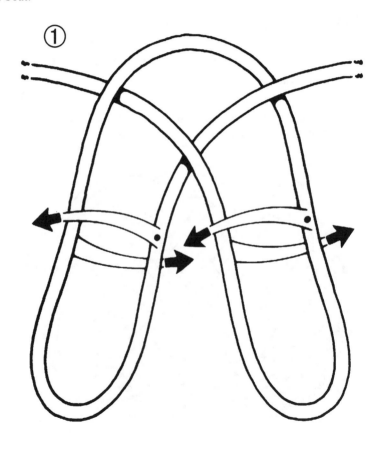

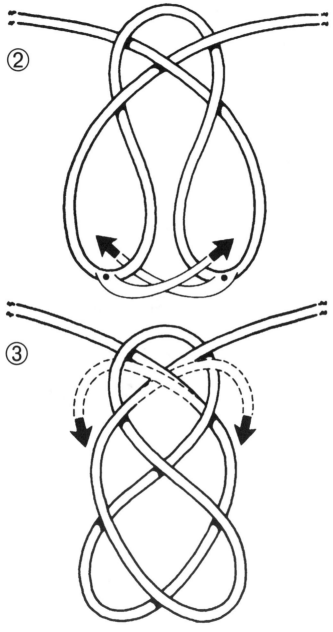

② ③

continued pg. 636

Ocean Plat

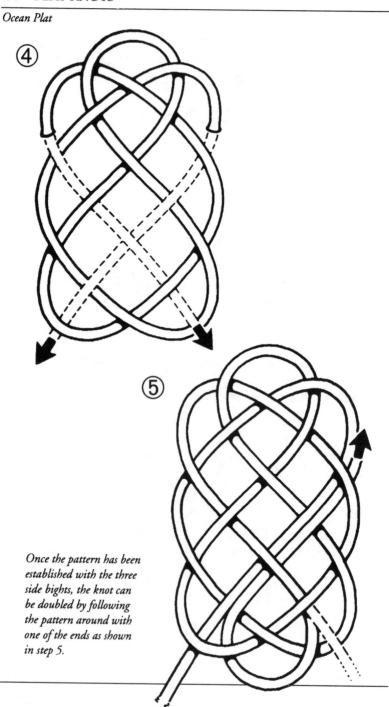

Once the pattern has been established with the three side bights, the knot can be doubled by following the pattern around with one of the ends as shown in step 5.

⑥

*The knot can be doubled or followed
around as many times as desired. It can
also be left loosely formed as shown above,
or it can be tightened and made solid
as in step 7.*

continued pg. 638

Ocean Plat

To finish, hide the ends by tucking them
into the weave on the underside of the knot.
If the knot is to be used as a mat, the whole structure
can be greatly strengthened by sewing together all
of the intersecting points with strong thread.

CHINESE KNOT

This rectangular flat knot is created by enlarging a Carrick Bend Knot. The Carrick Bend is tied using two cords, as in step 1, then gradually enlarged by alternately tucking over and under two diagonally opposite ends across the knot. To add to the already decorative appearance of this knot, the ends can be brought out of the four corners and finished with the other decorative knots, for example, Multiple Overhand Knots (see pg. 538), as in step 5.

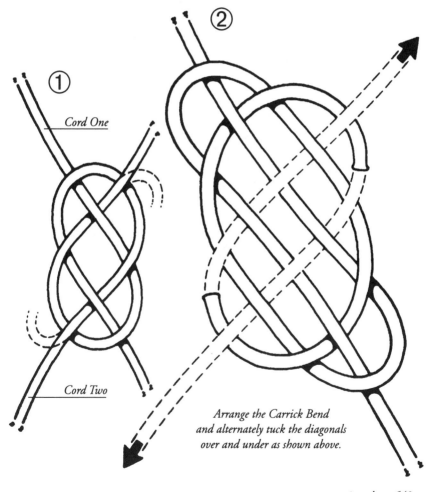

① Cord One

Cord Two

②

Arrange the Carrick Bend and alternately tuck the diagonals over and under as shown above.

continued pg. 640

Chinese Knot

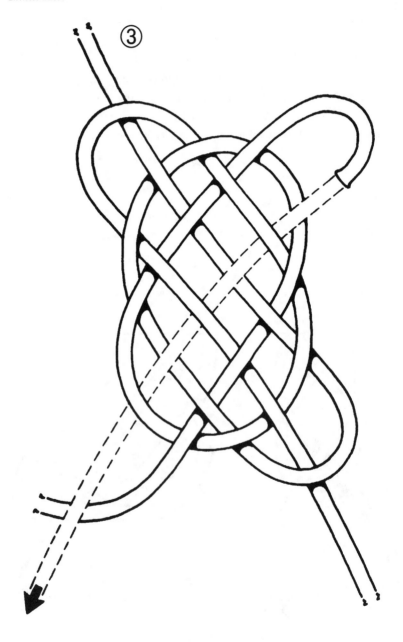

continued pg. 642

Chinese Knot

⑤

*To finish, arrange and work the knot into its final
form and add decorative stopper knots to
the four ends.*

8

APPLIED
DECORATIVE KNOTS

· ·

Decorative knots can be used individually or in elaborate combinations; they can be used for practical purposes or pure decoration. This chapter shows just a few examples of how to use decorative knots, but remember with the information contained in this book and a little imagination the possibilities are endless!

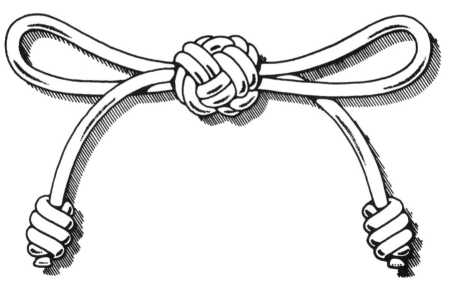

A Turk's Head Curtain Tieback

DECORATIVE BUTTONS

To further enhance the decorative appearance of Button Knots (see pg. 587), they can be attached to garments by using flat appliquéd knots known as "frogs." Each button is attached using two frogs — one creates a loop for the button hole and the other secures the button knot itself. The Turk's Head - Three Lead, Five Bight (see pg. 611) in its flat form would make a suitable frog, but increasing it to a seven bight knot, as illustrated here in steps 1, 2 and 3, gives it a more circular and decorative appearance. The finished assembly of two frogs and a Double Chinese Button Knot (see pg. 590) is shown in step 5.

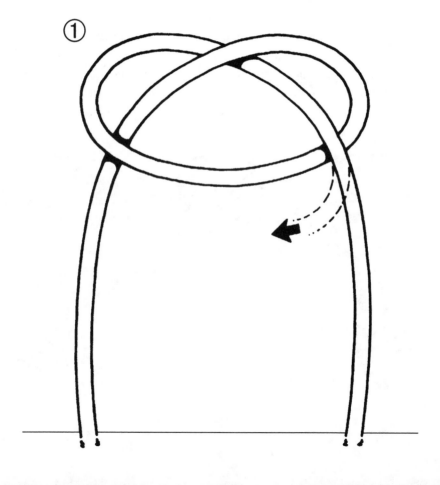

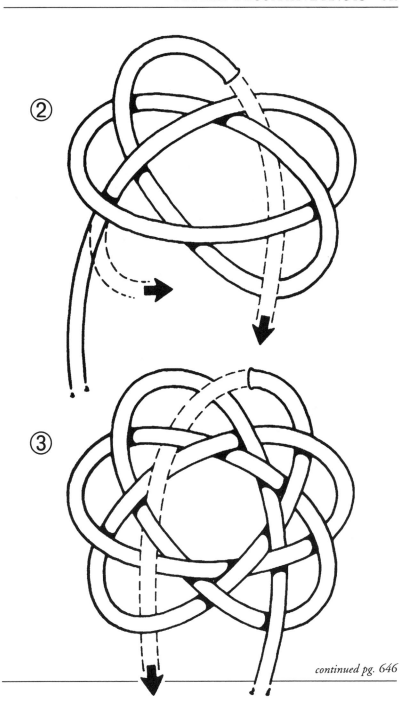

② ③

continued pg. 646

Decorative Buttons

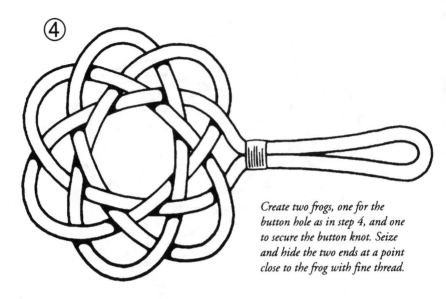

④

*Create two frogs, one for the
button hole as in step 4, and one
to secure the button knot. Seize
and hide the two ends at a point
close to the frog with fine thread.*

⑤

*To finish, secure a Double Chinese
Button Knot to one of the frogs. Bring together the two frogs
and position on the garment. Attach to the garment
by sewing with fine thread on the
underside of the frogs.*

Turk's Head Curtain Tieback

Expensive looking curtain tiebacks are surprisingly easy to make. Arrange a length of high quality cord, as in step 1, and seize it in the center with tape or thread as shown. Now, with a second piece of cord, tie a snug-fitting Turk's Head - Four Lead, Three Bight (see pg. 614) around the first piece of cord covering the seized area. To finish, as in step 2, tie the two ends with Multiple Overhand Knots (see pg. 538).

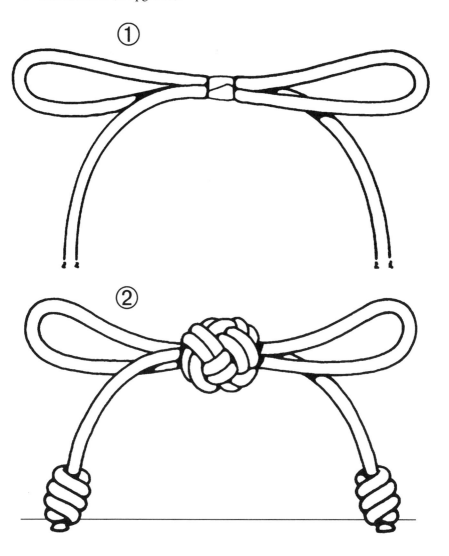

ROPE LADDER

This is a fine example of how decorative knotting can create an extremely useful piece of equipment. To tie a ladder of any substantial size is going to require a long length of rope, so provision for this should be made before starting. To start, take a length of rope, middle it, and tie a loop in the bight of the rope. In the example shown here, a Figure-Eight Loop has been used. Arrange the left end as in step 1, and pass the right end through, as shown, to start making a series of turns. Determine the width of the ladder rung and make as many turns as required. Finish the rung as shown in step 2 – keeping the turns tight and making sure the rung is secure on both sides. Now continue the process until the required number of rungs are achieved.

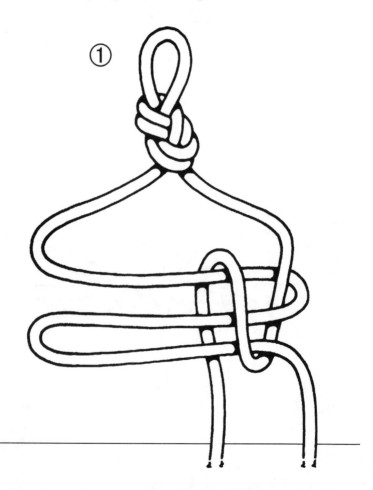

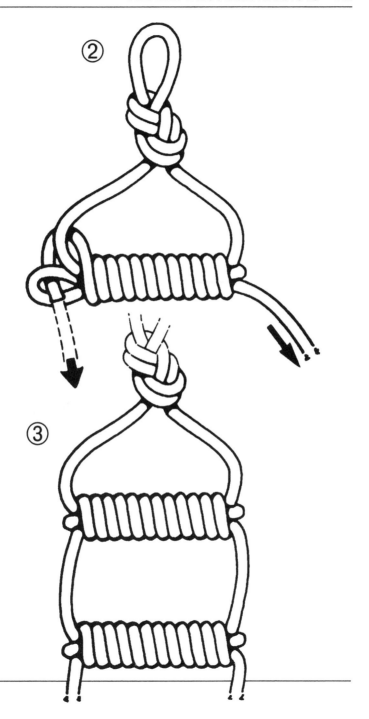

PLANT HOLDER

This is an example of how a series of knots can be tied together to construct an object – in this case a simple but effective plant holder. A certain amount of planning will be required beforehand; the holder should be roughly constructed around the pot first to establish the various lengths of cord or rope required, and you need to decide if the pot will be staying in the holder or needs to be taken out for regular maintenance, in which case this needs to be made possible within the construction. The main joints in this example are Reef Knots, as in steps 1 & 2, but a wide variety of knots could be used – for example the Carrick Bend (see pg. 639). Two eyes are seized in the top and bottom parts of the construction, as in steps 3 & 4, and the finished holder is shown in step 5.

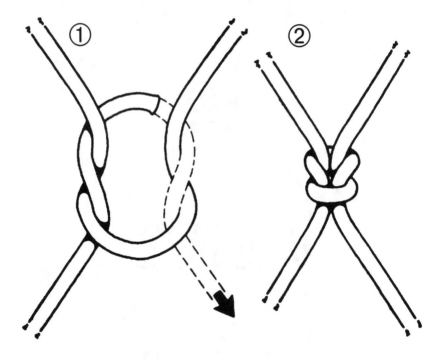

③

④

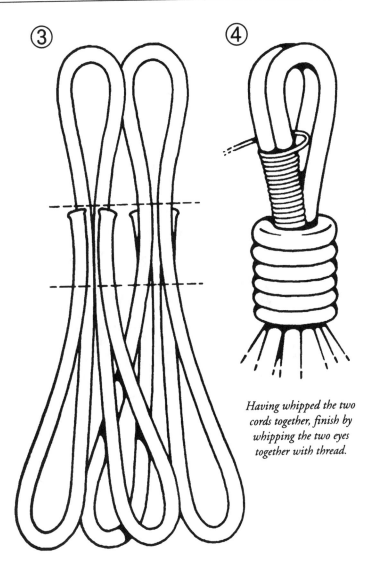

*Having whipped the two
cords together, finish by
whipping the two eyes
together with thread.*

*To create the top or bottom section, arrange two
lengths of cord as above, and seize them together as
shown in step 4, by using the same technique as
shown on page 16 for whipping the end of a rope.*

continued pg. 652

Plant Holder

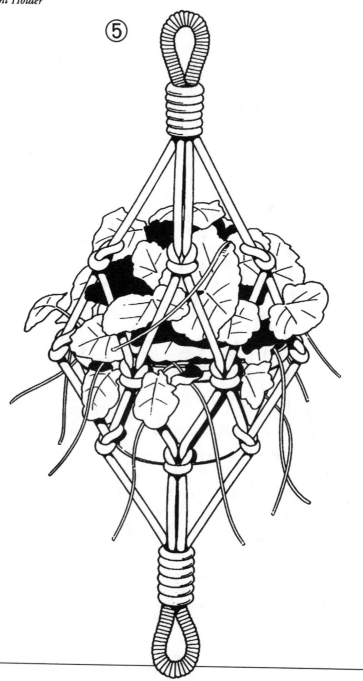

CHINESE DRAGONFLY

Since the mid-nineteenth century there has been a fascination, especially by jewelers, with creating the shapes of insects and butterflies by using various combinations of decorative knots. This Chinese Dragonfly has proved to be a very popular example; it is made up of a Chinese Button Knot (see pg. 588) and two True-Lover's Knots (see pg. 576).

GLOSSARY

Abseiling. A method of descending a rope using friction as a control.

Applique. A decoration or trimming that is sewn or otherwise fixed onto material.

Arbor. The center of a reel spool.

Astern. At or toward the rear part of a boat or the reversing maneuver of a vessel as in: *full speed astern!*

Backing line. High-breaking-strain monofilament or braided line used under the fly line on a reel to bulk out the spool. Also used as additional line when the fly line is stripped off the reel by a fish making a long run.

Belay. Anchor point on the rock face, being the position where a climber can secure himself to the rock and, by placing the ropes around his body, or to a belay device, can protect other climbers.

Bend. The action of tying two ropes together by their ends. Also the name given to the group of knots that are used to tie lines to each other or to some other object.

Bight. The slack section of the rope between the working end and the standing end. The term is particularly used when this section of the rope is formed into a loop or turned back on itself. Knots tied "in the bight" or "on the bight" do not require you to use the ends in the tying process.

Bollard. A large fixed post made of iron or wood for mooring a boat.

Bow. The front end of a boat.

Braid. To interweave several strands.

Braided Line. Line manufactured by interweaving several strands of material.

Breaking strength or strain. The manufacturer's estimate of the load that will cause a rope to part. This calculation is based on strength of a dry line under a steady pull; it generally takes no account of wetness, wear and tear, knots, or shock loading. Lines are weaker when worn, wet or knotted; the manufacturer's estimate cannot, therefore, be regarded as a safe working load.

Butt. The thicker part of a leader, usually monofilament, that is attached to the fly line.

Cable. A rope of large diameter: anchor warp or chain.

Cable-laid. Rope formed of three right-handed hawsers laid up left-handed to make a larger, nine-stranded rope or cable.

Chafe. To make or become worn or frayed by rubbing.

Chock. An artificial device designed to be inserted into a crack in the rock face and used as an anchor point.

Cleat. A T-shaped fitting on which a rope or line can be secured.

Cord. The name given to several tightly twisted yarns making a line with a diameter of less than ? inch.

Cordage. Collective name for ropes and cords; especially used to describe the ropes in a ship's rigging.

Core. The inner, or central, part found in ropes and sinnets of more than three strands, and in most braided lines. Formed from a bundle of parallel strands or loosely twisted yarn running the length of the rope, or the central part of a monkey's fist knot, inserted to add weight.

Descendeur. A friction brake device used in abseiling.

Double. To follow the lead strand of a decorative knot and additional circuit.

Dropper. Short length of monofilament that is joined or tied into the leader, usually monofilament, that is attached to the fly line.

Dynamic rope. A rope that stretches when under load. Main climbing ropes must be dynamic.

End. Generally, the end of a length of rope that is being knotted

Eye. A circle or loop attached or formed at the end of a hook or item of tackle, to which line is attached or a loop formed at the end of a length of rope.

Fancy knot. Any decorative knot including ones that have a practical use.

Fender. A cushion of flexible material, positioned on the sides of boats to prevent damage when tying up or mooring.

Fid. Tapered wooden pin used to work or loosen strands of rope.

Finish. To add the final touches or to make the final arrangement.

Fly line. A coated nylon, Dacron, or PVC line specifically developed to cast an artificial fly attached to a leader.

Follow the lead. To pass a cord along a path parallel to the first lead strand, usually in an over and under movement.

Fray. To unravel, especially the end of a piece of rope.

Free climbing. The practice of modern climbing, where no aid is used.

Frog. A flat appliquéd knot that is sewn or otherwise attached to garments or uniforms. Serves the purpose of securing a button knot and providing the button hole.

Grommet or **grummet.** A ring, usually made of metal or twisted rope, that is used to fasten the edge of a sail to its stay, hold an oar in place, etc.

Hawser. A rope or cable, five to twenty-four inches in circumference, large enough for towing or mooring.

Hawser-laid. A type of rope construction that uses a number of twisted strands.

Heaving Line. A line with a weighted knot tied at one end, that is attached to another heavier line and is thrown from boat to shore or to another vessel. The purpose of the heaving line is to draw behind it a heavier line that will be used for tying up or mooring.

Hitch. Knot made to secure a rope to a ring, spar, etc., or to another rope.

Karabiner. A metal linking device, with a sprung gate on one side so that ropes or tapes can be easily clipped in. A **screwgate karabiner** has a threaded sleeve enabling the gate to be locked shut.

Kernmantle. Modern climbing rope made from synthetic materials and having a core of parallel fibers contained in a braided sheath.

Lanyard. A short length of rope or cord made decorative with knots and sinnets. Used to secure personal objects; usually worn around the neck or attached to a belt.

Lay. The direction, right- or left-handed, of the twist in the strands that form a rope.

Lead. The direction the working end takes through a knot. When a knot is doubled, the lead is followed around by the working end for a second.

Leader The tapered length of nylon that forms the connection between a fly line and a fly. It may be tapered mechanically (knotless), or created by joining sections of line with reducing diameters.

Line. Generic name for cordage with no specific purpose, although it can describe a particular use (clothesline, fishing line, etc.).

Loop. Part of a rope that is bent so that it comes together across itself.

Lure. A term to describe artificial baits.

Make fast. To secure a rope line to a cleat, etc.

Middle (To). To establish the center of a piece of rope or cord by laying the two ends together.

Monofilament. Strong and flexible single-strand nylon line.

Nip. The binding pressure within a knot that stops it from slipping.

Over and under. Description of the weave in knots such as the Turk's Head.

Peg. Metal spike driven into the rock face for use as a belay.

Piton. A metal pin that can be driven into a crack in the rock face to form an anchor point.

Plain-laid rope. Three-strand rope laid (twisted) to the right.

Plait or **Plat.** Pronounced *plat*. To intertwine strands in a pattern.

Port. The left-hand side of a boat looking forward.

Prusik. A technique to climb the main rope using special knots or mechanical devices.

Reeve. The act of threading or passing a rope through an aperture such as a ring, block, or cleat.

Retractor. A spring-loaded spool of cord, usually pinned to clothing, to attach items such as scissors.

Rope. Strong, thick cord more than 1 inch in circumference made from twisted strands of fiber, wire, etc.

Route. The climb.

Rung. The crosspiece that forms a step of a ladder.

Running rigging. Rope or wire used to control the sails.

Seat or Seated. A term used to describe the process of knot formation.

Seizing. To bind two cords or ropes together.

Shank. The straight part of a hook.

Sinker. Any weight, usually lead, that is attached to a fishing line.

Sinnet or **Sennet.** Braided cordage (flat, round, or square), formed from three to nine cords.

S-laid rope. Left-hand-laid rope.

Sling. A loop of nylon tape or rope used to form anchors and belays.

Small stuff. Thin cordage, twine, string, rope, or line that has a circumference less than 1 inch, or a diameter of less than ? inch.

Snell. To tie a hook by wrapping line around the shank or straight part of the hook.

Spade end. The flattened end of a shank hook.

Splice. To join ends of rope by interweaving strands.

Standing end. The short are at the end of the standing part of the rope.

Standing part. The part of the rope that is fixed and under tension (as opposed to the free working end with which the knot is tied).

Stopper knot. Any terminal knot used to bind the end of a line, cord, or rope to prevent it from unraveling and also to provide a decorative end.

Strand. Yarns twisted together in the opposite direction to the yarn itself. Rope made from strands (rope that is not braided) is called laid line.

Swivel. An item of tackle used in the terminal rig to prevent twists in the line.

Tag end. The part of the line in which the knot is tied and then excesses trimmed off.

Taut. Tightly stretched.

Thread. A fine cord of twisted filaments—especially of cotton—used in sewing and weaving.

Tippet. The thin terminal section of the leader, to which the fly is tied.

Turn. One complete revolution of one line around another.

Twine. Thin line of various types for various uses, as in whipping twine, etc.

Tying on. How a climber ties himself to the rope or to the anchors.

UIAA. Union Internationale des Associations d'Alpinisme. An international body chiefly concerned with the improvement of safety standards in climbing and mountaineering.

Whipping. Tightly wrapping small stuff around the end of a cord or rope to prevent it from fraying.

Work (To). To draw up and shape a knot; to make the final arrangement.

Working end. The part of the rope or cord used actively in tying a knot. The opposite of the standing end.

Yarn. The basic element of rope or cord formed form artificial or synthetic filaments or natural fibers.

Z-laid rope. Right-hand-laid rope.

CONVERSION CHART

Note: These conversion factors are not exact. They are given only to the accuracy you're likely to need in everyday calculations.

Linear Measure

0.25 inch	=	0.6 cm
0.5 inch	=	1.25 cm
1 inch	=	2.54 cm
2 inches	=	5.08 cm
4 inches	=	10.16 cm
6 inches	=	15.25 cm
8 inches	=	20.32 cm
10 inches	=	25.40 cm
12 inches (1 foot)	=	30.48 cm
2 feet	=	0.61 m
3 feet (1 yard)	=	0.91 m
5 feet	=	1.52 m
10 feet	=	3.05 m

Temperature

Celsius		Fahrenheit
-17.8	=	0
-10	=	14
0	=	32
10	=	50
20	=	68
30	=	86
40	=	104
50	=	122
60	=	140
70	=	158
80	=	176
90	=	194
100	=	212

Measures of Weight

1 lb	=	450 g
2 lb	=	900 g
5 lb	=	2.25 kg
10 lb	=	4.5 kg
20 lb	=	9 kg
50 lb	=	23 kg
100 lb	=	46 kg

INDEX